George Eliot: *Middlemarch*

Casebook Series

GENERAL EDITOR: A. E. Dyson

Jane Austen: *Emma* DAVID LODGE
William Blake: *Songs of Innocence and Experience*
    MARGARET BOTTRALL
Emily Brontë: *Wuthering Heights* MIRIAM ALLOTT
Dickens: *Bleak House* A. E. DYSON
George Eliot: *Middlemarch* PATRICK SWINDEN
T. S. Eliot: *Four Quartets* BERNARD BERGONZI
T. S. Eliot: *The Waste Land* C. B. COX AND ARNOLD P. HINCHLIFFE
Henry Fielding: *Tom Jones* NEIL COMPTON
E. M. Forster: *A Passage to India* MALCOLM BRADBURY
Jonson: *Volpone* JONAS A. BARISH
John Keats: *Odes* G. S. FRASER
D. H. Lawrence: *Sons and Lovers* GĀMINI SALGĀDO
D. H. Lawrence: *'The Rainbow' and 'Women in Love'* COLIN CLARKE
Marlowe: *Doctor Faustus* JOHN JUMP
John Osborne: *Look Back in Anger* JOHN RUSSELL TAYLOR
Pope: *The Rape of the Lock* JOHN DIXON HUNT
Shakespeare: *Antony and Cleopatra* J. RUSSELL BROWN
Shakespeare: *Hamlet* JOHN JUMP
Shakespeare: *Henry IV Parts I and II* G. K. HUNTER
Shakespeare: *Henry V* MICHAEL QUINN
Shakespeare: *Julius Caesar* PETER URE
Shakespeare: *King Lear* FRANK KERMODE
Shakespeare: *Macbeth* JOHN WAIN
Shakespeare: *Measure for Measure* C. K. STEAD
Shakespeare: *The Merchant of Venice* JOHN WILDERS
Shakespeare: *Othello* JOHN WAIN
Shakespeare: *The Tempest* D. J. PALMER
Shakespeare: *Twelfth Night* D. J. PALMER
Shakespeare: *The Winter's Tale* KENNETH MUIR
Tennyson: *In Memoriam* JOHN DIXON HUNT
Virginia Woolf: *To the Lighthouse* MORRIS BEJA
Wordsworth: *Lyrical Ballads* ALUN R. JONES AND
    WILLIAM TYDEMAN
Wordsworth: *The Prelude* W. J. HARVEY AND RICHARD GRAVIL
Yeats: *Last Poems* JON STALLWORTHY

IN PREPARATION

Charlotte Brontë: *'Jane Eyre' and 'Villette'* MIRIAM ALLOTT
Coleridge: *The Ancient Mariner and Other Poems* ALUN R. JONES AND
    WILLIAM TYDEMAN
Conrad: *The Secret Agent* IAN WATT
Donne: *Songs and Sonnets* JULIAN LOVELOCK
James Joyce: *Portrait of the Artist as a Young Man* MORRIS BEJA
Milton: *Paradise Lost* A. E. DYSON
Milton: *Samson Agonistes* STANLEY FISH
Shakespeare: *Richard II* NICHOLAS BROOKE

George Eliot

Middlemarch

A CASEBOOK

EDITED BY

PATRICK SWINDEN

MACMILLAN

First published 1972 by
THE MACMILLAN PRESS LTD
London and Basingstoke
Associated companies in New York Toronto
Dublin Melbourne Johannesburg and Madras

SBN 333 02119 3 (hard cover)
SBN 333 05838 0 (paper cover)

Printed in Great Britain by
THE ANCHOR PRESS LTD
Tiptree, Essex

CONTENTS

SOURCES AND ACKNOWLEDGEMENTS

PART I

Extracts from correspondence and diaries, from *George Eliot's Life as related in her Letters and Journals*, ed. J. W. Cross (Blackwoods, 1885), and *The George Eliot Letters*, ed. G. S. Haight (Yale U.P., 1954–6). Reviews from [R. H. Hutton], 'The Melancholy of Middlemarch', *Spectator*, 1 June 1872, pp. 685–7; *Athenaeum*, 7 Dec 1872, pp. 725–6; W. L. Collins, *Blackwood's Edinburgh Magazine*, CXII (Dec 1872) 743–4; H. Lawrenny (Edith Simcox), *Academy*, 1 Jan 1873, pp. 1–3; Sidney Colvin, *Fortnightly Review*, 1 Jan 1873, pp. 142–7; Th. Bentzon, 'Le Roman de la Vie de Province en Angleterre', *Revue des Deux mondes*, no. 103 (Feb 1873) pp. 668–9, 678–9, 688–90; F. N. Broome, *The Times*, 7 Mar 1873, pp. 3–4; Henry James, *Galaxy*, XV (Mar 1873) 424–8, reprinted in *The House of Fiction*, ed. L. Edel (Hart-Davis, 1957) pp. 259–67; [R. H. Hutton], *British Quarterly Review*, LVII (1 Apr 1873) 407–23, 429.

PART 2

Leslie Stephen, 'George Eliot', *Cornhill Magazine*, XLIII (Feb 1881) 164–7; Bessie Rayner Belloc, *In a Walled Garden* (Ward & Downey, 1894) pp. 6, 12; W. D. Howells, 'George Eliot's Dorothea Brooke', in *Heroines of Fiction*, vol. II (Harper, 1901) pp. 74–8; W. C. Brownell, 'George Eliot', in *Victorian Prose Masters* (David Nutt, 1902) pp. 138–41; Leslie Stephen, '*Middlemarch*', in *George Eliot*, English Men of Letters Series (Macmillan, 1902) pp. 173–84; Oliver Elton, *A Survey of English Literature, 1830–1880*, vol. II (Edward Arnold, 1920) pp. 264–5; Virginia Woolf, 'George Eliot', *TLS*, XVIII (20 Nov 1919) 657–8, reprinted in *The Common Reader* (Hogarth Press, 1925) I 213; V. S. Pritchett, 'George Eliot', in *The Living Novel* (Chatto & Windus, 1947) pp. 88–94; Barbara Hardy, *The Novels of George Eliot* (Athlone Press, 1959) pp. 143–8; David Daiches,

George Eliot: 'Middlemarch' (Edward Arnold, 1963) pp. 47–8, 54–8; W. J. Harvey, *The Art of George Eliot* (Chatto & Windus, 1961) pp. 55–62, 143–8; Frank Kermode, 'Lawrence and the Apocalyptic Types', *Critical Quarterly Tenth Anniversary Number* (spring–summer 1968) pp. 26–35, reprinted in *Continuities* (Routledge & Kegan Paul, 1968) pp. 137–48.

PART 3
Arnold Kettle, 'George Eliot: *Middlemarch*', in *An Introduction to the English Novel*, I (Hutchinson, 1951) 160–77; Quentin Anderson, 'George Eliot in *Middlemarch*', in *The Penguin Guide to English Literature*, VI (1958) 274–93; W. J. Harvey, 'Introduction' to Penguin English Classics edition of *Middlemarch* (1966) pp. 7–22; Barbara Hardy, 'The Surface of the Novel: Chapter 30', in *Middlemarch: Critical Approaches* (Athlone Press, 1967) pp. 154–71; Laurence Lerner, 'Dorothea and the Theresa-Complex', in *The Truthtellers* (Chatto & Windus, 1967) pp. 249–69.

GENERAL EDITOR'S PREFACE

Each of this series of Casebooks concerns either one well-known and influential work of literature or two or three closely linked works. The main section consists of critical readings, mostly modern, brought together from journals and books. A selection of reviews and comments by the author's contemporaries is also included, and sometimes comments from the author himself. The Editor's Introduction charts the reputation of the work from its first appearance until the present time.

The critical forum is a place of vigorous conflict and disagreement, but there is nothing in this to cause dismay. What is attested is the complexity of human experience and the richness of literature, not any chaos or relativity of taste. A critic is better seen, no doubt, as an explorer than as an 'authority', but explorers ought to be, and usually are, well equipped. The effect of good criticism is to convince us of what C. S. Lewis called 'the enormous extension of our being which we owe to authors'. This Casebook will be justified only if it helps to promote the same end.

A single volume can represent no more than a small selection of critical opinions. Some critics have been excluded for reasons of space, and it is hoped that readers will follow up the further suggestions in the Select Bibliography. Other contributions have been severed from their original context, to which some readers may wish to return. Indeed, if they take a hint from the critics represented here, they certainly will.

A. E. DYSON

INTRODUCTION

'A treasure-house of detail, but...an indifferent whole.' That was Henry James's conclusion on *Middlemarch* when he reviewed it for *Galaxy* in March 1873. If he was right, he certainly flew in the face of evidence concerning the publication of the novel which we now have at our disposal. *Middlemarch* was George Eliot's sixth novel, published nine years after *Romola* and six years after *Felix Holt*. *Romola* was oddly reviewed, the profundity, nobility and above all the diligence of its author being commended at the same time as her straying beyond the bounds of English Midland rural life was wondered at, and the tediousness of the novel paid a glancing and hesitant acknowledgement. 'No reader of *Romola* will lay it down without admiration, and few without regret'; this opening sentence of the *Saturday Review* notice (25 July 1863) sums up the general feeling. At the same time the opening sentence of the *Westminster* article (October 1863) indicates the favour it found among the intelligentsia: 'It cannot be denied that *Romola* is less popular than its predecessors, but we do not hesitate to say that it is its author's greatest work.' Its successor proved a less dubious favourite with the reviewer and, we may suppose, with the public at large. Both were glad to be back among the English hedgerows, and neither seemed so bothered about the melodrama, improbability and legal paraphernalia as are *Felix*'s modern critics. These two novels set the seal on George Eliot's reputation as the foremost English novelist of her day. Her position with Lewes, combining with this high reputation and a consequent lack of dependence on sales, made it possible for her to think carefully about her next novel, to take great pains with the historical background material (as was also the case with *Romola*) and to consider the total structure of the story. Incidentally, it also enabled her to write *The Spanish Gipsy*.

George Eliot had been meditating *Middlemarch* since 1867. Indeed, in a sense, she had been meditating Dorothea's story for many more years than that. In her journal for 2 December 1870 she wrote that the subject of her new novel was one 'which has been recorded among my possible themes ever since I began to write fiction'. A. T. Kitchel and Jerome Beaty have each provided detailed accounts of the genesis of *Middlemarch* (see Bibliography), and W. H. Harvey conveniently summarises it in his Introduction to the Penguin edition. Very briefly, the *Middlemarch* we now have is a novel created out of the union of two unfinished fictions: the one, *Middlemarch*, a novel primarily about Lydgate; the other, 'Miss Brooke', a long story primarily about Dorothea. Although the latter deals with a theme George Eliot had been pondering since she began to write novels, *Middlemarch* was the first of the two to be started, in July–August 1869. On 11 September of that year the project lapsed, and the next thing we hear about George Eliot's fiction, on 2 December 1870, is that she is 'experimenting in a story' of Dorothea. By the end of the year she is well advanced with it and by the spring of 1871 she has decided to incorporate the *Middlemarch* material into the 'Miss Brooke' story. In doing this, she expands that story into what she now realises will be a long novel. Dr Harvey explains how Lewes suggested the idea of the bi-monthly parts so as to ensure that the expansiveness of the novel would not be cramped by limitations imposed even by the three-decker novel form. George Eliot and Henry James shared a tendency, acknowledged in some of James's prefaces to the New York edition of his work, to foreshorten their novels and rush their endings. But the bi-monthly plan also meant that the writing itself need not be so hurried (her next and last novel, *Daniel Deronda*, was published in monthly instalments). In any case, by the time Lewes arranged the terms of publication with *Blackwood's* she must have written over 150 pages, and her notebooks show that she had thought carefully about the general direction the narrative would take.

She also thought carefully about the structure of the half-volumes. Blackwood wrote to her on 20 July 1871 after receiving the second half-volume that 'our plan of publication is the right one as the two parts are almost distinct, each complete in itself. Indeed there will be complaints of the want of the continuous interest of a story.' George Eliot endorsed this view in her comments on the Fourth Book on 21 February 1872: 'It has caused me some uneasiness that the Third Part is two sheets less than the First. But Mr Lewes insisted that the death of old Featherstone was the right point to pause at, and he cites your approbation of the Part as a proof that effectiveness is secured in spite of diminished quantity.' How far this insistence on making of each Book a complete narrative sequence actually does interfere with the successful and natural development of the action over the spread of the whole novel, how far it does create a 'want of continuous interest', is a matter modern readers will settle for themselves. What we are concerned with now is how serial publication, and more especially this particular form of it, affected the approach to the novel in the reviews of George Eliot's contemporaries.

Most of these noted the firm design of the plotting, and assumed that, although published in instalments, the book had not been *written* serially. Again, Dr Harvey points out the importance of this fact in his essay on contemporary reviews of *Middlemarch*.[1] Three in particular – the *Examiner*, *Spectator* and *Athenaeum*[2] – reviewed each book as it came out as a half-volume, a measure of the status George Eliot had acquired by this time. All insisted upon the developing unity of the novel – 'there is no sign of a half-complete or altered design anywhere' (*Spectator*) – and the *Athenaeum* found the mode of publication 'injudicious' and 'intolerable', since it prevented the reader from appreciating the total structure. On occasion, however, we do find George Eliot adapting her story to meet 'the exigencies of the serial form'.

In one important respect the serialisation of *Middlemarch* in these long half-volumes did, perhaps advantageously, affect its readers' responses to the action in a way we can only dimly share; or, if we do share it, our sharing can be seldom so active or so eager. I mean the link between the fortunes of Lydgate and

Dorothea. It is obvious to us that there is a link and that it grows stronger as the novel progresses and as they have more to do with each other. But I suppose this link remains for us overwhelmingly thematic, a matter of comparison and contrast, whereas for the Victorians – speculating upon the possibilities open to their characters in the next instalment – it is likely to have been at least as much naïvely and hopefully actual. Would Dorothea eventually marry Lydgate rather than Ladislaw after Casaubon's death and the gradual breakdown of Lydgate's marriage with Rosamond? The reviewers clearly responded in this way. Thus the *Examiner* (3 February 1872) speculated on 'an artistic relationship already in course of being established between the two characters', and the *Edinburgh* (CXXXVII, 1873) was disappointed that Dorothea and Lydgate ('the real hero and heroine of the book') do not marry at the end.

The importance of such speculations upon the fortunes of characters in the novel can scarcely be exaggerated. Encouraged by serial publication, reviewers frequently went beyond the bounds of the books themselves to the real world into which the characters were presumed to move when the last pages had been read, and from which they so often entered the book, in mid-career, in the first place. Hence W. L. Collins in *Blackwood's* (December 1872) felt so intensely the 'mental agony' and 'bitter humiliation' of Bulstrode that he was 'inclined to take his arm as Lydgate does, and help him to his carriage'. We remember that fourteen years earlier George Eliot herself had more or less done this with Adam Bede in chap. xvii of her first novel, projecting herself into the narrative to take on a role as a character within her own story. The fact that in spite of the break in the illusion she did so satisfactorily as a participant makes vivid to us the 'lifelikeness' of the scenes and people. And this insistence on 'lifelikeness' is precisely what contemporaries admired most in *Middlemarch* and in George Eliot's other novels. Blackwood admired Part Two not least because the characters are 'true . . . to Nature' (20 July 1871). Joseph Munt Langford wrote to Blackwood about book III (11 March

1872) that, as for the characters, 'one feels them all to be true to life'. Of course, many of us value this 'naïve' response to character even now, however little we find in the modern novel to exercise it on; but we do not, or we try not to, let it jeopardise our critical approach to the work as a whole. The Victorians did not seem to mind quite so much. The critic in the *Saturday Review* (21 December 1872) doubted if Casaubon or Bulstrode are very effective in so far as they affect the plot. Even so, this is not important, because it is not the main ground of our interest in them – which is to enjoy them for what they are. The *Edinburgh Review* also selected Bulstrode for special attention: his is 'the most forcible portion of the story' even though it has 'little real bearing on any of the three groups of characters'. Both of these particular points of view were rightly rejected by many contemporary critics and are shared by few modern ones. I doubt whether any modern readers feel that either Casaubon or Bulstrode is an ineffective appendage to the plot. But it is an open question how far we apprehend them vividly in themselves, as our Victorian forebears did.

There were dissident voices respecting this whole matter of George Eliot's creation of 'lifelike' characters. For some, she was 'too analytic'. The *Examiner* (5 October 1872) noted her 'subtle power of showing the true function of sentiment in the process of mental development. She is the foremost novelist of our day, but she is even better as a psychologist than a novelist.' Perhaps the comparison here was supposed to work in George Eliot's favour. But there is no doubt about the *Spectator*'s attitude (30 March 1872): 'She dissects her own characters till she spoils the charm of some of them, and makes the humour of others of her conceptions too evident by subtle comment and elaborate analysis.' This dislike of elaborate analysis reminds us of slightly later attacks on James by reviewers like Saintsbury and Lena Milman,[3] which is rather odd considering the same critic's dislike of evident, although subtle, comment from above – in other words, just the kind of thing James set himself to dispense with through his battery of point-of-view and register techniques.

The review articles on *Middlemarch* show how conscious literary critics before the last quarter of the nineteenth century were
of the need to disguise the presence of the author in her fiction.
This is the other side of the coin to their delight in the free play
of character, and marks the beginnings of an important shift of
opinion since the days of *Adam Bede* and *The Mill on the Floss*.
So the *Spectator* in its next review (5 October 1872) felt that
'Her characters are so real that they have a life and body of
their own quite distinct from her criticism of them; and one is
conscious at times of taking part with the characters against
the author, and of accusing her of availing herself unfairly of
the privilege of the author, by adding a trait that bears out her
own *criticism* rather than her own imaginative conception.'
The *Edinburgh*, Edith Simcox, Colvin, and A. G. Segwick in
the *Atlantic Monthly* (April 1873) all pointed to the same habit,
with comments ranging from mild to severe disapproval. Dicey,
in the *Saturday Review* (31 December 1872), was probably the
most severe: 'the form of the story has made it impossible to
centre the reader's interest fixedly on any one character', but
'the mere annoyance at being constantly shifted from one scene
to another is a trifling consideration. A much more serious
evil of this constant shifting is that it prevents the author from
fully elaborating any one character, and from studying the
effect of the work as a whole.' The argument has moved from
objections to the commentating novelist to an attack on George
Eliot's basic habit of narrative – what was later to be called
the panoramic manner. The movement towards a Jamesian
system of registration and location of centres of consciousness
was well under way by this time, which is all the more reason
why we should respect James's own fair and judicious treatment
of *Middlemarch*.

The main contemporary objection to the novel was not,
however, an objection to its form. More often critics found
themselves at odds with what they took to be its 'melancholy'
view of life, 'that inconsequence and incompleteness in *Middlemarch* and its personages' discovered by the *Quarterly* (no. 134,
1873), which 'baffles and, we might say, defies criticism. . . .

What is the lesson of this book, what its conclusion, not that verbal one on the last page, but the logical inference when reading is done, and judgment would settle itself? . . . Towards what in earth and heaven does she beckon us on?' This is the burden of, so many otherwise respectful and approbatory reviews. It is most exhaustively, and probably most intelligently, taken up by R. H. Hutton in his (?) two reviews of *Middlemarch* in the *Spectator* and the *British Quarterly*, both of which I have felt it right to include in the first part of this book. But he is by no means alone in finding in *Middlemarch* what a critic in the *North American Review* (CXVI, 1873) called the 'prevailing pessi-mism of a generation'.

In the *Spectator* article (1 June 1872), Hutton's comments on this pessimism are very general, a matter of assessing the tone where they do not take the form of a discussion of Dorothea's character. Where they do take this form they are frequently illuminating in spite of their piety, which is of the decent, compassionate sort. Hutton questions whether 'any one lays the book down without an extra twinge of melancholy in his feeling'. Although sometimes he finds this melancholy respon-sible, and the author herself responsible, for cynicism and a tendency to enjoy 'jeering at human evil', on the whole he is convinced that it is as much an imposition for George Eliot as it is for her heroine. For Dorothea's 'faith' is 'exquisitely melancholy . . . the passion of a soul compelled always to give up prayer as too exhausting, because it seems the radiation of force into a vacuum, and yet retaining all the passionate love for higher guidance in which prayer too finds its source and justi-fication'. This strikes me as being a sympathetic account of Dorothea's dilemma, and of George Eliot's dilemma in creating her. Its weakness is that it singles out those aspects of Dorothea's character that are themselves a source of weakness when George Eliot chooses, or allows herself to countenance, behaviour on Dorothea's part which we should expect to be viewed ironically, or to be transformed into a kind of strength. Hutton shows him-self to be incapable of accepting what George Eliot tries to accept in the novel, that the religious impulsions in Dorothea's nature may be able to function 'ardently' quite outside of the particular religious schema which he wishes to impose around her. But George Eliot is herself at times uncertain, even 'pessimistic', about this – which makes Hutton less of a fool than his rhetoric declares him to be. It is a point which is taken up by most recent critics, either in studies of George Eliot's irony, or of her vision of society – which itself requires a study of the selectivity of her irony. We shall return to this later.

Hutton found himself on altogether firmer ground in his review of the completed book in the *British Quarterly* (1 April 1873). We have already seen that the *Quarterly* was unhappy with the 'verbal' conclusion of the Finale. Other critics noticed there what they took to be a statement about Dorothea's situation which contradicted much of what George Eliot had said elsewhere. The offending passage occurred towards the end of the Finale, in the penultimate paragraph, and emphasised the pressure to social conformity as a determining factor in Dorothea's behaviour. George Eliot herself must have felt that her commentary here had detracted from the readers' sense of Dorothea as a free agent whose conduct might be affected but not determined by events outside her control. So, in the first place, she crossed out some of the detail in the MS. and afterwards removed a particularly objectionable clause from the second edition (see Leslie Stephen's 1902 essay). Laurence Lerner deals with this in more detail, and with due regard to its implications, at the end of his essay on 'Dorothea and the Theresa-Complex'. But as early as 1873 we discover Hutton struggling with what George Eliot had written in the first edition, and finding that her 'set theory of melancholy realism' was responsible for this attempt at persuading herself that Dorothea's 'misadventures . . . were actually more oppressive and paralyzing than they really were'.

All of which brings us to Sidney Colvin who, to my mind, wrote the best contemporary review of the novel (the *Fortnightly*, 1 January 1873) outside of James. His article cannot be taken as a direct answer to Hutton since the dates of publication preclude that possibility. But Colvin anticipates the

points Hutton was to raise, not merely about the confusions of
the Finale, but also about the direction in which the novel as
a whole was felt to be tending. For his views the reader will
turn to the antepenultimate and penultimate paragraphs of
his essay and find there a clear and unbiased explanation of
the problem:

In her prelude and conclusion both, she seems to insist upon the
design of illustrating the necessary disappointment of a woman's
nobler aspirations in a society not made to second noble aspirations
in a woman. And that is one of the most burning lessons any writer
could set themselves [sic] to illustrate. But then, Dorothea does not
suffer in her ideal aspirations from yielding to the pressure of social
opinion. She suffers in them from finding that what she has done,
in marrying an old scholar in the face of social opinion, was done
under a delusion as to the old scholar's character. 'Exactly,' is
apparently the author's drift; 'but it is society which so nurtures
women that their ideals cannot but be ideals of delusion.'

But Colvin is not thoroughly satisfied with his explanation.
He thinks that if this is the author's main point then 'the prelude
and conclusion leave it still ambiguous'. He is not happy, as
Hutton was not happy, that George Eliot has properly 'placed'
the responsibility for what happens to Dorothea: what responsibility shall be attributed to society and what to herself? He
does not, however, go on to do what we might expect him to
do, namely to look closely at the relationship George Eliot has
established between herself and Dorothea, in an attempt to
locate the source of this evasion of contradiction – depending
whereabouts in the text we are reading – in the intermittent
identification of author and character. Discussion of this problem
was to be left to the twentieth century. It is doubly surprising
that Colvin did not do this (the ethics of reviewing the work of
a contemporary Victorian writer probably have much to do
with it), because he finds so much else in the novel that might
well spring from the same combination of confusion and bias:
his questioning of the comparisons and contrasts George Eliot
draws between Fred and Rosamond, and Rosamond and Celia,

for example. Here he detects an incipient and possibly actual
unfairness, a relaxation of criticism in respect of one character
but not in respect of another where circumstances seem to call
for the same treatment in each case. Edith Simcox in the
Academy (1 January 1873) noticed this habit of comparison and
contrast too, though she discovered no unfairness in the way it is
enforced. Colvin's article is altogether more shrewd. We might
note in passing that it could have been his comments on George
Eliot's habit of 'rousing' and 'attaching' her readers rather
than 'satisfying' them, coupled with her distinctions between
English and French modes of fiction, which prompted Thérèse
Bentzon's attack on *Middlemarch* (she had long before sought
and obtained permission to translate parts of the novel) in
the number of the *Revue des Deux Mondes* (no. 103, February
1873) the following month. If so, she provides us with a convenient link between Colvin and James, since her insistence on
George Eliot's inattention to matters of form and proportion,
her 'slavish imitations of life' which create a 'mere succession
of unconnected chapters', points forward to that Flaubertian
approach to the writing and appreciation of fiction with which
James appears to be fighting a running battle in the *Galaxy*.

I began this Introduction with James's celebrated comment
on *Middlemarch*, that it is a 'treasure-house of detail, but it is
an indifferent whole'. This appears to be damning with faint
praise, but in fact James is not so 'down' on *Middlemarch* as
this single sentence makes him seem to be. He is genuinely
appreciative of George Eliot's 'discursive' and 'expansive' manner. Concentration would have been inappropriate in her case,
because 'the author's purpose was to be a generous rural historian, and this very redundancy of touch, born of abundant
reminiscence, is one of the greatest charms of her work'.
However, this abundance does not, unfortunately, extend to
Dorothea. Her situation does not 'expand' to 'full capacity'.
'It is treated with too much refinement and too little breadth.'
There is the rub. Unlike Flaubert in *Madame Bovary*, possibly
even unlike himself in *The Portrait of a Lady* seven years later,
James believes that in Dorothea George Eliot has a heroine of

great potential, one in whom we are willing to take a persistent interest. But we are not allowed to persist. The 'expansiveness' and 'redundancy of touch' which James admires for itself gets in the way of a sufficiently full treatment of Dorothea. In spite of this, James notices the way in which the other plots help to bring out Dorothea. Take the comparison between her and Lydgate, for example: 'Each is a tale of matrimonial infelicity, but the conditions in each are so different and the circumstances so broadly opposed that the mind passes from one to the other with that supreme sense of the vastness and variety of human life, under aspects apparently similar, which it belongs only to the greatest novels to produce.' We shall do well to pause and ponder that passing reference to the 'vastness and variety of human life'. It is arguable whether many critics after James and the Victorians are as aware of it as they might be, or attach as great an importance to their awareness of it as they might do. When James goes on to disclose that *Middlemarch* 'sets a limit . . . to the development of the old-fashioned English novel', we begin to see how he is branching off on the Flaubert–Turgenev line where he will call *War and Peace* a 'loose and baggy monster' and write *The Golden Bowl*. The strictures against the omniscient but populous novelist which we came up against in the *Edinburgh* critic, Dicey and others, we rediscover here, in the midst of so much that is different. By 1890 we shall find the *Westminster* (vol. CXXXIV) defining that limit more closely than James did, though with reference to the evolving criteria of fiction which James was not exactly to codify, but for which at least he was to provide copy that later critics of the novel would use to draw up such a codification. George Eliot is here held responsible for 'the habit of telling us when anything is said, *how* it is said'. She tells us beforehand 'what is going on in the speaker's mind, analysing the whole process to the utter destruction of that charm and apparent unconsciousness and consequent surprise and credence which makes us feel that we are not assisting at a got-up show, but living an experience'.

Little wonder that, with *Middlemarch* a 'got-up show', a

guard action was to be fought in defence of George
utation throughout the 1880s and 1890s. But it was
novels whose claims were advanced. Leslie Stephen
and in the late novels the 'charm' that he found in
Adam ... le. George Saintsbury in his *Corrected Impressions* (1895)
thought *The Mill on the Floss* her best book, 'though it may not
contain her best scenes'. *Felix Holt* and *Middlemarch* are 'elaborate
studies of what seem to the author to be modern characters and
society – studies of immense effort and erudition . . . but on
the whole dead'. Not until Virginia Woolf's essay in the
TLS in 1919 did *Middlemarch* again take pride of place in an
intelligent critic's assessment of the novels; and that was so
generalised, such a brief mention, that the novel was still
overlooked by the reading public until it was rediscovered by
F. R. Leavis in his *Scrutiny* articles,[4] later incorporated in *The
Great Tradition* (1948).

We were not able, unfortunately, to reprint extracts from
The Great Tradition in this Casebook. Readers of *Middlemarch*,
however, would do well to turn to Dr Leavis's chapter on
George Eliot in that book. It contains some of his very best
criticism, acknowledging and demonstrating the greatness of
the novel, yet giving much of its space to an attack on the
assumption that Dorothea represents her author's strength
rather than her weakness. In other words, Dr Leavis took up
the issues raised by the novel where Colvin left them in 1873.
In doing so he was marking out the main area of critical disagreement for the next twenty years. Throughout *Middlemarch*,
he writes, 'George Eliot tends to identify herself with Dorothea,
though Dorothea is far from being the whole of George Eliot'.
There is a fair degree of uncertainty about this up to chap. 3
of the novel, at which point the flimsiness of the ironic perspective in which George Eliot tries to convince us that Dorothea
is being presented, is revealed for what it is. Here we are 'in
sight of unqualified self-identification'; the heroine is patently
'immune' from the irony functioning elsewhere. Later our
vision of Dorothea becomes the same as Will's vision of her in
the Vatican. We share his 'idealising' faculty, as we also share

her idealisation of him. And since Dorothea is at the moral centre of the novel, the self-indulgence George Eliot discloses in her presentation of her suggests a residual 'immaturity' in one who elsewhere shows herself to be one of the most adult novelists in the great tradition: 'We have an alternation between the poised impersonal insight of a finely tempered wisdom and something like the emotional confusions and self-importances of adolescence'. This is backed up with brief and pointed comments on important passages from the text.

A lot of modern criticism takes the form of a reply to Dr Leavis, insisting either that Dorothea is not the moral centre of the book his assessment of it takes her to be – the most competent example of this approach is probably contained in Dr Daiches's little book on *Middlemarch*; or that, granted she *is* the moral centre, she is not so unaware of her deficiencies (and, more important, Geoge Eliot is not so unaware of them) as Dr Leavis supposes she is – Derek Oldfield's contribution to Miss Hardy's symposium on *Middlemarch* takes this line. It seems to me, though, that the most successful attempt to justify George Eliot in the face of Dr Leavis's indictment takes up neither of these points of view. Laurence Lerner's recent essay in *The Truthtellers* happily accepts both that Dorothea is the moral centre and that her deficiencies are precisely those Dr Leavis says they are, but that to insist that they are indeed 'deficiencies' is to be guilty oneself of taking up a moral position apropos of the issues thrown up by the novel which is not itself unassailable: 'I think that Leavis is right and Daiches wrong about the balance of the book: Dorothea is its moral centre. But I think Leavis is wrong and George Eliot right about her soul-hunger.' He disagrees that the undoubted personal interest George Eliot takes in Dorothea is, in Dr Leavis's words, a 'deflecting' one. It all depends on how you value 'maturity' and how you value what Mr Lerner calls 'the Theresa-complex' – the impulsion to idealise one's own conduct and to change the society in which such forms of idealisation are confounded with immaturity. What has happened is that Dr Leavis 'has passed off his ethical disagreement as if it were a discovery of an artistic flaw'. This is certainly an ingenious answer. But is it a convincing one? For instance, how does it account for the superiority of Dorothea's 'confessional' scenes with Lydgate and with Rosamond in *Middlemarch* over similar scenes between Dinah Morris and Hetty Sorrel in *Adam Bede*? And how does it account for the uncomfortable feeling that many people have in reading *Middlemarch* that what was weak in such a scene from the earlier book is not entirely exorcised in the later, that Dinah and Dorothea share as much as they do not share, and that what they share is not entirely a strength and will in turn be largely responsible for the disaster of Daniel Deronda's presentation in his scenes with Gwendolen Harleth in George Eliot's next book? I think Dr Leavis's quotations from the text reveal the 'unreduced enclave of immaturity' he claims they reveal, that the uncertain play of irony around the figure of Dorothea shows that George Eliot was aware of this and unhappy at not being able to absorb it into more responsible forms of idealisation, and that this means we have an artistic and not an ethical problem to confront. Even so, there is a justice to be done to Dorothea's 'ardour' which Dr Leavis does not do, and it may well be that Mr Lerner's essay has done something to right the balance of our response to her.

The immaturity, if that is what it is, that Dr Leavis discovered in Dorothea, other critics have found not so much in any one particular character as in George Eliot's vision of society as it is displayed in *Middlemarch*. The most impressive of these approaches has been that of Dr Kettle, who observes a discrepancy between the author's sense of the 'contradictions within every action and situation' in her rendering of 'individual personal experiences' and her lack of it in her rendering of public ones. This accounts for her 'static' view of society, her inability to see not merely the power of society but the way it changes: 'though George Eliot hates *Middlemarch* she believes in its inevitability'. This in turn helps to explain the unsatisfactoriness other critics have felt about the presentation of Dorothea. Perhaps the equivocal role she plays in the novel can be attributed to George Eliot's defective sense of history as much as to the 'private indulgence' theory we have seen in Dr Leavis's essay. Dr Kettle's 'historical' approach offers him a Dorothea who 'represents that element in human experience for which in the determinist universe of mechanistic materialism there is no place – the need of man to change the world he inherits'. This emphatically is not to equate Dorothea's immaturity with the 'need of man to change the world', but to explain the author's handling of Dorothea's immaturity by drawing attention to George Eliot's refusal to come to terms with a Dorothea figure who might be quite realistically and at the same time ironically presented, *and* responsibly and actively opposed to *Middlemarch* and what it represents. But this is surely to say, after all, that George Eliot did not hate *Middlemarch* as much as Dr Kettle says she did.

Professor Kermode's piece is a part of a much longer essay on apocalypse in both *Middlemarch* and Lawrence's *Women in Love*. My own feeling is that it is elegantly confused: that to insist upon a movement of thought from political crisis to apocalypse of any kind is quite out of place in a discussion of this novel, and that the meanings of words have been stretched not a little to encompass two widely dissimilar novels within a single theoretical system. A 'humanised' or 'Feuerbachian' apocalypse is in my view not an apocalypse at all. It is a change from one social system to another – in this case gradual, partial and uncertain. If this is an important essay it is so by virtue of the fact that it testifies to the ability of many academic theorists to believe in the sophistry that muddled and undirected change is a viable form – in present-day Western societies perhaps the only viable form – of revolutionary action. As such, it probably tells us more about the forces of reaction and change in modern Britain than it does about *Middlemarch*.

With Professor Hardy and Dr Harvey the wheel has come full circle. Both attend closely to the surface of the novel. Both are intellectually aware of structural parallels and contrasts in *Middlemarch* which only a few of its contemporary critics had any grasp of at all. But with all their sophisticated techniques of analysis, what they are really after is that sense of life which all the Victorians from Collins to James seem to have had an instinctive feeling for in the novels of their own day. What they value in *Middlemarch* is, in Dr Harvey's words, 'that peculiarly open effect . . . that sense of life spreading out and continuing in time'. I think all the critics represented in the collection value this, and that in their different ways they are trying to account for it. It is certainly a good place to stop a critical survey and reopen the novel itself.

PATRICK SWINDEN

NOTES

1. In chap. 6 of Barbara Hardy's *Middlemarch: Critical Approaches* (1967) pp. 125-47.

2. *Examiner*, 2 Dec 1871, 3 Feb 1872, 30 Mar 1872, 8 June 1872, 27 July 1872, 5 Oct 1872, 7 Dec 1872; *Spectator*, 16 Dec 1871, 3 Feb 1872, 30 Mar 1872, 5 Oct 1872, 7 Dec 1872; *Athenaeum*, 2 Dec 1871, 3 Feb 1872, 30 Mar 1872, 1 June 1872, 27 July 1872, 7 Dec 1872.

3. See George Saintsbury, *Fortnightly Review*, XLIII (Jan 1888) 118; and Lena Milman, 'A Few Notes on Henry James', *Yellow Book*, VII (Oct 1895) 71-83.

4. See *Scrutiny*, XIII 4 (spring 1946) 268-71 and XIV 7 (summer 1946) 15-26.

PART ONE

Earlier Comments, 1869—1873

EXTRACTS FROM GEORGE ELIOT'S JOURNAL AND CORRESPONDENCE

George Eliot's Journal, 1 January 1869
I have set myself many tasks for the year. I wonder how many will be accomplished? – a novel called *Middlemarch*, a long poem on Timoleon, and several minor poems.

19 July 1869
Writing an introduction to *Middlemarch*.

23 July 1869
Meditated characters for *Middlemarch*.

2 August 1869
Began *Middlemarch*.

5 August 1869
This morning I finished the first chapter of *Middlemarch*.

1 September 1869
I meditated characters and conditions for *Middlemarch*, which stands still in the beginning of ch. iii.

11 September 1869
I do not feel very confident that I can make anything satisfactory of *Middlemarch*.

2 December 1870
I am experimenting in a story ['Miss Brooke'], which I began without any serious intention of carrying it out lengthily. It is a subject which has been recorded among my possible themes ever since I began to write fiction, but will probably take new shapes in the development.

31 December 1870
I have written only 100 pages – good printed pages – of a story which I began about the opening of November, and at present mean to call 'Miss Brooke'.

John Blackwood to George Eliot, 20 July 1871

I have read the second portion of *Middlemarch* with the greatest admiration. It is a most wonderful study of human life and nature. You are like a great giant walking about among us and fixing every one you meet upon your canvas. In all this life-like gallery that you put before us every trait in every character finds an echo or recollection in the reader's mind that tells him how true it is to Nature.

It was a disappointment at first not to find any of my old friends of the former part, all except Lydgate apparently entirely strangers, but as you beautifully express it we never know who are to influence our lives while 'Destiny stands by sarcastic with our dramatis personae folded in her hand'. The elaborate picture of the formation of Lydgate's character is powerfully relieved by the tremendous French adventure into which the wise young Doctor fell. It would be endless to try to refer to all the happy hits and turns. That sylph caught young and made perfect by Mrs Lemon is a great success, and I like poor Ned. Where did you hear those horsey men talking? Willie's room at George St opens from my room and I often hear the mysterious words of wisdom flowing between him and his horsey yeomany friends. You have caught the very tone.

The Farebrother family are delights, a perfect picture. Reading of all the various characters in this second volume – for it is really almost a volume – I had quite forgotten Mr Brooke, but I *knew his voice* the moment he came into the room at the meeting for the election of Chaplain. There is something uncommonly good about Mary Garth who has her 'peculiar temptations' not to accept 'good sense and good principle' 'ready mixed' and does feel it hard to think that she must be called 'an ugly thing' alongside of fair Rosamond.

I think our plan of publication is the right one as the two parts are almost distinct, each complete in itself. Indeed there will be complaints of the want of the continuous interest of a story, but this does not matter where all is so fresh and true to life. Each group that you introduce is a complete little book or study in itself.

George Eliot to John Blackwood, 24 July 1871

Mr Lewes has been saying that it may perhaps be well to take
in a portion of Part II at the end of Part I. But it is too early for
such definite arrangements. I don't see how I can leave anything out, because I hope there is nothing that will be seen to
be irrelevant to my design, which is to show the gradual action
of ordinary causes rather than exceptional, and to show this in
some directions which have not been from time immemorial
the beaten path – the Cremorne walks and shows of fiction.
But the best intentions are good for nothing until execution
has justified them. And you know I am always compassed about
with fears. I am in danger in all my designs of parodying dear
Goldsmith's satire on Burke, and think of refining when novel
readers only think of skipping.

George Eliot's Journal, 1 December 1871

This day the first part of *Middlemarch* was published. I ought by
this time to have finished the fourth part, but an illness . . . has
robbed me of two months.

29 January 1872

I have finished the fourth part – i.e. the second volume of
Middlemarch. The first part, published on December 1, has been
excellently well received; the second part will be published the
day after to-morrow.

John Blackwood to G. H. Lewes, 3 February 1872

Part II will more than sustain the reputation of Part I and
as for Part III it is transcendant. I cannot imagine anything of
its kind more neat than the capture of Lydgate. It is done with
such fine touches, is so simple and *so true*. Who does not remember at battledore the effect of stooping at the same moment
with a fair friend to pick up the fallen shuttlecock? I remember
one case in particular when if the tear had been there as well as
the smile I would have been done for at a very early stage in life.

Joseph Munt Langford to John Blackwood, 11 March 1872

The Third Book of *Middlemarch* seems to me first-rate – as

good as anything she has written. The number and variety of characters each clear and distinct and standing on its own legs are perfectly marvellous; – down to the Vet and Mr Bowyer 'hoping somebody will invite him to dinner' one feels them all to be *true to life*. The death of old Featherstone is most powerful. She is wonderful in the faculty, when she has to be forcible, of getting at the right word and phrase directly and without beating about the bush for strong language. There is no hesitation or doubt when the blow has to be struck at the imagination. The humorous touches are delicious – what a group the family in waiting is. One thing I do not like is the habit of putting her characters at a distance as if to look at them and then making remarks on them.

George Eliot to Sara Hennell, 22 March 1872
Owing to my loss of two months in illness and my infirm health ever since, I have not yet finished the writing of *Middlemarch*.

George Eliot to Alexander Main, 29 March 1872
Try to keep from forecast of Dorothea's lot, and that sort of construction beforehand which makes everything that actually happens a disappointment. I need not tell you that my book will not present my own feeling about human life if it produces on readers whose minds are really receptive the impression of blank melancholy and despair. I can't help wondering at the high estimate made of *Middlemarch* in proportion to my other books. I suppose the depressed state of my health makes my writing seem more than usually below the mark of my desires, and I am too anxious about its completion – too fearful lest the impression which it might make (I mean for the good of those who read) should turn to nought – to look at it in mental sunshine.

John Blackwood to George Eliot, 29 April 1872
I inclose some memoranda of *Middlemarch* Book III which show that there is a pleasing movement going on although not so rapid as one could wish.

George Eliot's Journal, 1 January 1873

At the beginning of December, the eighth and last book of
Middlemarch was published, the three final numbers having
been published monthly.

George Eliot to Charles Ritter, 11 February 1873

From what you say about public criticism, you will understand
why Mr Lewes keeps all reviews of my book away from me. If
he reads them himself, he only gives me an occasional quotation
which he thinks will cheer me by its exceptional insight. But
he has not yet seen the article in the *Revue des Deux Mondes* to
which you refer.[1] Though *Middlemarch* seems to have made a
deep impression in our own country, and though the critics are
as polite and benevolent as possible to me, there has not, I
believe, been one really able review of the book in our newspapers and periodicals.

NOTE

1. Th. Bentzon, 'Le Roman de la vie de province en angleterre',
Revue des Deux Mondes, no. 103 (Feb 1873), pp. 667–90. See below,
pp. 56–60. Ritter wrote of 'la sottise épaisse des critiques (voir
l'absurde article dans la *Revue des Deux Mondes* sur *Middlemarch*)'.

CONTEMPORARY REVIEWS

[R. H. HUTTON?] *Spectator*, 1 June 1872

We all grumble at *Middlemarch*; we all say that the action is slow, that there is too much parade of scientific and especially physiological knowledge in it, that there are turns of phrase which are even pedantic, and that occasionally the bitterness of the commentary on life is almost cynical; but we all read it, and all feel that there is nothing to compare with it appearing at the present moment in the way of English literature, and not a few of us calculate whether we shall get the August number before we go for our autumn holiday, or whether we shall have to wait for it till we return. And yet does it really add to the happiness of its readers or not? We feel that we cannot do without it, that the criticisms on life given by our great novelist, and the pictures of life given by our great critic, are criticisms and pictures such as acquire a double value from the very fact that the criticisms are tested by such an insight and imagination as hers, and the pictures criticised by a judgment so fine and balanced as hers; – but we question whether any one lays the book down without either an extra tinge of melancholy in his feeling, or in its place, a combative disposition to challenge the tendency and dispute the fidelity of tone of the pictures he has been studying. It is not in any degree true that the incidents are specially melancholy. On the contrary, the story is not at all of a gloomy description, and there are characters in it which the reader enjoys as he enjoys a gleam of warm sunshine on a dull October day, – especially that of Caleb Garth, the happy, eager, unworldly land-surveyor. Then, again, there are pictures showing a humour so large and delicate that that laughter which really brightens the spirits breaks out even if we are alone, – especially the picture of the slip-shod-minded bachelor landowner, Mr Brooke, with his weakness for an economical administration of his estate, his odds and ends of ideas, his desultory 'documents' on all sorts of subjects of which he hopes to see something effective made some day, his disposition to dabble in Liberalism, his easy-going, easily daunted ambition, and his indolent restlessness. Mr Brooke, and Mrs Cadwallader, – the crisp-minded, witty, worldly, aristocratic rector's wife, – are enough to cheer the reader of any story, however intellectual, even if we were not always coming in for whiffs of dry humour from other quarters, – from the genial, dubious-minded, whist-playing vicar, for instance, as well as from what George Eliot insists on calling the 'low people' of the story. Still, in spite of these snatches of warm sunshine, and of the frequent springs of delightful humour, – at the end of almost every part and every chapter, if not nearly every page, there comes an involuntary sigh. George Eliot never makes the world worse than it is, but she makes it a shade darker. She paints the confusions of life no worse than they are, but she steadily discourages the hope that there is any light for us behind the cloud. She is large in her justice to the visible elements in human nature, but she throws cold water with a most determined hand on the idealism, as she evidently thinks it, which interprets by faith what cannot be interpreted by sympathy and sight.

For instance, in this new June part, – the ablest yet issued, – nothing can be more melancholy than the language of her final criticism on old Featherstone, not so much for its implied belief that there are plenty of human beings without any good at all left in them, as for the hint she throws out that it is those with the truest and deepest knowledge of man such as she and men of equal endowments possess, who have most reason to believe this, while the opposite belief, – the belief in 'the soul of goodness in things evil', – is due to the idealism of merely theoretic opinion. 'If any one will here contend,' she says, 'that there must have been traits of goodness in old Featherstone, I will not presume to deny this; but I must observe that goodness is of a modest nature, easily discouraged, and when much elbowed in early life by unabashed vices, is apt to retire into extreme privacy, so that it is more easily believed in by those who construct a selfish old gentleman theoretically, than by those who form the narrower judgments based on his personal acquaintance.' The sneer there against the idealists increases instead of diminishing the melancholy impression produced. It seems to say not merely that the truest insight sees much more of unalloyed evil in the world than the sentimentalism of the day chooses to suppose, but that, after all, it does not very much matter, – that a sarcasm is quite as suitable, by way of attack on such a popular sentimentalism, as a grave and reluctant refutation. From George Eliot such a tone really jars us. Let her say, if she will, what no one has a better right to say with authority, that there are many characters so selfish as not to show a trace of anything good; but she should hardly say it with the taunting air of one who despises the world for its credulity.

Perhaps, however, the deepest symptom of melancholy in this book is the disposition so marked in it to draw the most reflective and most spiritual characters as the least happy. It is not a new thing for George Eliot to draw clergymen of large, tolerant, charitable character, with no great belief in dogma, and not a little secret uneasiness as to their position as spiritual teachers; but she always takes care that the larger the nature and the more spiritual the charity, the less is there any appearance of real rest and satisfaction of spirit. There are two clergymen of this class in *Middlemarch*, Mr Cadwallader, and Mr Farebrother, both of them men of large nature and good hearts, but Mr Farebrother, certainly the abler and wiser and more genuinely religious of the two, is certainly also, as the authoress constantly makes you feel, the least happy. She is always touching gently and compassionately Mr Farebrother's slight moral weaknesses, – his preference for comfortable drawing-rooms and whist, especially whist at which he can make certain small but steady winnings, over the duties of his calling, – his eagerness for the salary of the hospital chaplaincy, for the salary rather than for the work which should earn the salary; – and she takes pains to give the impression of spiritual *wistfulness*, rather than faith, as the hidden centre of the vicar's Christianity. But the most remarkable thread of spiritual melancholy in the book constitutes the real end for which it is written, – the picture of Dorothea's beautiful and noble, but utterly unsatisfied and unresting character, and the illustration of the wreck of happiness which results from her unguided spiritual cravings. In one of the most beautiful, but also one of the most melancholy passages of this new part, Dorothea Casaubon confesses her faith, and how little she can lean on any divine power external to herself for its fulfilment. The private belief, she says, to which she clings as her only comfort, is 'that by desiring what is perfectly good, even when we don't quite know what it is and cannot do what we would, we are part of the divine power against evil, – widening the skirts of light, and making the struggle narrower'. And she goes on, 'Please not to call it [this faith] by any name. You will say it is Persian, or something else geographical. It is my life. I have found it out, and cannot part with it. I have always been finding out my religion since I was a little girl. I used to pray so much; now I hardly ever pray. I try not to have desires merely for myself, because they may not be good for others, and I have too much already.' That is exquisitely truthful and exquisitely melancholy, – the passion of a soul compelled almost to give up prayer as too exhausting, because it seems the radiation of force into a vacuum, and yet retaining all the passionate love for higher guidance in which prayer finds its source and its justification. And just as Dorothea finds no real access of spiritual strength in the religious life, beyond that which expresses itself in her desire for a religious life, so her unhappy, narrow-hearted husband finds no remedy for his own smallness of life, for his jealousy, in the religious ideas which he accepts. He reflects that his recent seizure – a heart-seizure – might not mean an early death, that he might still have twenty years of work left in him to prove to the critics – Messrs Carp and Company – who had ridiculed his mighty preparations for small achievements, that they had been mistaken. 'To convince Carp of his mistake,' says our author, 'so that he would have to eat his own words with a good deal of indigestion, would be an agreeable accident of triumphant authorship, which the prospect of living to future ages on earth, and to all eternity in Heaven, could not exclude from contemplation. Since thus the prevision of his own ever-enduring bliss could not nullify the bitter savours of irritated jealousy and vindictiveness, it is the less surprising that the probability of transient earthly bliss for other persons, when he himself should have entered into glory, had not a potently sweetening effect. If the truth should be that some undermining disease was at work within him, there might be large opportunity for some people to be the happier when he was gone; and if one of those people should be Will Ladislaw, Mr Casaubon objected so strongly, that it seemed as if the annoyance would make part of his disembodied existence.' There you get again, not only the melancholy, but the harsh, caustic tone, – the tone which the author takes when she is disparaging a faith which she thinks vulgar as well as untrue, – the jeering tone in which she says, in describing the creatures of prey who attended old Featherstone's funeral, 'When the animals entered the Ark in pairs, one may imagine that allied species made much private remark on each other, and were tempted to think that so many forms feeding on the same store of fodder were eminently superfluous, as tending to diminish the rations. (I fear that the part played by the vultures on that occasion would be too painful for Art to represent, those birds being disadvantageously naked about the gullet, and apparently without rites and ceremonies.)' Sentences such as these give an occasional impression that George Eliot really likes jeering at human evil, which it is most painful to imagine in one who has so noble and so high a conception of good. One almost gathers that she regards the large speculative power she possesses as itself a source of pure unhappiness. The happiest creatures she draws are those who are most able, like Caleb Garth or Adam Bede, to absorb their whole minds and sink their whole energies in limited but positive duties of visible utility. Go a little higher in the scale to a being like Dorothea, full of nobility of the highest kind, but without a definite practical sphere, and compelled to lavish her life on spiritual efforts to subdue her own enthusiasm, her throbbing, inward yearning for a higher life, and we are in a world of unhappiness.

where rest is never found. But the height of this unhappiness comes out in the authoress's own comments on the universe and its structure, including in that structure its religions. She takes side gallantly and nobly with the power that wars against evil. The hope that she can do something on that side is part of her life. She has found it out, and cannot part with it. But she has a very poor hope of the issue. She sees evil, and sees it not seldom even unmixed with good in the hearts around her, and scoffs at the attempt to suppose that they are better than they seem. She sees narrowness so oppressive to her that she is constantly laughing a scornful laugh over it, and despairing of any better euthanasia for it than its extinction. And all this makes her bitter. She clings to the nobler course, but she cannot repress discordant cries at the disorder of the universe and the weakness of the painfully struggling principle of good. She is a melancholy teacher, – melancholy because sceptical; and her melancholy scepticism is too apt to degenerate into scorn.

Athenaeum, 7 December 1872
If we have a fault to find in *Middlemarch,* it is that it is almost *too* laboured. Good as are the points, and telling as is their humour, they yet show far too clearly the *labor limae.* They have been written and re-written, polished and re-polished, until they glitter almost painfully. When Mrs Cadwallader says that Casaubon's great soul is a great bladder for dried peas to rattle in, and when she adds to this the further remark that a drop of his blood was put under a magnifying glass, and it was all semicolons and parentheses, we cannot resist a certain sense of effort. It is possible to take even too much pains, and not sufficiently to hide the symptoms of our art. Paradoxical as it may seem to say so, *Middlemarch* would probably have pleased most of us more than it does if it had been written in a greater hurry.

[w. l. collins] *Blackwood's Edinburgh Magazine,* December 1872
There is one observation which strikes us more forcibly in reading these volumes than in any others which have come to

us from the same hand. It is the power which the writer shows in awakening, not only our interest in, but our sympathies with, nearly all the prominent characters in the full drama of the story. In most novels, there is at least some one creation of the author's fancy on whose brightness a shadow is seldom allowed to fall, in whose cause we become partisans, and whose greatest weaknesses are cleverly excused. Or, if the hero or heroine are not so near perfection in the outset, some discipline or other is introduced in the course of the story, which in the end completes and purifies the character. And in some sense, if the novelist is to be regarded as a moral teacher, this seems in accordance with the fitness of things. But such is by no means the principle upon which the author of *Middlemarch* works. We find in these volumes nothing of the conventional hero or heroine. As, even in the most disagreeable characters, we are shown in almost every instance the good that is working in them fitfully here and there, so in the portraits of the favourites the shadows are not left out. The only personages in the story with whom we are never angry or disappointed are those in whom we are never called upon to take any very lively interest – who have not character enough to involve contradictions, – such as Sir James Chettam and Celia. Dorothea provokes us continually in the first book, until we scarcely pity her, though we can foresee much of the result, when she marries Casaubon; there is an Epicurean selfishness about Lydgate, in spite of his nobler aspirations, which makes us feel that the lower form of selfishness in others from which he is made to suffer has in it something of retributive justice; Ladislaw is full of weaknesses and irresolution. On the other hand, there is no one who acts thoroughly the 'villain' in the piece; Rosamond, who most rouses our indignation, is after all more contemptible than hateful; there is no one in whose frustrated designs the virtuous reader (what a tribute it is to the divinity of righteousness that we all become so virtuous when we sit down to read!) feels the sort of triumph which David proclaims over his enemies. Casaubon, with all his pedantic narrowness, is, perhaps, the most pathetic conception in the book; and when Bulstrode is at last exposed and makes his miserable exit, so intensely have we been made to feel the mental agony and bitter humiliation of the man, that we are inclined to take his arm, as Lydgate does, and help him to his carriage. The creatures are all so intensely human, even in their baser aspects, that in spite of that sevenfold shield of virtue behind which we shelter ourselves, as has been said, when we sit in judgment on the characters of fiction, an honest conscience hesitates to cast the stone. . . .

[EDITH SIMCOX] *Academy*, 1 January 1873
Middlemarch marks an epoch in the history of fiction in so far as its incidents are taken from the inner life, as the action is developed by the direct influence of mind on mind and character on character, as the material circumstances of the outer world are made subordinate and accessory to the artistic presentation of a definite passage of mental experience, but chiefly as giving a background of perfect realistic truth to a profoundly imaginative psychological study. The effect is as new as if we could suppose a *Wilhelm Meister* written by Balzac. In *Silas Marner*, *Romola*, and the author's other works there is the same power, but it does not so completely and exclusively determine the form in which the conception is placed before us. In *Silas Marner* there is a natural and obvious unity in the life of the weaver, but in *Romola* – where alone the interest is at once as varied and as profound as in *Middlemarch* – though the historic glories of Florence, the passions belonging to what, as compared with the nineteenth century, is an heroic age, are in perfect harmony with the grand manner of treating spiritual problems, yet the realism, the positive background of fact, which we can scarcely better bear to miss, has necessarily some of the character of an hypothesis, and does not inspire us with the same confidence as truths we can verify for ourselves. For that reason alone, on the mere point of artistic harmony of construction, we should rate the last work as the greatest; and to say that *Middlemarch* is George Eliot's greatest work is to say that it has scarcely a superior and very few equals in the whole wide range of English fiction.

As 'a study of provincial life', if it were nothing more, *Middlemarch* would have a lasting charm for students of human nature in its less ephemeral costumes; besides the crowds of men and women whom we have all known in real life, where, however, to our dimmer vision, they seemed less real and life-like than in the book, the relations between the different clusters, the proportions in which the different elements mix, the points of contact and the degree of isolation in the different ranks; the contented coexistence of town and county, the channels of communication between the two always open and yet so rarely used, the effect of class distinctions in varying the mental horizon and obliging the most matter-of-fact observer to see a few things in perspective, – all the subtle factors which make up the character of a definite state of society are given with inimitable accuracy and fulness of insight. The picture in its main outlines is as true of the England of to-day or the England of a hundred years ago as of the England of the Reform agitation. The world as we know it has its wise and good, its fools and hypocrites scattered up and down a neutral-tinted mass in much the same proportion as at Middlemarch. The only difference is that they are not so plainly recognisable, and this is perhaps the reason that a first perusal of the book seems to have an almost oppressive effect on ordinary readers, somewhat as little children are frightened at a live automaton toy. It is not natural to most men to know so much of their fellow-creatures as George Eliot shows them, to penetrate behind the scenes in so many homes, to understand the motives of ambiguous conduct, to watch 'like gods knowing good and evil' the tangled course of intermingled lives, the remote mainsprings of impulse and the wide-eddying effects of action. Even with the author's assistance it is not easy to maintain the same height of observant wisdom for long, and since the intricacy of the subject is real, a feeling of even painful bewilderment in its contemplation is not entirely unbecoming.

But the complicated conditions of so seemingly simple a thing as provincial life are not the main subject of the work. The busy idleness of Middlemarch, its trade, its politics, its vestry meetings, and its neighbouring magnates, only form the background of relief to two or three spiritual conflicts, the scenery amongst which two or three souls spend some eventful years in working out their own salvation and their neighbours', or in effecting, with equal labour, something less than salvation for both. The story of these conflicts and struggles is the thread which unites the whole, and sympathy with its incidents is the force that reconciles the reader to the unwonted strain upon his intellectual faculties already noticed; and to the yet further effort necessary to recognise the fact that the real and the ideal sides of our common nature do coexist in just such relations, and with just such proportionate force as the author reveals. For, without this admission, it is impossible to appreciate the full literary and artistic perfection of the work as a whole; some readers may delight spontaneously in the author's moral earnestness, and only admire her satirical insight, while others delight in her satire and coldly admit the excellence of the moral purpose; but the two are only opposite aspects of the same large theory of the universe, which is at once so charitable and so melancholy that it would be fairly intolerable (although true) without the sauce of an unsparing humour.

Middlemarch is the story of two rather sad fatalities, of two lives which, starting with more than ordinary promise, had to rest content with very ordinary achievement, and could not derive unmixed consolation from the knowledge, which was the chief prize of their struggles, that failure is never altogether undeserved. One of the original mottoes to the first book gives the clue to what follows:

> *1st Gent.* Our deeds are fetters that we forge ourselves.
> *2nd Gent.* Ay, truly; but I think it is the world
> That brings the iron:

but as the action proceeds a further consciousness gathers shape: 'It always remains true that if we had been greater circumstances would have been less strong against us'; which is still more simply expressed in Dorothea's 'feeling that there was always something better which she might have done, if she had only been better and known better'. The two failures, however, have little in common but their irrevocable necessity. From one point of view, Dorothea's is the most tragical, for the fault in her case seems to be altogether in the nature and constitution of the universe; her devotion and purity of intention are altogether beautiful, even when, for lack of knowledge, they are expended in what seems to be the wrong place, but it is a sad reflection that their beauty must always rest on a basis of illusion because there is no right place for their bestowal. Except in the chapter of her marriages Dorothea is a perfect woman, but for a perfect woman any marriage is a *mésalliance*, and as such, 'certainly those determining acts of her life were not ideally beautiful'. But we can as little tell as the Middlemarchers 'what else that was in her power she ought rather to have done'. If she had had no illusions she might have been a useful Lady Bountiful, managing her own affairs like Goethe's Theresa, a personage who inspires but mediocre interest, and might have married Mrs Cadwallader's philanthropic Lord Triton without suspicion of *mésalliance*: but then she would not have been Dorothea, not the impetuous young woman with 'a heart large enough for the Virgin Mary', whose sighs, when she thinks her lover is untrue, are breathed for 'all the troubles of all the people on the face of the earth'. The world must be ugly for her power of seeing it as it is not to be beautiful, just as men's lives must be sad and miserable to call for the exercise of her infinite charity. Still the illusions are sweet and the charity beneficent, and since women like Dorothea are content to live only for others, life may offer occasions enough for self-sacrifice to compensate them for the natural impossibility of shaping an ideally perfect course through the multitudinous imperfections of real existence. It would be ungenerous to accept such a fate for them without reluctance, and therefore some sadness must always mix with our thoughts of the historic and unhistoric Dorotheas of the world; but it is also true that the moral force exercised by such characters can no more be wasted than any physical impulse, and that, without the disinterested virtue of the few, the conflicting appetites of a world of Rosamonds would make life impossible. To keep society alive is perhaps a worthier mission than to cheer the declining years of Mr Casaubon; but to do more than keep it alive, to make it a fit home for future Dorotheas, the present supply of such missionaries would have to be increased; and they are born, not made. Perhaps the strongest example of the author's instinctive truthfulness is that she never loses sight of the limits to the exercise of the power which she represents so vividly and values so highly. A life's growth of empty egotism like Mr Casaubon's cannot be melted in a year of marriage, even to Dorothea; with a generous example close before her, Rosamond can be almost honest for once at little expense, but she can no more change her character than her complexion or the colour of her eyes, or than she can unmake the whole series of circumstances which have made her life less negatively innocent than Celia's. A little more selfishness, a little more obstinacy, a little less good fortune, and especially life in a just lower moral atmosphere, make all the difference between a pretty, prosaic, kittenish wife and a kind of well-conducted domestic vampire. It is by such contrasts as these that George Eliot contrives to preach tolerance even while showing with grim distinctness the ineffaceableness of moral distinctions and the unrelenting force of moral obligations. If virtue is a matter of capacity, defect only calls for pity; but defects which we do not venture to blame may be none the less fatal to the higher life, while the smallest shoot of virtue, if the heavens and earth chance to be propitious to its growth, may spread into a stately tree.

Such at least is the inference suggested by another contrast, that between Lydgate and Fred, for though marriage appears the 'determining act' in their lives also, it is itself determined by certain essential points of character and disposition. Fred's honest boyish affection for a girl who is a great deal too good for him brings its own reward, as that kind of virtue often will; there was enough self-abandonment in it to deserve a generous answer, and in the long-run people generally get their deserts. The failure of Lydgate's intellectual aspirations, as the consequence of a marriage contracted altogether at the bidding of his lower nature, is of course much more elaborately treated than Fred's simple 'love-problem'. Unlike most of the other characters, Lydgate does not become thoroughly intelligible till the last number of the work has been read in connection with the first: then he appears as a masculine counterpart to Dorothea with the relative proportions of head and heart reversed. But while it was abstractedly impossible for Dorothea to be altogether wise, without detriment to the peculiar and charming character of her goodness, there was nothing but concrete human infirmity to prevent Lydgate from combining the mind of Bichat and the morals of Fred Vincy. Instead of such a compound the actual and very human Lydgate is one of those men whose lives are cut in two, whose intellectual interests have no direct connection with their material selves, and who only discover the impossibility of living according to habit or tradition when brought by accident or their own heedlessness face to face with difficulties that require thought as well as resolution. There was not room in the life he contemplated for a soul much larger than Rosamond's, and it may be doubted whether the Rosamond he wished for would not, by a merely passive influence, have been as obstructive to his wide speculations, for he was just, though not expansive, and the duties entailed by one act of weakness may multiply and branch as much as if they were of a valuable stock. On the other hand, if the scientific ardour had been more absorbing, he might have gone on his own way, crushing all poor Rosamond's little schemes of opposition, and then she would have been the victim instead of the oppressor, but his character would have been as far from ideal excellence as before. The interest culminates when Lydgate, entangled with the consequences of his own and other people's wrongdoing, finds in Dorothea the beneficent influence that spends itself in setting straight whatever is not constitutionally crooked, but he has also of course found out by then that the events which led him to cross her path were the same that had proved fatal to his aspirations; the enlarged sympathies were gathered during the process that paralysed his original activity. The story of a man 'who has not done what he once meant to do' has always a strong element of pathos, but when what he meant to do was not in itself impossible, like the realisation of Dorothea's visions, there remains a twofold consolation; if possible in itself, and yet not done as proposed, it must have been impossible to the proposer, and therefore his failure is free from blame, while disappointment of his hopes, though painful, cannot be regarded as an unmitigated evil, since such fallen aspirations as Lydgate's are still something it is better to have had than to be altogether without. Natural fatality and the logic of facts are made to persuade us that all regrets are unpractical except the most unpractical of all – 'if we had only known better and been better' – but the first step towards solving a problem is to state it; and one of the many merits of *Middlemarch* is that it shows the inadequacy of all other less arduous short cuts to the reformation of society. Ordinary mortals who are not fatalists have no excuse for calling a book sad which makes the redress of every one's wrongs rest in the last resort with themselves; while people whose idea of the world is already as gloomy as it well can be, cannot fail to derive some consolation from the thought that George Eliot's wider knowledge and juster perceptions find here and there a little to admire as well as much everywhere to laugh at. . . .

[SIDNEY COLVIN] *Fortnightly Review*, 1 January 1873
Fifteen months of pausing and recurring literary excitement are at an end; and *Middlemarch*, the chief English book of the immediate present, lies complete before us. Now that we have the book as a whole, what place does it seem to take among the rest with which its illustrious writer has enriched, I will not say posterity, because for posterity every present is apt in turn to prove itself a shallow judge, but her own generation and us who delight to honour her?

In the sense in which anything is called ripe because of fulness and strength, I think the last of George Eliot's novels is also the ripest. *Middlemarch* is extraordinarily full and strong, even among the company to which it belongs. And though I am not sure that it is the property of George Eliot's writing to satisfy, its property certainly is to rouse and attach, in proportion to its fulness and strength. There is nothing in the literature of the day so rousing – to the mind of the day there is scarcely anything so rousing in all literature – as her writing is. What she writes is so full of her time. It is observation, imagination, pathos, wit and humour, all of a high class in themselves; but what is more, all saturated with modern ideas, and poured into a language of which every word bites home with peculiar sharpness to the contemporary consciousness. That is what makes it less safe than it might seem at first sight to speak for posterity in such a case. We are afraid of exaggerating the meaning such work will have for those who come after us, for the very reason that we feel its meaning so pregnant for ourselves. If, indeed, the ideas of to-day are certain to be the ideas of to-morrow and the day after, if scientific thought and the positive synthesis are indubitably to rule the world, then any one, it should seem, might speak boldly enough to George Eliot's place. For the general definition of her work, I should say, is precisely this – that, among writers of the imagination, she has taken the lead in expressing and discussing the lives and ways of common folks – *votum, timor, ira, voluptas* – in terms of scientific thought and the positive synthesis. She has walked between two epochs, upon the confines of two worlds, and has described the old in terms of the new. To the old world belong the elements of her experience, to the new world the elements of her reflection on experience. The elements of her experience are the 'English Provincial Life' before the Reform Bill – the desires and alarms, indignations and satisfactions, of the human breast in county towns and villages, farms and parsonages, manor-houses, counting-houses, surgeries, streets and lanes, shops and fields, of midlands unshaken in their prejudices and unvisited by the steam-engine. To the new world belong the elements of her reflection; the many-sided culture which looks back upon prejudice with analytical amusement; the philosophy which declares the human family deluded in its higher dreams, dependent upon itself, and bound thereby to a closer if a sadder brotherhood; the habit in regarding and meditating physical laws, and the facts of sense and life, which leads up to that philosophy and belongs to it; the mingled depth of bitterness and tenderness in the human temper of which the philosophy becomes the spring.

Thus there is the most pointed contrast between the matter of these English tales and the manner of their telling. The matter is antiquated in our recollections, the manner seems to anticipate the future of our thoughts. Plenty of other writers have taken humdrum and narrow aspects of English life with which they were familiar, and by delicacy of perception and justness of rendering have put them together into pleasant works of literary art, without running the matter into a manner out of direct correspondence with it. But this procedure of George Eliot's is a newer thing in literature, and infinitely harder to judge of, than the grey and tranquil harmonies of that other mode of art. For no writer uses so many instruments in riveting the interest of the cultivated reader about the characters, and springs of character, which she is exhibiting. First, I say, she has the perpetual application of her own intelligence to the broad problems and conclusions of modern thought. That, for instance, when Fred Vincy, having brought losses upon the Garth family, feels his own dishonour more than their suffering, brings the reflection how *we are most of us brought up in the notion that the highest motive for not doing a wrong is something irrespective of the beings who would suffer the wrong*. That again, a few pages later, brings the humorous allusions to Caleb Garth's classification of human employments, into business, politics, preaching, learning, and amusement, as one which *like the categories of more celebrated men, would not be acceptable in these more advanced times*. And that makes it impossible to describe the roguery of a horse-dealer without suggesting that he *regarded horse-dealing as the finest of the arts, and might have argued plausibly that it had nothing to do with morality*.

Next, this writer possesses, in her own sympathetic insight into the workings of human nature, a psychological instrument which will be perpetually displaying its power, its subtlety and

trenchancy, in passages like this which lays bare the working of
poor Mrs Bulstrode's faithful mind upon the revelation of her
husband's guilt: 'Along with her brother's looks and words,
there darted into her mind the idea of some guilt in her husband.
Then, under the working of terror, came the image of her
husband exposed to disgrace; *and then, after an instant of scorching
shame in which she only felt the eyes of the world, with one leap of her
heart she was at his side in mournful but unreproaching fellowship with
shame and isolation.*' Of the same trenchancy and potency, equally
subtle and equally sure of themselves, are a hundred other
processes of analysis, whether applied to serious crises – like
that prolonged one during which Bulstrode wavers before the
passive murder which shall rid him of his one obstacle as an
efficient servant of God – or to such trivial crises as occur in the
experiences of a Mrs Dollop or a Mrs Taft, or others who, being
their betters, still belong to the class of 'well-meaning women
knowing very little of their own motives'. And this powerful
knowledge of human nature is still only one of many instruments
for exposing a character and turning it about. What the character itself thinks and feels, exposed by this, will receive a simul-
taneous commentary in what the modern analytic mind has to
remark upon such thoughts and feelings: see a good instance in
the account (at page 98 of book III) of Mr Casaubon's motives
before marriage and experiences after it.

Then, the writer's studies in science and physiology will
constantly come in to suggest for the spiritual processes of her
personages an explanation here or an illustration there. For a
stroke of overwhelming power in this kind, take what is said
in one place of Bulstrode – that 'he shrank from a direct lie
with an intensity disproportionate to the number of his more
indirect misdeeds. *But many of these misdeeds were like the subtle
muscular movements which are not taken account of in the consciousness,
though they bring about the end that we fix in our minds and desire. And
it is only what we are vividly conscious of that we can vividly imagine to
be seen by Omniscience.*'

And it is yet another instrument which the writer handles
when she seizes on critical points of physical look and gesture

in her personages, in a way which is scientific and her own. True, there are many descriptions, and especially of the beauty and gestures of Dorothea – and these are written with a peculiarly loving and as it were watchful exquisiteness – which may be put down as belonging to the ordinary resources of art. But look at Caleb Garth; he is a complete physiognomical study in the sense of Mr Darwin, with the 'deepened depression in the outer angle of his bushy eyebrows, which gave his face a peculiar mildness'; with his trick of 'broadening himself by putting his thumbs into his arm-holes', and the rest. Such are Rosamond's ways of turning her neck aside and patting her hair when she is going to be obstinate. So, we are not allowed to forget 'a certain massiveness in Lydgate's manner and tone, corresponding with his physique'; nor indeed, any point of figure and physiognomy which strike the author's imagination as symptomatic. Symptomatic is the best word. There is a medical strain in the tissue of the story. There is a profound sense of the importance of physiological conditions in human life. But further still, I think, there is something like a medical habit in the writer, of examining her own creations for their symptoms, which runs through her descriptive and narrative art and gives it some of its peculiar manner.

So that, apart from the presence of rousing thought in general maxims and allusions, we know now what we mean when we speak of the fulness and strength derived, in the dramatic and narrative part of the work, from the use of so many instruments as we have seen. Then comes the question, do these qualities satisfy us as thoroughly as they rouse and interest? Sometimes I think they do, and sometimes not. Nothing evidently can be more satisfying, more illuminating, than that sentence which explained, by a primitive fact in the experimental relations of mind and body, a peculiar kind of bluntness in the conscience of the religious Bulstrode. And generally, wherever the novelist applies her philosophy or science to serious purposes, even if it may be applied too often, its effect seems to me good. But in lighter applications I doubt if the same kind of thing is not sometimes mistaken. The wit and humour of this writer every one of us knows and has revelled in; I do not think these want to gain body from an elaborate or semi-scientific language. In the expression of fun or common observation, is not such language apt to read a little technical and heavy, like a kind of intellectual slang? I do not think the delightful fun about Mrs Garth and Mary and the children gains by it. I doubt if it is in place when it is applied to the mental processes of Mrs Dollop or Mr Bambridge. And when, for example, we are asked to consider what would have happened if Fred Vincy's 'prophetic soul had been urged to particularise', that is what I mean by something like a kind of intellectual slang.

But all this only concerns some methods or processes of the writer, picked from random points in the development of her new story and its characters. What of these in themselves? Well, there comes back the old sense, of a difference to the degree to which we are roused, attached, and taught, and the degree to which we are satisfied. The book is full of high feeling, wisdom, and acuteness. It contains some of the most moving dramatic scenes in our literature. A scene like that of Dorothea in her night of agony, a scene like that in which the greatness of her nature ennobles for a moment the smallness of Rosamond's, is consummate alike in conception and in style. The characters are admirable in their vigour and individuality, as well as in the vividness and fulness of illustration with which we have seen that they are exhibited. Dorothea with her generous ardour and ideal cravings; Mr Brooke with his good-natured viewy incoherency and self-complacence; Celia with her narrow worldly sense seasoned by affectionateness; Chettam with his honourable prejudices; Ladislaw with his dispersed ambitions, and the dispositions and susceptibilities of his origin; Casaubon with his learning which is lumber, his formalism and inaccessibility of character, his distrust of himself and other people; Lydgate with his solid ambitions which fail, and his hollow which succeed; Rosamond 'with that hard slight thing called girlishness', and all the faults which can underlie skin-deep graces; Bulstrode with the piety designed in vain to propitiate the chastisement of destiny; the witty unscrupulous rattle of

Mrs Cadwallader; the Garth household, the Farebrother household, the Vincys, the country bankers and country tradesmen, the rival practitioners, the horse-dealer, the drunkard who is the ghost of Bulstrode's ancient sin – all these are living and abiding additions to every one's circle of the familiar acquaintances that importune not. But as one turns them over in one's mind or talk, them and their fortunes in the book, with laughter or sympathy or pity or indignation or love, there will arise all sorts of questionings, debatings, such as do not arise after a reading which has left the mind satisfied. One calls in question this or that point in the conduct of the story; the attitude which the writer personally assumes towards her own creations; the general lesson which seems to underlie her scheme; above all, the impression which its issue leaves upon oneself.

The questions one asks are such as, within limits like these, it would be idle to attempt to solve, or even to state, except in the most fragmentary way. Are not, for instance, some points in the story a little coarsely invented and handled? At the very outset, is not the hideous nature of Dorothea's blind sacrifice too ruthlessly driven home to us, when it ought to have been allowed to reveal itself by gentler degrees? Is it not too repulsive to talk of the moles on Casaubon's face, and to make us loathe the union from the beginning? Is not the formalism and dryness of Casaubon's nature a little overdone in his first conversation and his letter of courtship? Or again, is not the whole intrigue of Ladislaw's birth and Bulstrode's guilt, the Jew pawnbroker and Raffles, somewhat common and poor? The story is made to hinge twice, at two important junctures, upon the incidents of watching by a death-bed. Is that scant invention, or is it a just device for bringing out, under nearly parallel circumstances, the opposite characters of Mary Garth and of Bulstrode – her untroubled and decisive integrity under difficulties, his wavering conscience, which, when to be passive is already to be a murderer, permits itself at last in something just beyond passiveness? Or, to shift the ground of question, does not the author seem a little unwarrantably hard upon some of her personages and kind to others? Fred and Rosamond Vincy, for instance – one would have said there was not so much to choose. The author, however, is on the whole kind to the brother, showing up his faults but not harshly, and making him in the end an example of how an amiable spendthrift may be redeemed by a good man's help and a good girl's love. While to the sister, within whose mind 'there was not room enough for luxuries to look small in', she shows a really merciless animosity, and gibbets her as an example of how an unworthy wife may degrade the career of a man of high purposes and capacities. Celia, too, who is not really so very much higher a character, the author makes quite a pet of in comparison, and puts her in situations where all her small virtues tell; and so on. Minute differences of character for better or worse may justly be shown, of course, as producing vast differences of effect under the impulsion of circumstances. Still, I do not think it is alto-gether fancy to find wanting here the impartiality of the creators towards their mind's offspring.

Then, for the general lesson of the book, it is not easy to feel quite sure what it is, or how much importance the author gives it. In her prelude and conclusion both, she seems to insist upon the design of illustrating the necessary disappointment of a woman's nobler aspirations in a society not made to second noble aspirations in a woman. And that is one of the most burning lessons which any writer could set themselves to illustrate. But then, Dorothea does not suffer in her ideal aspirations from yielding to the pressure of social opinion. She suffers in them from finding that what she has done, in marrying an old scholar in the face of social opinion, was done under a delusion as to the old scholar's character. 'Exactly,' is appar-ently the author's drift; 'but it is society which so nurtures women that their ideals cannot but be ideals of delusion.' Taking this as the author's main point (and I think prelude and conclusion leave it still ambiguous), there are certainly passages enough in the body of the narrative which point the same remon-strance against what society does for women. '*The shallowness of a water-nixie's soul may have a charm till she becomes didactic*': that describes the worthlessness of what men vulgarly prize in women. '*In the British climate there is no incompatibility between scientific insight and furnished lodgings. The incompatibility is chiefly between scientific ambition and a wife who objects to that kind of residence.*' That points to the rarity of a woman, as women are brought up, who prefers the things of the mind to luxury. ' *"Of course she is devoted to her husband," said Rosamond, implying a notion of necessary sequence which the scientific man regarded as the prettiest possible for a woman.*' That points with poignant irony to the science, as to the realities of society and the heart, of men whose science is solid in other things.

It is perhaps in pursuance of the same idea that Dorothea's destiny, after Casaubon has died, and she is free from the consequences of a first illusory ideal, is not made very brilliant after all. She cannot be an Antigone or a Theresa. She marries the man of her choice, and bears him children; but we have been made to feel all along that he is hardly worthy of her. There is no sense of triumph in it; there is rather a sense of sadness in a subdued and restricted, if now not a thwarted, destiny. In this issue there is a deep depression; there is that blending of the author's bitterness with her profound tenderness of which I have already spoken. And upon this depends, or with it hangs together, that feeling of uncertainty and unsatisfiedness as to the whole fable and its impression which remains with the reader when all is done. He could spare the joybells – the vulgar upshot of happiness for ever after – Sophia surrendered to the arms of her enraptured Jones – if he felt quite sure of the moral or intellectual point of view which had dictated so chastened and subdued a conclusion. As it is, he does not feel clear enough about the point of view, the lesson, the main moral and intellectual outcome, to put up with that which he feels to be uncomfortable in the combinations of the story, and flat in the fates of friends and acquaintances who have been brought so marvellously near to him.

That these and such like questionings should remain in the mind, after the reading of a great work of fiction, would in ordinary phrase be said to indicate that, however great the other qualities of the work, it was deficient in qualities of art.

The fact is, that this writer brings into her fiction so many new
elements, and gives it pregnancy and significance in so many
unaccustomed directions, that it is presumptuousness to pronounce in that way as to the question of art. Certainly, it is
possible to write with as little illusion, or with forms of disillusion
much more cynical, as to society and its dealings and issues,
and yet to leave a more harmonious and definite artistic
impression than is here left. French writers perpetually do so.
But then George Eliot, with her science and her disillusion,
has the sense of bad and good as the great French literary
artists have not got it, and is taken up, as they are not, with the
properly moral elements of human life and struggling. They
exceed in all that pertains to the passions of the individual;
she cares more than they do for the general beyond the individual. That it is by which she rouses – I say rouses, attaches, and
elevates – so much more than they do, even if her combinations
satisfy much less. Is it, then, that a harmonious and satisfying
literary art is impossible under these conditions? Is it that a
literature, which confronts all the problems of life and the world,
and recognises all the springs of action, and all that clogs the
springs, and all that comes from their smooth or impeded
working, and all the importance of one life for the mass, – is
it that such a literature must be like life itself, to leave us sad
and hungry?

TH. BENTZON *Revue des Deux Mondes*, February 1873
The 'Prelude' to George Eliot's latest work, announcing that
what is to be presented is the study of one of those forceful
spirits which up to now she has not felt herself ready to paint,
is full of good intentions. It would appear that the lady novelist
who has already put her celebrated but pseudonymous signature
to several books remarkable for their stylistic vigour and profound observation of character is to abjure the approach for
which we have so often taken her to task – an approach which
takes the form of obstinately evading the exceptional, of searching out truth in the common crowd, not only as a result of
her untiring preoccupation with bringing out the beauty of

the ordinary things of life, but also of her open hostility to anything resembling heroism, the ideal. Even if the average man, beset by all sorts of hardships and trivialities depicted in microscopic detail, had aroused our interest under the name of Adam Bede – the actual novel of that name a masterpiece of realism without vulgarity – it might be dangerous to exaggerate certain facets of his character and circumstances. In subsequent novels by the author of *Adam Bede*, the study of realistic truth has more than once stifled whatever passion there was; her delicate, patient analysis has become tiring and prolix; the dispassionateness (always a little aloof and condescending), according to which weaknesses were represented as strengths, has ended by making the reader indifferent to characters whom he doesn't know whether to love or hate, and doesn't feel inclined to trouble to find out.

George Eliot has led one to believe that she was going to emerge from these generalisations by portraying a modern Protestant St Theresa who, in the gallery of her fiction as it stood, would produce the effect of a figure of Raphael strayed unaccountably among those Flemish or Dutch portraits which stand out more than anything else by the precision of their copying and their detail. 'Miss Brooke possessed that kind of beauty which seems to be thrown into relief by poor dress . . .' [there follows a long quotation from the first paragraph of *Middlemarch*]. Why not admit it? Secretly we are hoping to discover in *Middlemarch* the reflection of a soul and a life which, whilst escaping the attentions and curiosity of the public at large, *we* know to be quite exceptional. It is with this secret hope that we have opened this first of eight volumes, dated the beginning of last year – since they have come out month by month or at even longer intervals. To give a better picture of our disappointment, we shall trace the progress of the three-pronged intrigue which develops along with an obtrusive crowd of secondary characters who from time to time, though for no apparent reason, acquire a very great importance.

[There follows a précis of the plot of books i and ii, ending with a description of the Middlemarch townsfolk.] . . . Here we come across a peculiar painting of manners and characters, clearly marked with that very English quality – so English as to be virtually untranslatable, the 'quaintness', a *mélange* of wit, grace and originality. Nevertheless, these *hors d'œuvres* make plain once more the basic defect of an approach to fiction which consists entirely of reproducing each succeeding episode, each passing character, with nothing more than photographic precision, so to speak. Even the finest photograph, however clear, however penetrating it may be, is still inferior to a painting created with an eye to structure and unity of effect.

If the author had left out the secondary characters, who do not in any way advance the main plot, the novel would have been half the length, since most of the townsfolk of Middlemarch seem to put in an appearance only so as to give the Casaubons time to get to Rome, where we find them thoroughly disenchanted with each other – which it was not difficult to foresee. . . .

Why is it one never is satisfied, one never can be satisfied, after reading a novel by George Eliot? The English critic replies that her achievement does not lie in her ability to *satisfy*, but in her ability to rivet the reader's attention to what she writes; and that her work is not to blame if it leaves us, like life itself, sad and still hungry. Very well! But we must reply to this with the question: must art then be no more than an exact and slavish imitation of life?

Middlemarch comprises three novels, only one of which – the story of Fred Vincy and Mary Garth – shows us contented people who have demanded very little of their lives. . . . Their kind of modest happiness – without excitement, without intoxication, without ecstasy – is the only happiness, it seems, that is really possible, the only one that is to be desired; it defines by contrast the failed destinies of more exacting spirits. After her first cruel mistake, does not Dorothea allow her life, which should have been consecrated to the whole of humanity, to be absorbed within the life of one other person? Does not Lydgate, who, like her, wanted to put all his powers into a vast project for the good of his fellow men, become the plaything and victim of a woman without heart or intelligence, ignorant of the harm she does, who ruins his career and destroys his confidence in himself? . . . Certainly, George Eliot lacks neither ability, knowledge, wit (few English writers have the advantage of her on this score), style (even though we could point out one or two blemishes here and there – the abuse of medical and physiological expressions, for example), nor invention; there are all of these things in this enormous novel, in the 'genre' scenes – which will stand up to very close and attentive reading – as much as in the most dramatic sequences. One hardly dares to criticise the election scenes for being over-long, they have so much else to recommend them in their accurate, caustic examination of human ambition and weakness, and above all their mixture of judicious good feeling and prudent non-commitment where the issue of political reform and social improvement arises; but these noble, weighty qualities, forceful and sensitive as they might be, are not enough to make up for a flagrant offence against the essential rules of art: *Middlemarch* is made up of a succession of unconnected chapters, following each other at random – with the result that the final effect is one of an incoherence which nothing can justify. Perhaps the blame should be laid at the door of its serial publication, the most venial inconvenience of which is that it exhausts the reader. At any rate, to reconcile us to provincial life, particularly drab and tedious in England, it would have been necessary that this study should be only the background to a picture that was interesting and all the more lively by contrast. To merit the title of great novelist, George Eliot must come to realise that the first condition of producing beauty is to attend to the overall structure of the work at hand before bothering oneself over ornamentation, and that perfection of detail is no compensation for absence of a well-thought-out design; just as the real cannot properly be said to exist outside of its relation with the ideal, however hard one may try to make it do so. It has been said often enough, but it cannot be said too often, that the ideal is not something set over above nature: it is itself a part of the whole truth, an indispensable part of all work aspiring to a sufficiently high standard. It is because she has misunderstood this immortal precept; because, at the behest of a private whim, she has given pride of place to observation rather than imagination, to an inexorable analysis rather than sensibility, passion or fantasy, that George Eliot will not be numbered among those novelists of the very highest rank.

[F. N. BROOME] *The Times*, 7 March 1873
Thought and expression is everywhere exact and acute, and the explanations and solutions of moods, feelings, mental processes, and circumstances are clear and true. Through the four volumes we feel that the story moves like the forces of a General who has made all his dispositions beforehand, and has left nothing to chance. It is a thoroughly worked out and prepared conception which is being unfolded to us page by page. We do not watch the fashioning of the plot and the modelling of the characters; we detect no second thoughts and alterations, the writing of the books has merely been as the drawing of a curtain, and work is turned and shown to us which has been finished in the mind.

HENRY JAMES *Galaxy*, March 1873
Middlemarch is at once one of the strongest and one of the weakest of English novels. Its predecessors as they appeared might have been described in the same terms; *Romola* is especially a rare masterpiece, but the least *entraînant* of masterpieces. *Romola* sins by excess of analysis; there is too much description and too little drama; too much reflection (all certainly of a highly imaginative sort) and too little creation. Movement lingers in the story, and with it attention stands still in the reader. The error in *Middlemarch* is not precisely of a similar kind, but it is equally detrimental to the total aspect of the work. We can well remember how keenly we wondered, while its earlier chapters unfolded themselves, what turn in the way of form the story would take – that of an organized, moulded, balanced composition, gratifying the reader with a sense of design and construction, or a mere chain of episodes, broken into accidental lengths and unconscious of the influence of a plan. We expected

the actual result, but for the sake of English imaginative literature which, in this line is rarely in need of examples, we hoped for the other. If it had come we should have had the pleasure of reading, what certainly would have seemed to us in the immediate glow of attention, the first of English novels. But that pleasure has still to hover between prospect and retrospect. *Middlemarch* is a treasure-house of detail, but it is an indifferent whole.

Our objection may seem shallow and pedantic, and may even be represented as a complaint that we have had the less given us rather than the more. Certainly the greatest minds have the defects of their qualities, and as George Eliot's mind is preëminently contemplative and analytic, nothing is more natural than that her manner should be discursive and expansive. 'Concentration' would doubtless have deprived us of many of the best things in the book – of Peter Featherstone's grotesquely expectant legatees, of Lydgate's medical rivals, and of Mary Garth's delightful family. The author's purpose was to be a generous rural historian, and this very redundancy of touch, born of abundant reminiscence, is one of the greatest charms of her work. It is as if her memory was crowded with antique figures, to whom for very tenderness she must grant an appearance. Her novel is a picture – vast, swarming, deep-coloured, crowded with episodes, with vivid images, with lurking master-strokes, with brilliant passages of expression; and as such we may freely accept it and enjoy it. It is not compact, doubtless; but when was a panorama compact? And yet, nominally, *Middlemarch* has a definite subject – the subject indicated in the eloquent preface. An ardent young girl was to have been the central figure, a young girl framed for a larger moral life than circumstance often affords, yearning for a motive for sustained spiritual effort and only wasting her ardour and soiling her wings against the meanness of opportunity. The author, in other words, proposed to depict the career of an obscure St Theresa. Her success has been great, in spite of serious drawbacks. Dorothea Brooke is a genuine creation, and a most remarkable one when we consider the delicate material in which she is

wrought. George Eliot's men are generally so much better than
the usual trousered offspring of the female fancy, that their
merits have perhaps overshadowed those of her women. Yet
her heroines have always been of an exquisite quality, and
Dorothea is only that perfect flower of conception of which her
predecessors were the less unfolded blossoms. An indefinable
moral elevation is the sign of these admirable creatures; and
of the representation of this quality in its superior degrees the
author seems to have in English fiction a monopoly. To render
the expression of a soul requires a cunning hand; but we seem
to look straight into the unfathomable eyes of the beautiful
spirit of Dorothea Brooke. She exhales a sort of aroma of
spiritual sweetness, and we believe in her as in a woman we
might providentially meet some fine day when we should find
ourselves doubting of the immortality of the soul. By what
unerring mechanism this effect is produced – whether by fine
strokes or broad ones, by description or by narration, we can
hardly say; it is certainly the great achievement of the book.
Dorothea's career is, however, but an episode, and though
doubtless in intention, not distinctly enough in fact, the central
one. The history of Lydgate's *ménage*, which shares honours
with it, seems rather to the reader to carry off the lion's share.
This is certainly a very interesting story, but on the whole it
yields in dignity to the record of Dorothea's unresonant woes.
The 'love-problem', as the author calls it, of Mary Garth, is
placed on a rather higher level than the reader willingly grants
it. To the end we care less about Fred Vincy than appears to
be expected of us. In so far as the writer's design has been to
reproduce the total sum of life in an English village forty years
ago, this commonplace young gentleman, with his somewhat
meagre tribulations and his rather neutral egotism, has his
proper place in the picture; but the author narrates his fortunes
with a fullness of detail which the reader often finds irritating.
The reader indeed is sometimes tempted to complain of a
tendency which we are at loss exactly to express – a tendency to
make light of the serious elements of the story and to sacrifice
them to the more trivial ones. Is it an unconscious instinct or is

it a deliberate plan? With its abundant and massive ingredients *Middlemarch* ought somehow to have depicted a weightier drama. Dorothea was altogether too superb a heroine to be wasted; yet she plays a narrower part than the imagination of the reader demands. She is of more consequence than the action of which she is the nominal centre. She marries enthusiastically a man whom she fancies a great thinker, and who turns out to be but an arid pedant. Here, indeed, is a disappointment with much of the dignity of tragedy; but the situation seems to us never to expand to its full capacity. It is analysed with extraordinary pentration, but one may say of it, as of most of the situations in the book, that it is treated with too much refinement and too little breadth. It revolves too constantly on the same pivot; it abounds in fine shades, but it lacks, we think, the great dramatic *chiaroscuro*. Mr Casaubon, Dorothea's husband (of whom more anon), embittered, on his side, by matrimonial disappointment, takes refuge in vain jealousy of his wife's relations with an interesting young cousin of his own and registers this sentiment in a codicil to his will, making the forfeiture of his property the penalty of his widow's marriage with this gentleman. Mr Casaubon's death befalls about the middle of the story, and from this point to the close our interest in Dorothea is restricted to the question, will she or will [she] not marry Will Ladislaw? The question is relatively trivial and the implied struggle slightly factitious. The author has depicted the struggle with a sort of elaborate solemnity which in the interviews related in the two last books tends to become almost ludicrously excessive. The dramatic current stagnates; it runs between hero and heroine almost a game of hair-splitting. Our dissatisfaction here is provoked in a great measure by the insubstantial character of the hero. The figure of Will Ladislaw is a beautiful attempt, with many finely completed points; but on the whole it seems to us a failure. It is the only eminent failure in the book, and its defects are therefore the more striking. It lacks sharpness of outline and depth of colour; we have not found ourselves believing in Ladislaw as we believe in Dorothea, in Mary Garth, in Rosamond, in Lydgate, in Mr

Brooke and Mr Casaubon. He is meant, indeed, to be a light creature (with a large capacity for gravity, for he finally gets into Parliament), and a light creature certainly should not be heavily drawn. The author, who is evidently very fond of him, has found for him here and there some charming and eloquent touches; but in spite of these he remains vague and impalpable to the end. He is, we may say, the one figure which a masculine intellect of the same power as George Eliot's would not have conceived with the same complacency; he is, in short, roughly speaking, a woman's man. It strikes us as an oddity in the author's scheme that she should have chosen just this figure of Ladislaw as the creature in whom Dorothea was to find her spiritual compensations. He is really, after all, not the ideal foil to Mr Casaubon which her soul must have imperiously demanded, and if the author of the *Key to all Mythologies* sinned by lack of order, Ladislaw too has not the concentrated fervour essential in the man chosen by so nobly strenuous a heroine. The impression once given that he is a *dilettante* is never properly removed, and there is slender poetic justice in Dorothea's marrying a *dilettante*. We are doubtless less content with Ladislaw, on account of the noble, almost sculptural, relief of the neighbouring figure of Lydgate, the real hero of the story. It is an illustration of the generous scale of the author's picture and of the conscious power of her imagination that she has given us a hero and heroine of broadly distinct interests – erected, as it were, two suns in her firmament, each with its independent solar system. Lydgate is so richly successful a figure that we have regretted strongly at moments, for immediate interests' sake, that the current of his fortunes should not mingle more freely with the occasionally thin-flowing stream of Dorothea's. Toward the close, these two fine characters are brought into momentary contact so effectively as to suggest a wealth of dramatic possibility between them; but if this train had been followed we should have lost Rosamond Vincy – a rare psychological study. Lydgate is a really complete portrait of a *man*, which seems to us high praise. It is striking evidence of the altogether superior quality of George Eliot's imagination that, though elaborately represented, Lydgate should be treated so little from what we may roughly (and we trust without offence) call the sexual point of view. Perception charged with feeling has constantly guided the author's hand, and yet her strokes remain as firm, her curves as free, her whole manner as serenely impersonal, as if, on a small scale, she were emulating the creative wisdom itself. Several English romancers – notably Fielding, Thackeray, and Charles Reade – have won great praise for their figures of women: but they owe it, in reversed conditions, to a meaner sort of art, it seems to us, than George Eliot has used in the case of Lydgate; to an indefinable appeal to masculine prejudice – to a sort of titillation of the masculine sense of difference. George Eliot's manner is more philosophic – more broadly intelligent, and yet her result is as concrete or, if you please, as picturesque. We have no space to dwell on Lydgate's character; we can but repeat that he is a vividly consistent, manly figure – powerful, ambitious, sagacious, with the maximum rather than the minimum of egotism, strenuous, generous, fallible, and altogether human. A work of the liberal scope of *Middlemarch* contains a multitude of artistic intentions, some of the finest of which become clear only in the meditative after-taste of perusal. This is the case with the balanced contrast between the two histories of Lydgate and Dorothea. Each is a tale of matrimonial infelicity, but the conditions in each are so different and the circumstances so broadly opposed that the mind passes from one to the other with that supreme sense of the vastness and variety of human life, under aspects apparently similar, which it belongs only to the greatest novels to produce. The most perfectly successful passages in the book are perhaps those painful fireside scenes between Lydgate and his miserable little wife. The author's rare psychological penetration is lavished upon this veritably mulish domestic flower. There is nothing more powerfully real than these scenes in all English fiction, and nothing certainly more *intelligent*. Their impressiveness and (as regards Lydgate) their pathos is deepened by the constantly low key in which they are pitched. It is a tragedy based on unpaid butchers' bills, and the urgent need for small economies.

G.E.M.—C

The author has desired to be strictly real and to adhere to the facts of the common lot, and she has given us a powerful version of that typical human drama, the struggles of an ambitious soul with sordid disappointments and vulgar embarrassments. As to her catastrophe we hesitate to pronounce (for Lydgate's ultimate assent to his wife's worldly programme is nothing less than a catastrophe). We almost believe that some terrific explosion would have been more probable than his twenty years of smothered aspiration. Rosamond deserves almost to rank with Tito in *Romola* as a study of a gracefully vicious, or at least of a practically baleful nature. There is one point, however, of which we question the consistency. The author insists on her instincts of coquetry, which seems to us a discordant note. They would have made her better or worse – more generous or more reckless; in either case more manageable. As it is, Rosamond represents, in a measure, the fatality of British decorum.

In reading, we have marked innumerable passages for quotation and comment; but we lack space and the work is so ample that half a dozen extracts would be an ineffective illustration. There would be a great deal to say on the broad array of secondary figures, Mr Casaubon, Mr Brooke, Mr Bulstrode, Mr Farebrother, Caleb Garth, Mrs Cadwallader, Celia Brooke. Mr Casaubon is an excellent invention; as a dusky *repoussoir* to the luminous figure of his wife he could not have been better imagined. There is indeed something very noble in the way in which the author has apprehended his character. To depict hollow pretentiousness and mouldy egotism with so little of narrow sarcasm and so much of philosophic sympathy, is to be a rare moralist as well as a rare story-teller. The whole portrait of Mr Casaubon has an admirably sustained grayness of tone in which the shadows are never carried to the vulgar black of coarser artists. Every stroke contributes to the unwholesome, helplessly sinister expression. Here and there perhaps (as in his habitual diction), there is a hint of exaggeration; but we confess we like fancy to be fanciful. Mr Brooke and Mr Garth are in their different lines supremely genial creations; they are drawn with the touch of a Dickens chastened and intellectualized. Mrs Cadwallader is, in another walk of life, a match for Mrs Poyser, and Celia Brooke is as pretty a fool as any of Miss Austen's. Mr Farebrother and his delightful 'womankind' belong to a large group of figures begotten of the superabundance of the author's creative instinct. At times they seem to encumber the stage and to produce a rather ponderous mass of dialogue; but they add to the reader's impression of having walked in the Middlemarch lanes and listened to the Middlemarch accent. To but one of these accessory episodes – that of Mr Bulstrode, with its multiplex ramifications – do we take exception. It has a slightly artificial cast, a melodramatic tinge, unfriendly to the richly natural colouring of the whole. Bulstrode himself – with the history of whose troubled conscience the author has taken great pains – is, to our sense, too diffusely treated; he never grasps the reader's attention. But the touch of genius is never idle or vain. The obscure figure of Bulstrode's comely wife emerges at the needful moment, under a few light strokes, into the happiest reality.

All these people, solid and vivid in their varying degrees, are members of a deeply human little world, the full reflection of whose antique image is the great merit of these volumes. How bravely rounded a little world the author has made it – with how dense an atmosphere of interests and passions and loves and enmities and strivings and failings, and how motley a group of great folk and small, all after their kind, she has filled it, the reader must learn for himself. No writer seems to us to have drawn from a richer stock of those long-cherished memories which one's later philosophy makes doubly tender. There are few figures in the book which do not seem to have grown mellow in the author's mind. English readers may fancy they enjoy the 'atmosphere' of *Middlemarch*; but we maintain that to relish its inner essence we must – for reasons too numerous to detail – be an American. The author has commissioned herself to be real, her native tendency being that of an idealist, and the intellectual result is a very fertilizing mixture. The constant presence of thought, of generalizing instinct, of *brain*, in a word,

nd her observation, gives the latter its great value and her
le manner its high superiority. It denotes a mind in which
imagination is illumined by faculties rarely found in fellowship
with it. In this respect – in that broad reach of vision which
would make the worthy historian of solemn fact as well as
wanton fiction – George Eliot seems to us among English
romancers to stand alone. Fielding approaches her, but to our
mind, she surpasses Fielding. Fielding was didactic – the author
of *Middlemarch* is really philosophic. These great qualities imply
corresponding perils. The first is the loss of simplicity. George
Eliot lost hers some time since; it lies buried (in a splendid
mausoleum) in *Romola*. Many of the discursive portions of
Middlemarch are, as we may say, too clever by half. The author
wishes to say too many things, and to say them too well; to
recommend herself to a scientific audience. Her style, rich and
flexible as it is, is apt to betray her on these transcendental
flights; we find, in our copy, a dozen passages marked 'obscure'.
Silas Marner was a delightful tinge of Goldsmith – we may
almost call it: *Middlemarch* is too often an echo of Messrs
Darwin and Huxley. In spite of these faults – which it seems
graceless to indicate with this crude rapidity – it remains a very
splendid performance. It sets a limit, we think, to the development of the old-fashioned English novel. Its diffuseness, on
which we have touched, makes it too copious a dose of pure
fiction. If we write novels so, how shall we write History? But
it is nevertheless a contribution of the first importance to the
rich imaginative department of our literature.

[R. H. HUTTON?] *British Quarterly Review*, 1 April 1873
George Eliot has never displayed more imaginative and intellectual power than in this her latest and, in some important
respects, her richest tale. There is more passion and more lofty
conception in *Adam Bede*, more affluence of the provincial
grotesques of English rural life in *The Mill on the Floss*, more
beauty in *Silas Marner*, more curious intellectual subtlety in
Romola; but none of them can really compare with *Middlemarch*
for delicacy of detail and completeness of finish – completeness

as regards not only the individual figures, but the whole picture
of the rural society delineated – and for the breadth of life
brought within the field of the story. It is, no doubt, as a mere
story, inferior both to *Adam Bede* and to *Silas Marner*, the latter
a perfect little gem of its kind, in which the author has done
what is so rare with her – sacrificed something of her own deep
feeling of the unsatisfactoriness of real life to the ideal demand
for 'poetical justice', by rounding off the events somewhat more
ideally than human lots are usually rounded off, in harmony
with the author's and reader's inward sense of moral fitness,
and scarcely in harmony with the average teaching of vigilant
observation. And, yet, even in *Silas Marner*, she has left a
certain spring of unhealed and undeserved pain to remind us
of the deep unsatisfactoriness of human things; in the catastrophe of *Adam Bede*, we hardly know whether she has not left
more rankling pain than satisfaction; and in *Romola*, the sense
of foiled aims and wrecked purposes unquestionably predomin-
ates, so that we can hardly help thinking she was drawn to the
subject of *Romola*, by perceiving a certain similarity between
the spiritual illusions of the age of the great Dominican heretic
and our own – a similarity which enables her to paint a great
historical theme in her own favourite melancholy tone, without
any violence to nature. And, now, in *Middlemarch*, George
Eliot has set herself, from the very beginning, to illustrate her
own profound conviction that the noblest aims, however faithfully and simply pursued, are apt to be wrecked, at least to
outward seeming, in this our modern age of distracted life.
She sets herself to paint by no means a tragedy, but what she
herself describes as 'a life of mistakes, the offspring of a certain
spiritual grandeur, ill-matched with the meanness of opportunity'. And what she loses in beauty and in grandeur of effect
by this deliberate aim, she seems to gain in ease, and in the
obviously greater accordance between her array of intellectual
and moral assumptions, and her artistic treatment of them. You
feel that the inmost mind of the writer is reflected, not merely
in the criticisms and the casual observations of the tale, but in
the tale itself; you feel throughout the painful sincerity which

underlies both the humour and the sarcasm; you feel the desolateness of the formative thought as well as the root of its bitterness, and yet you never cease to feel the author's extraordinary fidelity to her own moral aims. *Middlemarch* is, as the preface (unfortunately called a 'prelude') pretty plainly confesses, a sort of pictorial indictment of modern society for the crippling conditions it imposes on men and women, especially women, of high ideal enthusiasm. In consequence of the very aim of the tale, it could hardly be a satisfying imaginative whole, either tragic or otherwise; for the object is to paint not the grand defeat, but the helpless entanglement and miscarriage, of noble aims; to make us see the eager stream of high purpose, not leaping destructively from the rock, but more or less silted up, though not quite lost, in the dreary sands of modern life.

The very nature of this conception, while it ensures a certain vein of melancholy and even bitterness in the story, gives George Eliot's genius a fuller play than it has ever yet had for its predominant realism, and also for that minute knowledge of the whole moral field of modern life which alone tests the strength of a realistic genius. It was impossible to show how ideal aims could be frustrated and overborne by the mere *want of room* for them and the crowd of pettier thoughts and hopes in the society in which they were conceived, without a broad canvas and great variety of grouping; and this is exactly where George Eliot excels. . . . She can draw not merely eccentric characters, but perfectly simple and normal characters of to-day, with all the humour and truth that Scott reserved for his special studies. She has Miss Austen's accuracy and instinct combined with a speculative sympathy with various grooves of thought which gives depth to the minutiæ of real life, and which enables her to interest the intellect of her readers, as well as to engross their imagination. And these great powers have never been brought out with anything like the full success achieved in *Middlemarch*. As our author's object in this tale is to show the paralysis, and the misleading diversions from its natural course, which a blunt and unsympathetic world prepares for the noblest ideality of feeling that is not in sympathy with it, it was essential for her to give such a solidity and complexity to her picture of the world by which her hero's and heroine's idealism was to be more or less tested and partly subjugated, as would justify the impression that she understood fully the character of the struggle. We doubt if any other novelist who ever wrote could have succeeded equally well in this melancholy design, could have framed as complete a picture of English county and county-town society, with all its rigidities, jealousies, and pettiness, with its thorough good-nature, stereotyped habits of thought, and very limited accessibility to higher ideas, and have threaded all these pictures together by a story, if not of the deepest interest, still admirably fitted for its peculiar purpose of showing how unplastic is such an age as ours to the glowing emotion of an ideal purpose.

For melancholy, profoundly melancholy, both in aim and execution, *Middlemarch* certainly is; not that either hero or heroine dies within its limits; on the contrary, the only deaths are deaths of people profoundly indifferent or disagreeable to the reader. And the heroine, though she makes a sad blunder in her first marriage, marries the only man she has ever loved at the end of the tale. Nay, there is another love affair, which eventually prospers well, running through the tale; and the only characters of any moment which are left in a certain cheerless solitude at the close, are those of the young surgeon who has married the woman of his choice, but found the choice a fatal mistake for himself, and of the middle-aged and very Broad Church vicar, who shows to much more advantage in giving up his love than he could have shown in urging it, and who is made the occasion of giving us, perhaps, the only really satisfying emotion which the story excites. The melancholy of the story consists not in the catastrophes of fortune, but in the working out of the only design with which the author set out – the picture 'of the cygnet reared uneasily among the ducklings in the brown pond, and who never finds the living stream in fellowship with its own oary-footed kind'; in the delineation of what George Eliot (with a sentimentalism and disposition to 'gush', of which she is hardly ever guilty) calls the 'loving heart-beats and sobs after an unattained goodness', which 'tremble off and are dispersed among hindrances instead of centering in some long-recognisable deed'. The object of the book is gained by showing in Dorothea's case that a rare nature of the most self-forgetting kind, and the most enthusiastic love for the good and beautiful, is rather more likely to blunder, in its way through the world, than one of much lower moral calibre – which is probable enough; but also by showing that this rare nature does not find any satisfying inward life to compensate these blunders, and turn them into the conditions of purer strength and less accidental happiness – which we should have thought impossible; and again in Lydgate's case, by showing that an ardent love for truth – of the purely intellectual kind – is liable to be betrayed, by the commonplace good nature with which it is often combined, into a paralyzing contact with sordid cares and domestic trials – which, again, is probable enough; but also by showing that this love of truth is not transmuted into any higher moral equivalent through the noble and genuine self-denial of the sacrifice made for another's good – which, again, we should have held to be impossible. That Lydgate, marrying as he did, and with his wholesome nature, should before long have merged the gratification of his disinterested, speculative passion in the necessity of considering the happiness of his shallow-natured wife, is most true to nature. That, in pursuing that course from the high and right motive from which, on the whole, he pursued it, he should have gained no new power over either her or himself, but should have become bitter on his side, and left her as vain and shallow as he found her, is, we trust, not true to nature, but a picture due to that set theory of melancholy realism which George Eliot evidently regards as the best substitute for faith. It is only here and there, in the rare glimpses she gives us of the solitude of Dorothea's heart, that this radical deficiency of faith is carried, as it seems to us, into any touch untrue to what we know of real life. It does so come out, we think, in one or two descriptions of Dorothea's secret struggles, and in the bitter tone in which the close of Lydgate's career is described. Generally,

however, nothing can be more truthful or less like preconceived
theory than the pictures of provincial life in this wonderful
book. But not the less does this deep distrust of 'the Supreme
Power', who, in the words of the 'prelude' to *Middlemarch*, has
fashioned the natures of women 'with inconvenient indefiniteness', give a certain air of moral desolation to the whole book,
and make us feel how objectless is that network of complicated
motives and grotesque manners, of which she gives us so
wonderfully truthful a picture – objectless as those strange
scrawlings on the bare mountain side which, mistaken when
seen from a distance for the handwriting of some gigantic
power, turn out when approached to be the mere tracks of old
destructive forces, since diverted into other channels – the
furrows of dried-up torrents or the grooves of exhausted glaciers.

By far the most remarkable *effort* in *Middlemarch* – we are by
no means sure that the success is quite in proportion to the
effort, though the success is great, and one which only a mind
of great genius could have attained – is, of course, the sketch of
Dorothea Brooke (as she is at the beginning of the tale),
Dorothea Casaubon (as she is throughout its greater portion),
Dorothea Ladislaw (as she is at its close). One sees, on looking
back over the tale, that it was an essential of George Eliot's
purpose to make this high-minded and enthusiastic girl marry
twice, and in *neither* case make an 'ideal' marriage, though the
second is an improvement on the first. The author, indeed,
attempts at the close to ascribe the first mistake partly to causes
which she had never before indicated, and in so doing makes,
as we think, a faulty criticism on her own creation. She attenu-
ates Dorothea's own responsibility for her first marriage after
a fashion hardly consistent either with the type of the character
itself, or with the story as it has been told.

Dorothea [we are told] was spoken of to a younger generation as
a fine girl, who married a sickly clergyman, old enough to be her
father, and in little more than a year after his death gave up her
estate to marry his cousin – young enough to have been his son, with
no property, and not well-born. Those who had not seen anything of

Dorothea usually observed that she could not have been 'a nice woman', else she would not have married either the one or the other. Certainly those determining acts of her life were not ideally beautiful. They were the mixed result of young and noble impulse struggling under prosaic conditions. Among the many remarks passed on her mistakes, it was never said in the neighbourhood of Middlemarch that such mistakes could not have happened if the society into which she was born had not smiled on propositions of marriage from a sickly man to a girl less than half his own age, on modes of education which make a woman's knowledge another name for motley ignorance, on rules of conduct which are in flat contradiction with its own loudly-asserted beliefs. While this is the social air in which mortals begin to breathe, there will be collisions such as those in Dorothea's life, where great feelings will take the aspect of error, and great faith the aspect of illusion. For there is no creature whose inward being is so strong that it is not greatly determined by what lies outside it. A new Theresa will hardly have the opportunity of reforming a conventual life, any more than a new Antigone will spend her heroic piety in daring all for the sake of a brother's burial; the medium in which their ardent deeds took shape is for ever gone. But we insignificant people, with our daily words and acts, are preparing the lives of many Dorotheas, some of which may present a far sadder sacrifice than that of the Dorothea whose story we know. Her finely-touched spirit had still its fine issues, though they were not widely visible. Her full nature, like that river of which Alexander broke the strength, spent itself in channels which had no great name on the earth. But the effect of her being on those around her was incalculably diffusive; for the growing good of the world is partly dependent on unhistoric acts; and that things are not so ill with you and me as they might have been, is half owing to the number who lived faithfully a hidden life, and rest in unvisited tombs.

Now, the remark as to the world's 'smiling on a proposition of marriage from a sickly man to a girl less than half his own age', really has no foundation at all in the tale itself. When Mr Brooke, Dorothea's uncle, weakly carries Mr Casaubon's offer to Dorothea, he accompanies it with as much slipshod dissuasion as it is possible for so helpless a nature to use. Dorothea's sister Celia hears of it with an ill-disguised horror of disgust, which bitterly offends Dorothea. If the rector's wife, Mrs Cadwallader, represents county opinion (and who could represent it better?), the whole society disapproved it. Would George Eliot have orphan girls protected against the weakness of such uncles as Mr Brooke by the Court of Chancery, or would she like to see a law fixing the maximum difference of ages permissible between husband and wife? We hardly see how Dorothea could have been better protected against her first mistake than the picture of social life in Middlemarch represents her as having actually been protected. We note this point only because we find in this passage a trace that George Eliot is, on reviewing her own work, a little dissatisfied with her own picture of the 'prosaic conditions' to which she ascribes Dorothea's misadventures; and that she tries to persuade herself that they were actually more oppressive and paralyzing than they really were. It is obvious, we think, that Dorothea's character was one of much more impetuous self-assertion, of much more adventurous and self-willed idealism than this passage would suggest. She is painted from the first as groping her way with an imperious *disregard* of the prevailing conventional ideas, – ideas quite too mean and barren for the guidance of such a nature, – and as falling, in consequence of that imperious disregard, into her mistake – the mistake being due about equally to her hasty contempt for the existing social standards of conduct, and to her craving for nobler standards not supplied. It was rather the ambitious idealism and somewhat wilful independence of Dorothea's nature than any want of a sound general opinion about the matter, which is represented as leading her into the mistake of her marriage with the pedantic bookworm, Mr Casaubon; and George Eliot is hardly fair to the society she has herself so wonderfully portrayed, when she throws the responsibility of Dorothea's first great mistake upon it. In the early part of the tale, George Eliot clearly intended to charge the society around Dorothea with sins of omission rather than sins of commission; with having no noble aims to which such a nature as Dorothea's could dedicate itself with any satisfaction, rather than with failing to have a certain 'bottom of good sense', which might have saved her from her blunder, if she could but have shared it without losing anything in ideal purpose by sharing it. But in her final criticism of her heroine our author, in her desire to apologize for her, has wavered a little in her conception, and, instead of charging her failure, as at the start, on 'the meanness of opportunity', has charged it on the positive distortion of the social morality by which she was surrounded – a distortion which in her own picture she had not only forgotten to draw, but had carefully proved not to exist. This little inconsistency is important only as showing that George Eliot had unconsciously, in the course of her story, aggravated the faults of the society against which she brings her indictment both at the beginning and the close – a tendency which attaches more or less to her very negative spiritual philosophy. Faith is wanted to make people perfectly candid about the blots in human ideals. A frequent tendency may be noted in those who find no anchor for faith, to throw upon some abstract offender like 'society' the faults they see in those who most satisfy their longing for perfection. It is only profound belief in God which prevents us from indulging a certain amount of moral superstition about our human ideals, or as one may almost call them, the idols of one's conscience.

Nevertheless, after all such deductions, the character of Dorothea is very noble, after an original type. She is introduced to us as an enthusiastic girl, with high impulses which were a little unintelligible to the people around her, 'a young lady of some birth and fortune, who knelt suddenly down on a brick floor by the side of a sick labourer, and prayed fervidly as if she thought herself living in the time of the Apostles; who had strange whims of fasting like a Papist, and of sitting up at night to read old theological books'; who indulged herself in riding, 'in spite of some conscientious qualms'; for 'she felt that she enjoyed it in a pagan sensuous way, and always looked forward to renouncing it'. She is 'open, ardent, and not in the least self-admiring'; a purist in her dislike of ornament for herself, but ever eager to indulge her sister (Celia) in it, though somewhat astonished by her taste, and obliged to apologize for her to her own mind, by the remark that 'souls have complexions', as well as skins; and that 'what will suit one will not suit another'. The scene to which we allude, the first in the book, gives a most skilful artistic portrait of Dorothea's enthusiastic and mystic and slightly haughty, though generous nature. . . .

Now it is the main idea of this book to work out the mal-adaptation, as it were, of this fresh, disinterested, and spiritual-minded girl, to the world into which she was born; to show that instead of giving her a full natural channel for her enthusiasm, and opening to her a career as large as her heart and mind, it, for a time at least, absorbed her great qualities in futile and fruitless efforts, which left hardly any one but herself the better for them; that it made her the victim of a sort of irony of destiny, gave her no chance of marriage with the one man – living in her neighbourhood and in circles where they frequently crossed each other's paths – whom she could perhaps have helped to something great and noble, and left her, even at the close, in no position better adapted to her rare qualities than that of the wife of a clever, mercurial, petulant young politician, not without good in him, but without any signal need of the help of such a woman as this, a woman who, as his wife, came to be 'only known in a certain circle as a wife and mother'. Yet no one who knows George Eliot will suppose that this history is meant to throw any doubt on the intrinsic value of high moral qualities. However negative our author's spiritual creed may be, her ethics are always noble. She makes us feel with ever-increasing force, as the story goes on, the intrinsic grandeur of Dorothea's capacity for self-forgetfulness, sympathy, and love. The story does not end without one signal triumph of the purity of her unselfish purpose over poorer and meaner natures, a triumph painted in a scene that deserves to rank for power beside that in which Dinah wins her victory over Hetty's guilty heart in *Adam Bede*. But while true as ever to her own passionate love of a deep and inward morality, our author is evidently anxious in these pages to show how ill-suited this world is to detect the highest natures that find their way into it, and to use them for the highest ends. Dorothea's desire to devote herself to someone wiser and deeper than herself, leads her into marrying the Rev. Edward Casaubon, a middle-aged, reserved, vain, and dry clergyman, given to laborious researches into a somewhat vague science, Comparative Mythology, for the full treatment of which he does not possess the adequate Oriental learning, nor even access to the German authorities who had made that learning their own. He acts upon Dorothea as a mere moral sponge, to absorb all the finer juices of her nature without being the happier or the better for them, – rather, perhaps, the more irritable, and the worse. Her intellectual brightness, her power of perceiving that he himself distrusts his own power for his task, daunts him, and makes him feel under a sort of intellectual surveillance. Her ardent sympathy with his poor cousin, Mr Ladislaw, and wish to befriend him, make Mr Casaubon jealous, and dimly conscious of his own narrowness of nature. Her desire to share his deepest life makes him painfully conscious that he has no deepest life to be shared. Her ardour is a reproach to his formalism. Her enthusiasm is bewildering to his self-occupation. They lead together a life of mutual disappointment, in which her self-forgetful compassion for his broken health and his fear of intellectual wreck, gradually overpowers her own regrets, and she is on the very eve of promising him to carry out after his death, from his voluminous notes, his hopeless intellectual design, – without the slightest remaining faith, on her part, in its value, – when his sudden death relieves her of the necessity of making the fatal promise. Nothing can be finer than the picture of their mutual relations to each other; his reserved pride, her disappointed tenderness; his formal kindness and suspicious vigilance for his wife's distrust of his powers, her sickness of heart when she first begins to understand that his work will come to nothing, and to desire to give him a sympathy he cannot and will not receive. It is a picture such as no one but George Eliot could draw. And the delicate touch with which it is concluded, when she declines, after his death, to carry out his plan according to the 'Synoptical Tabulation for the use of Mrs Casaubon' found in his desk, is one of those signal marks of great genius in which, even taken alone, you would at once discern the master-hand. His 'Synoptical Tabulation' she 'carefully enclosed and sealed, writing within the envelope, "*I could not use it. Do you not see now that I could not submit my soul to yours, by working hopelessly at what I have no belief in? – Dorothea.*" Then she deposited the paper in her own desk.' Here we see that great need of Dorothea for distinctness of feeling, which separates her from so many idealists of the same type. Instead of shrinking from the subject of the trust her dead husband wished to repose in her, and which she could not accept, she felt the need to put down distinctly for him, even though his presence was only imagined, the answer of her heart. She could not leave him without an answer altogether. But she could not but refuse what he had asked. As a whole, the picture, however, is, and is meant to be, one of moral *waste*, – of a rich, and generous, and buoyant nature wasted on one which was only rendered restless and exhausted by intercourse with her. Nor is the picture of Dorothea's relation to Mr Casaubon's young cousin, Mr Ladislaw, whom her husband forbade her, by his will, to marry on pain of his property going away from her, at all a moral compensation. It is true that his love for her is ardent, though not self-forgetful; but her interest in him is chiefly due to Mr Casaubon's indifference and apparent injustice, and her love begins only after her attention is painfully called to the subject by the revelation of her husband's suspicions in his will. She lavishes herself on Will Ladislaw as a sort of generous compensation for his own relation's coldness to him; and one feels, and is probably meant to feel acutely, that here, too, it is 'the meanness of opportunity', and not intrinsic suitability, which determines Dorothea's second comparatively happy marriage. The world around her is a sponge to absorb Dorothea's great qualities, without profiting by them and without providing any adequate sphere for their expansion and their refinement.

It may be said that in one signal and final instance, George Eliot has given Dorothea the victory over the selfishness of others through the victory over herself; and so, at the end of her tale, has left her beautiful heroine enveloped in the imagination of the reader in a pure and radiant glory. And it is perfectly true that in this one instance she shows a spiritual grandeur *not* 'ill-matched with the meanness of opportunity', but on the contrary, well-matched with the nobleness of opportunity, and so far satisfying, even to the imagination. But even in the instance to which we refer, there is a void which it is impossible not to feel – an intentional and painful void in the background of the picture, which leaves upon us the oppressive sense that Dorothea's fine religious nature had no inward spiritual object on which to feed itself, no object in relation to which its invisible growth would be assured and permanent even when the outward world failed to call into full play her stores of spiritual compassion. But to justify this remark, we must say something of the wonderful pendant or companion picture to Dorothea, Rosamond Vincy, afterwards Rosamond Lydgate.

No one has ever so drawn the cruelty that springs from pure thinness and shallowness of nature, and yet given that cruelty so delicate and feminine an embodiment, as George Eliot has contrived to give it in her marvellous picture of Rosamond. This exquisitely-painted figure is the deadliest blow at the common assumption that limitation in both heart and brain is a desirable thing for women, that has ever been struck. The first impression is of grace, gentleness, propriety, conventional sense, soft tenacity of purpose, and something even that almost looks like tenderness. We refer to the time when Rosamond first falls in love with Lydgate. The reader is even a little disposed at this time to resent the author's evident scorn for Rosamond, and almost to take her part against the critic who seems to have hardened her heart against her own creation. But as the story proceeds, when Rosamond is married, when Lydgate gradually falls into money difficulties, and his graceful wife shows herself not only not able to give him sympathy, but constrained, apparently by her mere poverty of nature, to turn her heart away from him, and even to intrigue against his plans, the picture becomes painfully real and convincing. The reader has no power to doubt its fidelity. The cruelty of a shallow heart in woman has been painted a hundred times on its active side – in its love of power, its delight in admiration, its malicious vivacity. But it has never, as far as we know, been painted entirely in its passive phase – its absolute incompressibility – like the incompressibility of water itself – its cold aversion to any one, however conventionally dear, who, after being expected to be a source of pride and lustre, turns out to be in need of active sacrifices and of some spontaneousness of sympathy. Rosamond's helpless *finesse*, and mild, but stony-hearted irresponsiveness to her husband's appeals, her unashamed insincerity, her unyielding passiveness, and her perfect confidence in the wisdom of her own wishes in spite of her total inability to understand what is necessary to be understood, make up a startling picture of the unconscious but cruel inexorability of feminine selfishness, and of fair incapacity to understand and feel. The art which has contrasted this picture of Rosamond with that of Dorothea it is not easy to overpraise. [There follows a long quotation from chap. 80 of the novel, describing the steps by which Dorothea comes to her decision to 'see and save Rosamond'.]

This picture leaves a sense of want in the mind of the reader that survives even the powerful and pathetic scene of Dorothea's victory over Rosamond, a scene that, as we have already said, challenges comparison with that in which Dinah succeeds in touching Hetty's heart in *Adam Bede*. There is left upon us that for which the previous course of the tale had been preparing us, a conviction not only that Dorothea's life had been crippled by a 'meanness of opportunity' sadly ill-matched with her spiritual grandeur, but also that that 'meanness of opportunity' had been gradually extending inwards, as well as imprisoning her from outside. There is no such thing as inward 'meanness of opportunity' to one who has a life hidden in God as well as a life spent upon the world. That is a resource and a refuge, the grandeur of which is always on the increase, and is sometimes greatest of all when the outward field of opportunity is poorest. With this inward source of joy for Dorothea, one might have left her, even if Will Ladislaw had really failed her, with composure, with that sense of rest which even Greek tragedy, with its far fainter spiritual insights, always gives. But, without it, to know that she married after her first husband's death the young man whom her own generosity had first taught her to love, that she was recognized 'in a certain circle as a wife and mother', and that she fascinated all who really came to know her, and even by poor shallow Rosamond was never mentioned with depreciation, is a poor, ungracious, and unhappy close to a delineation of great power. 'Meanness of opportunity' does not really win the victory – Dorothea is too noble for that; but it does, in the picture at least, finally circumscribe and cripple a spirit of rare beauty and strength. Dorothea not only fails to express herself in 'a constant unfolding of far-resonant action'; we feel also that she fails to reach the constant unfolding of mute but far expatiating faith. She is noble to all whom she closely touches; but she is denied a great life within as well as without. It is true that the Divine Spirit lives in her, but she does not live in Him. She has not the joy, though she has the strength of the spiritual life. She has not the sweetness, though she has the good guidance of the life of purity and self-denial. The 'meanness' of external opportunity is, in fact, far more fatal to her than it could be to any equally noble nature with the life of faith freely open before it, for opportunities arising out of her external life are for her the only opportunities; she has no escape from the failing of her heart and flesh to one of whom she can say 'He is the strength of my heart and my portion for ever'. The 'meanness of opportunity' could have no more cruel triumph. . . .

That *Middlemarch* is a great and permanent addition to George Eliot's fame and to the rich resources of English literature we have no doubt. A book of more breadth of genius in conception, of more even execution, is hardly to be found in our language. No doubt it is a little tame in plot, but for that the depth of its purpose and the humour of its conversations sufficiently atone. The melancholy at the heart of it, no criticism of course can attenuate, for that is of its essence. George Eliot means to draw noble natures struggling hard against the currents of a poor kind of world, and without any trust in any invisible rock higher than themselves to which they can entreat to be lifted up. Such a picture is melancholy in its very conception. That in spite of this absence of any inward vista of spiritual hope, and in spite of the equally complete absence of any outward vista of 'far-resonant action', George Eliot should paint the noble characters in which her interest centres as clinging tenaciously to that *caput mortuum* into which Mr Arnold has so strangely reduced the Christian idea of God – 'a stream of tendency, not ourselves, which makes for righteousness', – and has never even inclined to cry out 'let us eat and drink, for to-morrow we die', is a great testimony to the ethical depth and purity of her mind. And it will add to the interest of *Middlemarch* in future generations, when at length this great wave of scepticism has swept by us, and 'this tyranny is overpast', that in pointing to it as registering the low-tide mark of spiritual belief among the literary class in the nineteenth century, the critics of the future will be compelled to infer from it that, even during that low ebb of trust in the supernatural element of religion, there was no want of ardent belief in the spiritual obligations of purity and self-sacrifice, nor even in that 'secret of the Cross' which, strangely enough, survives the loss of the faith from which it sprang.

PART TWO

Some Opinions and Criticism, 1874–1968

SOME OPINIONS AND CRITICISM

LESLIE STEPHEN: 'Hardly Charming'
When George Eliot returned to her proper ground, she did not regain the old magic. *Middlemarch* is undoubtedly a powerful book, but to many readers it is a rather painful book, and it can hardly be called a charming book to any one. The light of common day has most unmistakably superseded the indescribable glow which illuminated the earlier writings . . . it may certainly be said both of *Romola* and *Middlemarch* that they have some merits of so high an order that the defects upon which I have dwelt are felt as blemishes, not as fatal errors. If there is some misunderstanding of the limits of her own powers, or some misconception of true artistic conditions, nobody can read them without the sense of having been in contact with a comprehensive and vigorous intellect, with high feeling and keen powers of observation. Only one cannot help regretting the loss of that early charm. In reading *Adam Bede*, we feel first the magic, and afterwards we recognise the power which it implies. But in *Middlemarch* we feel the power, but we ask in vain for the charm. Some such change passes over any great mind which goes through a genuine process of development. It is not surprising that the reasoning should to some extent take the place of intuitive perception; and that experience of life should give a sterner and sadder tone to the implied criticism of human nature. We are prepared to find less spontaneity, less freshness of interest in the little incidents of life, and we are not surprised that a mind so reflective and richly stored should try to get beyond the charmed circle of its early successes, and to give us a picture of wider and less picturesque aspects of human life. But this does not seem to account sufficiently for the presence of something jarring and depressing in the later work.

(from *Cornhill Magazine*, 1881)

BESSIE RAYNER BELLOC: 'The Plaint of a Lost Ideal'
The *girl* is real enough; it is her chances which she and her
biographer seem to me to have singularly missed, probably
because the very weight and worth of English Dissenters forty
or fifty years ago secluded them from all society but their own.
. . . In truth *Middlemarch* is to me as a landscape seen in the
twilight; *au teint grisâtre.* It is from first to last the plaint of a
lost ideal. I do not think it even a true rendering of life as it
was lived in England sixty years ago. It would be easy to
account for this by saying that the writer had lost 'the wider
hope'. I prefer not to do it. Such an explanation is, indeed, so
obviously true as that in a country town the most strenuous
belief, the most unflagging work, is religious. But the scepticism
of *Middlemarch* also extends to things social and human.

(from *In a Walled Garden,* 1894)

W. D. HOWELLS: 'Akin to *War and Peace*'
Outlines, I have called these sketches of Dorothea, and perhaps
she is never more than outlined. The inferior nature can be
fully shown, because it is of a material which can be palpably
handled without loss or hurt; but in the superior nature there
is something elusive, something sensitive that escapes or perishes
under the touch, and leaves the exhaustive study a dumb image
and not a speaking likeness. Rosamond Vincy can be decanted
to the dregs, and be only more and more Rosamond; but if
you pour out all Dorothea her essence flies from you in a vital
aroma. She seems hardly to be contained in the story of her life,
but to exist mainly somewhere outside of it. That story is indeed
very slight, and without the incidents that lend themselves to
remembrance as powerful dramatic moments, though it is of
such a fatal pathos. It is reportably that of a magnanimous
young girl who falls in love with the notion of being the help-
meet of an eminent scholar because she believes in the importance of his work to the world, and in her own fitness to be of
use to him in it, and so marries a dull, passionless pedant of
mean soul and mistaken mind, who forces her out of his life
from first to last because there is no room in it for any but his

paltry self. The tragedy of Edward Casaubon is that he has undertaken work inconceivably beyond his powers, and that to a real scholarship his devoted labors are worse than useless: but his wife's tragedy is that he himself is a greater error, a sadder solecism, than even these. He cannot see her divine good-will any more than he can feel value in the facts with which his learning deals; it is the law of his narrow being that he must forbid almost her sympathy, restrict her help to the merest mechanical effect, and scarcely suffer her the efficiency of a trained nurse, when his health fails. It is to be said in his defence that he cannot admit her to his inner life because he has none, and if on that mere outside which is his whole being, he is cold and jealous and repellent, that he was made so and cannot help it. But Dorothea's fate is not the less cruel because it is his fate, too; and she is all the greater because she rises above it, not constantly, but finally.

In her case, as in the case of Lydgate, we see a meaner nature making a noble nature its prey, but Dorothea is more enduringly built than Lydgate, or else she is more favored by chance. Perhaps it is scientifically accurate to say this rather than the other thing, for Rosamond outlives Lydgate instead of dying and releasing him to new chances, while Casaubon suddenly, in the most critical moment, dies of heart failure and leaves Dorothea free. . . .

This end, with whatever skill it is managed, must be confessed a mechanical means of extricating Dorothea from her difficulty. It is to be condemned for that, and it is to be regretted that George Eliot had not had the higher courage of her art, and the clearer vision of her morality, and shown Dorothea capable of breaking a promise extorted from her against her reason and against her heart. It was from Ladislaw and her chance of happiness with him that her husband would have withheld her, and she could not have been more recreant to his will in being recreant to her word.

Her marriage to Ladislaw at last is one of the finest things, and one of the truest things in a book so great that it almost persuades one to call it the greatest in English fiction. It is not because *Middlemarch* is an immense canvas, thronged with such a multitude of marvellously distinguished and differenced figures, that it so richly represents life. Other huge novels have been of as great scope and greater dramatic effect; but *Middlemarch* alone seems to me akin in spiritual power to *War and Peace*. It is in its truth to motives as well as results that it is so tremendously convincing. After a lapse of years one comes to it not with a sense of having overmeasured it before, but with the perception that one had not at first realized its grandeur. It is as large as life in those moral dimensions which deepen inwardly and give the real compass of any artistic achievement through the impression received. There are none of its incidents that I find were overestimated in my earlier knowledge of them; and there are some that are far greater than I had remembered. I have had especially to correct my former judgment – I am not sure that it was mine at first hand – of the character of Ladislaw and his fitness to be Dorothea's lover. I had thought him a slight, if not a light man, a poorish sort of Bohemian, existing by her preference, in the reader's tolerance, and perhaps, as her husband, half a mistake. But in this renewed acquaintance with him, I must own him a person of weight by those measures which test the value of precious stones or precious metals: an artist through and through, a man of high courage and high honor, and of a certain social detachment which leaves him free to see the more easily and honestly himself. Dorothea made great and sorrowful mistakes through her generous and loyal nature; but Ladislaw was one of her inspirations: a centre of truth in which her love and her duty, otherwise so sadly at odds, could meet and be at peace.

(from *Heroines of Fiction*, vol. II, 1901)

w. c. brownell: 'Recesses of the Commonplace'
Middlemarch any one can praise. It is probably the 'favorite novel' of most 'intellectual' readers among us – at least those who are old enough to remember its serial appearance. It is, indeed, a half-dozen novels in one. Its scale is cyclopaedic, as

I said, and it is the microcosm of a community rather than a story concerned with a unified plot and set of characters. And it is perhaps the writer's fullest expression of her philosophy of life. . . .

This world was not to her the pure spectacle it is to the pure artist, nor even the profoundly moving and significant spectacle it is to the reflective and philosophic artist. Its phenomena were not *disjecta membra* to be impressionistically reproduced or combined in agreeable and interesting syntheses. They were data of an inexorable moral concatenation of which it interested her to divine the secret. What chiefly she sought in them was the law of cause and effect, the law of moral fatality informing and connecting them. Since the time of the Greek drama this law has never been brought out more eloquently, more cogently, more inexorably or – may one not say, thinking of Shakespeare? – more baldly. But at the same time she makes human responsibility perfectly plain. No attentive reader can hope for an acquittal at her hands in virtue of being the plaything of destiny. She is more than mindful, also, of the futilities as well as the tragedies of existence, and, indeed, gives them a tragic aspect. *Middlemarch*, for example, read in the light – the sombre light – of its preface, is a striking showing of her penetration into the recesses of the commonplace, and of the else undiscovered deeps which there reward her subtlety; with the result, too, of causing the reader to reflect on infinity, as he does after a look through the telescope or microscope – an effect only to be produced by a master. But in neither the tragic nor the trifling does she engage the freedom of the individual, and if she shows the victim in the toils of fate, she shows also with relentless clearness how optionally he got there. Her central thought is the tremendous obligation of duty. Duty is in a very special way to her 'the law of human life'. The impossibility of avoiding it, the idleness of juggling with it, the levity of expecting with impunity to neglect it, are so many facets of her persistent preoccupation. The fatality here involved she states and enforces on every occasion. . . . The 'note' appears again and again. It is a diapason whose slow and truly solemn vibrations, communi-

cated to their own meditations, all of her thoughtful readers
must recall.

(from *Victorian Prose Masters*, 1902)

LESLIE STEPHEN: 'A Satire on the Modern World'
The immediate success of *Middlemarch* may have been propor-
tioned rather to the author's reputation than to its intrinsic
merits. It certainly lacks the peculiar charm of the early work,
and one understands why the *Spectator* should have been led to
say that George Eliot was 'the most melancholy of authors'.
The conclusion was apparently softened to meet this objection.
There is not much downright tragedy, but the general impression is unmistakably sad. This, however, does not prevent
Middlemarch from having, in some ways, even a stronger interest
than its companions. George Eliot was now over fifty, and the
book represents the general tone of her reflection upon life and
human nature. By that age most people have had some rather
unpleasant aspects of life pretty strongly forced upon their
attention; and George Eliot, though she made it a principle to
take things cheerfully, had never had much of the buoyancy
which generates optimism. She was not, she used to say, either
an optimist or a pessimist, but a 'meliorist' – a believer that
the world could be improved, and was perhaps slowly improving,
though with a very strong conviction that the obstacles were
enormous and the immediate outlook not specially bright.
Some people, it seems, attributed her sadness to her creed,
though I fancy that, in such matters, creed has much less to do
with the matter than temperament. So sensitive a woman,
working so conscientiously and with so many misgivings, could
hardly make her imaginary world a cheerful place of residence.
Middlemarch is primarily a portrait of the circles which had been
most familiar to her in youth, and its second title is 'a study of
provincial life'. Provincial life, however, is to exemplify the
results of a wider survey of contemporary society. One peculi-
arity of the book is appropriate to this scheme. It is not a story,
but a combination of at least three stories – the love affairs of
Dorothea and Casaubon, of Rosamond Vincy and Lydgate, and

of Mary Garth and Fred Vincy, which again are interwoven with the story of Bulstrode. The various actions get mixed together as they would naturally do in a country town. Modern English novelists seem to have made up their mind that this kind of mixture is contrary to the rules of art. I am content to say that I used to find some old novels written on that plan very interesting. It is tiresome, of course, if a reader is to think only of the development of the plot. But when the purpose is to get a general picture of the manners and customs of a certain social stratum, and we are to be interested in all the complex play of character and the opinions of neighbours, the method is appropriate to the design. The individuals are shown as involved in the network of surrounding interests which affects their development. *Middlemarch* gives us George Eliot's most characteristic view of such matters. It is her answer to the question, What on the whole is your judgment of commonplace English life? for 'provincialism' is not really confined to the provinces. Without trying to put the answer into a single formula, and it would be very unjust to her to assume that such a formula was intended, I may note one leading doctrine:

'An eminent philosopher among my friends,' she says, with a characteristically scientific illustration, 'who can dignify even your ugly furniture by lifting it into the serene light of science, has shown me this pregnant little fact. Your pier-glass, an extensive surface of polished steel made to be rubbed by a housemaid, will be minutely and multitudinously scratched in all directions; but place now against it a lighted candle as a centre of illumination, and the scratches will seem to arrange themselves in a fine series of concentric circles round that little sun. It is demonstrable that the scratches are going everywhere impartially, and it is only your candle which produces the flattering illusion of a concentric arrangement, its light falling into an exclusive optical selection. These things are a parable' – showing the effect of egoism. It may also represent the effect of a novelist's mental preoccupation. Many different views of human society may be equally true to fact; but the writer, who has a particular 'candle', in the shape of a favourite principle, produces a spontaneous unity by its application to the varying cases presented. The personages who carry out the various plots of *Middlemarch* may be, as I think they are, very lifelike portraits of real life, but they are seen from a particular point of view. The 'prelude' gives the keynote. We are asked to remember the childish adventure of Saint Theresa setting out to seek martyrdom in the country of the Moors. Her 'passionate, ideal nature demanded an epic life . . . some object which would reconcile self-despair with the rapturous consciousness of life beyond self. . . . She ultimately found her epos in the reform of a religious order.' There are later-born Theresas, who had 'no epic life with a constant unfolding of far-resonant action'. They have had to work amid 'dim lights and tangled circumstances'; they have been 'helped by no coherent social faith and ardour which could perform the function of knowledge for the ardently thrilling soul'. They have blundered accordingly; but 'here and there is born a Saint Theresa, foundress of nothing, whose loving heart-beats and sobs after an unattained goodness tremble off, and are dispersed among hindrances, instead of centering on some long recognisable deed'. We are to see how such a nature manifests itself – no longer in the remote regions of arbitrary fancy, but in the commonplace atmosphere of a modern English town. In Maggie Tulliver and in Felix Holt we have already had the struggle for an ideal; but in *Middlemarch* there is a fuller picture of the element of stupidity and insensibility which is apt to clog the wings of aspiration. The Dodsons, among whom Maggie is placed, belong to the stratum of sheer bovine indifference. They are not only without ideas, but it has never occurred to them that such things exist. In *Middlemarch* we consider the higher stratum, which reads newspapers and supports the Society for the Diffusion of Useful Knowledge, and whose notions constitute what is called enlightened public opinion. The typical representative of what it calls its mind is Mr Brooke, who can talk about Sir Humphry Davy, and Wordsworth, and Italian art, and has a delightful facility in handling the small change of conversation which has ceased to possess any intrinsic value. Even his neighbours can see that he is a fatuous humbug, and do not care to veil their blunt common-sense by fine phrases. But he discharges the functions of the Greek chorus with a boundless supply of the platitudes which represent an indistinct foreboding of the existence of an intellectual world.

Dorothea, brought up with Mr Brooke in place of a parent, is to be a Theresa struggling under 'dim lights and entangled circumstances'. She is related, of course, both to Maggie and to Romola, though she is not in danger of absolute asphyxiation in a dense bucolic atmosphere, or of martyrdom in the violent struggles of hostile creeds. Her danger is rather that of being too easily acclimatised in a comfortable state of things, where there is sufficient cultivation and no particular demand for St Theresas. She attracts us by her perfect straightforwardness and simplicity, though we are afraid that she has even a slight touch of stupidity. We fancy that she might find satisfaction, like other young ladies, in looking after schools and the unhealthy cottages on her uncle's estate. Still, she has a real loftiness of character, and a disposition to take things seriously, which make her more or less sensible of the limitations of her circle. She has vague religious aspirations, looks down upon the excellent country gentleman, Sir James Chettam, and fancies that she would like to marry the judicious Hooker, or Milton in his blindness. We can understand, and even pardon her, when she takes the pedant Casaubon at his own valuation, and sees in him 'a living Bossuet, whose work would reconcile complete knowledge with devoted piety, a modern Augustine who united the glories of doctor and saint'.

Dorothea's misguided adoration is, I think, very natural, but it is undeniably painful, and many readers protested. The point is curious. George Eliot declared that she had lived in much sympathy with Casaubon's life, and was especially gratified when someone saw the pathos of his career. No doubt there is a pathos in devotion to an entirely mistaken ideal. To spend a life in researches, all thrown away from ignorance of what has been done, is a melancholy fate. One secret of Casaubon's blunder was explained to his wife during the honeymoon. He had not –

as Ladislaw pointed out – read the Germans, and was therefore
groping through a wood with a pocket compass where they had
made carriage roads. But suppose that he had read the last
authorities? Would that have really mended matters? A deeper
objection is visible even to his own circle. Solid Sir James
Chettam remarks that he is a man 'with no good red blood in
his body', and Ladislaw curses him for 'a cursed white-blooded
pedantic coxcomb'. Their judgment is confirmed by all that
we hear of him. He marries, we are told, because he wants
'female tendance for his declining years. Hence he determined
to abandon himself to the stream of feeling, and perhaps was
surprised to find what an exceedingly shallow rill it was.' His
petty jealousy and steady snubbing of his wife is all in character.
Now we can pity a man for making a blunder, and perhaps, in
some sense, we ought to 'pity' him for having neither heart nor
passion. But that is a kind of pity which is not akin to love.
Dorothea's mistake was not that she married a man who had
not read German, but that she married a stick instead of a man.
The story, the more fully we accept its truthfulness, becomes
the more of a satire against young ladies who aim at lofty ideals.
It implies a capacity for being imposed upon by a mere outside
shell of pretence. Then we have to ask whether things are made
better by her subsequent marriage to Ladislaw? That equally
offended some readers, as George Eliot complained. Ladislaw
is almost obtrusively a favourite with his creator. He is called
'Will' for the sake of endearment; and we are to understand him
as so charming that Dorothea's ability to keep him at a distance
gives the most striking proof of her strong sense of wifely duty.
Yet Ladislaw is scarcely more attractive to most masculine
readers than the dandified Stephen Guest. He is a dabbler in
art and literature; a small journalist, ready to accept employ-
ment from silly Mr Brooke, and apparently liking to lie on a
rug in the houses of his friends and flirt with their pretty wives.
He certainly shows indifference to money, and behaves himself
correctly to Dorothea, though he has fallen in love with her on
her honeymoon. He is no doubt an amiable Bohemian, for
some of whose peculiarities it would be easy to suggest a living

original, and we can believe that Dorothea was quite content with her lot. But that seems to imply that a Theresa of our days has to be content with suckling fools and chronicling small beer. We are told, indeed, that Ladislaw became a reformer – apparently a 'philosophical radical' – and even had the good luck to be returned by a constituency who paid his expenses. George Eliot ought to know; but I cannot believe in this conclusion. Ladislaw, I am convinced, became a brilliant journalist who could write smartly about everything, but who had not the moral force to be a leader in thought or action. I should be the last person to deny that a journalist may lead an honourable and useful life, but I cannot think the profession congenial to a lofty devotion to ideals. Dorothea was content with giving him 'wifely help'; asking his friends to dinner, one supposes, and copying his ill-written manuscripts. Many lamented that 'so rare a creature should be absorbed into the life of another', though no one could point out exactly what she ought to have done. That is just the pity of it. There was nothing for her to do; and I can only comfort myself by reflecting that, after all, she had a dash of stupidity, and that more successful Theresas may do a good deal of mischief.

The next pair of lovers gives a less ambiguous moral. Lydgate, we are told, though we scarcely see it, was a man of great energy, with a high purpose. His ideal is shown by his ambition to be a leader in medical science. In contrast to Casaubon, he is thoroughly familiar with the latest authorities, and has a capacity for really falling in love. Unfortunately, Rosamond Vincy is a model of one of the forms of stupidity against which the gods fight in vain. Being utterly incapable of even understanding her husband's aspirations, fixing her mind on the vulgar kind of success, and having the strength of will which comes from an absolute limitation to one aim, she is a most effective torpedo, and paralyses all Lydgate's energies. He is entangled in money difficulties; gives up his aspirations; sinks into a merely popular physician, and is sentenced to die early of diphtheria. A really strong man, such as Lydgate is supposed to be, might perhaps have made a better fight against the temptation and escaped that slavery to a pretty woman which seems to have impressed George Eliot as the great danger to the other sex. But she never, I think, showed more power than in this painful history. The skill with which Lydgate's gradual abandonment of his lofty aims is worked out without making him simply contemptible, forces us to recognise the truthfulness of the conception. It is an inimitable study of such a fascination as the snake is supposed to exert upon the bird: the slow reluctant surrender, step by step, of the higher to the lower nature, in consequence of weakness which is at least perfectly intelligible. George Eliot's 'psychological analysis' is here at its best; if it is not surpassed by the power shown in Bulstrode. Bulstrode, too, has an ideal of a kind; only it is the vulgar ideal which is suggested by a low form of religion. George Eliot shows the ugly side of the beliefs in which she had more frequently emphasised the purer elements. But still she judges without bitterness; and gives, perhaps, the most satisfactory portrait of the hypocrisy which is more often treated by the method of savage caricature. If he is not as amusing as a Tartuffe or a Pecksniff, he is marvellously lifelike. Nothing can be finer than the description of the curious blending of motives and the ingenious self-deception which enables Bulstrode to maintain his own self-respect. He is afraid of exposure by the scamp who has known his past history. 'At six o'clock he had already been long dressed, and had spent some of his wretchedness in prayer, pleading his motives for averting the worst evil if in anything he had used falsity and spoken what was not true before God. For Bulstrode shrank from a direct lie with an intensity disproportionate to the number of his direct misdeeds. But many of those misdeeds were like the subtle muscular movements which are not taken account of in the consciousness, though they bring about the end that we fix our mind on and desire. And it is only what we are naïvely conscious of that we can vividly imagine to be seen by Omniscience.' The culminating scene in which Bulstrode comes to the edge of murder, and, though he does not kill his enemy, refrains from officiously saving life, is the practical application of the principles; and one is half inclined to think that there was some excuse for the proceeding.

It is, I think, to the force and penetration shown in such passages that *Middlemarch* owes its impressiveness. It shows George Eliot's reflective powers fully ripened and manifesting singular insight into certain intricacies of motive and character. There is, indeed, a correlative loss of the early power of attractiveness. The remaining pair of lovers, Mary Garth and Fred Vincy, the shrewd young woman and the feeble young gentleman whom she governs, do not carry us away; and Caleb Garth, though he is partly drawn from the same original as Adam Bede, is unimpeachable, but a faint duplicate of his predecessor. The moral most obviously suggested would apparently be that the desirable thing is to do your work well in the position to which Providence has assigned you, and not to bother about 'ideals' at all. *Il faut cultiver notre jardin* is an excellent moral, but it comes more appropriately at the end of *Candide* than at the end of a story which is to give us a modern Theresa.

This, I think, explains the rather painful impression which is made by *Middlemarch*. It is prompted by a sympathy for the enthusiast, but turns out to be virtually a satire upon the modern world. The lofty nature is to be exhibited struggling against the circumambient element of crass stupidity and stolid selfishness. But that element comes to represent the dominant and overpowering force. Belief is in so chaotic a state that the idealist is likely to go astray after false lights. Intellectual ambition mistakes pedantry for true learning; religious aspiration tempts acquiescence in cant and superstition; the desire to carry your creed into practice makes compromise necessary, and compromise passes imperceptibly into surrender. One is tempted to ask whether this does not exaggerate one aspect of human tragicomedy. The unity, to return to our 'parable', is to be the light carried by the observer in search of an idealist. In *Middlemarch* the light shows the aspirations of the serious actors, and measures their excellence by their capacity for such a motive. The test so suggested seems to give a rather onesided view of the world. The perfect novelist, if such a being existed, looking upon human nature from a thoroughly impartial and scientific point of view, would agree that such aspirations are rare and obviously impossible for the great mass of mankind. People, indisputably, are 'mostly fools', and care very little for theories of life and conduct. But, therefore, it is idle to quarrel with the inevitable or to be disappointed at its results; and, moreover, it is easy to attach too much importance to this particular impulse. The world, somehow or other, worries along by means of very commonplace affections and very limited outlooks. George Eliot, no doubt, fully recognises that fact, but she seems to be dispirited by the contemplation. The result, however, is that she seems to be a little out of touch with the actual world, and to speak from a position of philosophical detachment which somehow exhibits her characters in a rather distorting light. For that reason *Middlemarch* seems to fall short of the great masterpieces which imply a closer contact with the world of realities and less preoccupation with certain speculative doctrines. Yet it is clearly a work of extraordinary power, full of subtle and accurate observation; and gives, if a melancholy, yet an undeniably truthful portraiture of the impression made by the society of the time upon one of the keenest observers, though upon an observer looking at the world from a certain distance, and rather too much impressed by the importance of philosophers and theorists.

(from *George Eliot*, 1902)

OLIVER ELTON: 'No Plan, but no Confusion'
[*Middlemarch*] is almost one of the great novels of the language. A little more ease and play and simplicity, a little less of the anxious idealism which ends in going beyond nature, and it might have been one of the greatest. Some of the figures, like Ladislaw, are mere pasteboard; but there is still a dense throng of persons whom we all might have known, perhaps too well. Some of the men whose inner crises are described with most labour and travail are the least real; such are the pedant Mr Casaubon and the banker Bulstrode. But the whole is like some piece of experience that we might wish to but cannot forget.

There is no plan, but there is no confusion. The 'three love-problems' are held firmly in hand. Dorothea, Lydgate, the Garth and Vincy families, meet and part, they pair and quarrel, they suffer and resign themselves, in what the authoress well calls an embroiled medium – say a kind of birdlime – yet solidly and distinctly; and the illusion holds out. The insignificant, like Fred Vincy, are made happy; the superior natures suffer. If they prospered, there would be no story: who could write a novel about the Brownings? George Eliot insists on making such persons suffer, above all in marriage. 'Retribution', said Lord Acton, 'is the constant theme and motive of her art.' Lord Acton did not exactly mean this in commendation; he held, himself, that 'virtue on earth is not much happier than crime'. However that may be, the retribution, in George Eliot's last two stories, is a visitation upon matrimonial blindness or folly, and not on crime. The folly of Dorothea in choosing Mr Casaubon is not made quite credible, and the immense pains taken in explaining it may betray a certain sense of the difficulty. But once the fact is granted, we foresee from the first the slow march of tragic disappointment. 'No one would ever know what she thought of a wedding journey to Rome.' The case is worse with Dr Lydgate, who wishes to become a second Bichat; it is worse, because his crampfish of a wife outlives him; whereas Mr Casaubon does die and makes room for Ladislaw. . . . *Middlemarch* is a precious document for the provincial life of that time, vaguely astir with ideas, but promptly sinking back into its beehive routine.

(from *A Survey of English Literature, 1830–1880*, vol. II, 1920)

VIRGINIA WOOLF: 'For Grown-up People'
To the reader who holds a large stretch of her early work in view it will become obvious that the mist of recollection gradually withdraws. It is not that her power diminishes, for, to our thinking, it is at its highest in the mature *Middlemarch*, the magnificent book which with all its imperfections is one of the few English novels written for grown-up people.

(from *The Times Literary Supplement*, 20 Nov 1919)

v. s. pritchett: 'No Hysteria . . . so much Determination'

No Victorian novel approaches *Middlemarch* in its width of reference, its intellectual power, or the imperturbable spaciousness of its narrative. It is sometimes argued by critics of contemporary literature that a return to Christianity is indispensable if we are to produce novels of the Victorian scale and authority, or indeed novels of any quality at all; but there are the novels of unbelievers like George Eliot and Hardy to discountenance them. The fact is that a wide and single purpose in the mind is the chief requirement outside of talent; a strong belief, a strong unbelief, even a strong egoism will produce works of the first order. If she had any religious leanings, George Eliot moved towards Judaism because of its stress on law; and if we think this preference purely intellectual and regard worry, that profoundly English habit of mind, as her philosophy, the point is that it was congenital, comprehensive worry. A forerunner of the psychologists, she promises no heaven and threatens no hell; the best and the worst we shall get is Warwickshire. Her world is the world of will, the smithy of character, a place of knowledge and judgments. So, in the sense of worldly wisdom, is Miss Austen's. But what a difference there is. To repeat our earlier definition, if Miss Austen is the novelist of the ego and its platitudes, George Eliot is the novelist of the idolatries of the super-ego. We find in a book like *Middlemarch*, not character modified by circumstance only, but character first impelled and then modified by the beliefs, the ambitions, the spiritual objects which it assimilates. Lydgate's schemes for medical reform and his place in medical science are as much part of his character as is his way with the ladies. And George Eliot read up her medical history in order to get his position exactly right. Dorothea's yearning for a higher life of greater usefulness to mankind will stay with her all her days and will make her a remarkable but exasperating woman; a fool for all her cleverness. George Eliot gives equal weight to these important qualifications. Many Victorian novelists have lectured us on the careers and aspirations of their people; none, before George Eliot, showed us the unity of intellect, aspiration and nature in action. Her judgment on Lydgate as a doctor is a judgment on his fate as a man:

He carried to his studies in London, Edinburgh and Paris the conviction that the medical profession as it might be was the finest in the world; presenting the most perfect interchange between science and art; offering the most direct alliance between intellectual conquest and the social good. Lydgate's nature demanded this combination: he was an emotional creature, with a flesh and blood sense of fellowship, which withstood all the abstractions of special study. He cared not only for 'Cases', but for John and Elizabeth, especially Elizabeth.

The Elizabeth, who was not indeed to wreck Lydgate's life, but (with far more probability) to corrupt his ideas and turn him into the smart practitioner, was Rosamond, his wife. Yet, in its own way, Rosamond's super-ego had the most distinguished ideals. A provincial manufacturer's daughter, she too longed idealistically to rise; the desire was not vulgar until she supposed that freedom from crude middle-class notions of taste and bearing could only be obtained by marriage to the cousin of a baronet; and was not immoral until she made her husband's conscience pay for her ambitions. The fountain, George Eliot is always telling us, cannot rise higher than its source.

Such analyses of character have become commonplace to us. When one compares the respectable Rosamond Lydgate with, say, Becky Sharp, one sees that Rosamond is not unique. Where *Middlemarch* is unique in its time is in George Eliot's power of generalisation. The last thing one accuses her of is *unthinking* acceptance of convention. She seeks, in her morality, the positive foundation of natural law, a kind of Fate whose measures are as fundamental as the changes of the seasons in nature. Her intellect is sculptural. The clumsiness of style does not denote muddle, but an attempt to carve decisively. We feel the clarifying force of a powerful mind. Perhaps it is not naturally powerful. The power may have been acquired. There are two George Eliots: the mature, experienced, quiet-humoured Midlander who wrote the childhood pages of *The Mill on the Floss*; and the naïve, earnest and masterly intellectual with her half-dozen languages and her scholarship. But unlike the irony of our time, hers is at the expense not of belief, but of people. Behind them, awful but inescapable to the eye of conscience, loom the statues of what they ought to have been. Hers is a mind that has grown by making judgments – as Mr Gladstone's head was said to have grown by making speeches.

Middlemarch resumes the observation and experience of a lifetime. Until this book George Eliot often strains after things beyond her capacity, as Dorothea Casaubon strained after a spiritual power beyond her nature. But now in *Middlemarch* the novelist is reconciled to her experience. In Dr Casaubon George Eliot sees that tragedy may paralyse the very intellect which was to be Dorothea's emancipation. Much of herself (George Eliot said, when she was accused of portraying Mark Pattison) went into Casaubon, and I can think of no other English novel before or since which has so truthfully, so sympathetically and so intimately described the befogged and grandiose humiliations of the scholar, as he turns at bay before the vengeance of life. Casaubon's jealousy is unforgettable, because, poisonous though it is, it is not the screech of an elderly cuckold, but the voice of strangled nature calling for justice. And notice, here, something very characteristic; George Eliot's pity flows from her moral sense, from the very seat of justice, and not from a sentimental heart.

Middlemarch is the first of many novels about groups of people in provincial towns. They are differentiated from each other not by class or fortune only, but by their moral history, and this moral differentiation is not casual, it is planned and has its own inner hierarchy. Look at the groups. Dorothea, Casaubon and Ladislaw seek to enter the highest spiritual fields – not perhaps the highest, for us, because, as we have seen, the world of George Eliot's imagination was prosaic and not poetic – still, they desire, in their several ways, to influence the standards of mankind. There is Lydgate, who is devoted to science and ex-pects to be rewarded by a career. He and his wife are practical people, who seek power. The pharisaical Bulstrode, the banker, expects to rise both spiritually and financially at once, until he sits on the right hand of God, the Father; a businessman with a bad conscience, he is the father of the Buchmanites and of all success-religions. The Garths, being country people and outside this urban world, believe simply in the virtue of work as a natural law and they are brought up against Fred Vincy, Rosamond's brother. He, as a horsey young man educated beyond his means, has a cheerful belief in irresponsible Style and in himself as a thing of pure male beauty with a riding crop. We may not accept George Eliot's standards, but we can see that they are not conventional, and that they do not make her one-sided. She is most intimately sympathetic to human beings and is never sloppy about them. When Vincy quarrels with Bulstrode about Fred's debts, when Casaubon's jealousy of Ladislaw secretes its first venom, when Lydgate tries vainly to talk about money to his wife or Fred goes to his erratic old uncle for a loan, vital human issues are raised. The great scenes of *Middlemarch* are exquisite, living transpositions of real moral dilemmas. Questions of principle are questions of battle; they point the weapons of the human comedy, and battle is not dull. In consequence, George Eliot's beliefs are rarely boring, because they are energies. They correspond to psychological and social realities, though more especially (on the large scale) to the functions of the will; they are boring only when, in the Victorian habit, she harangues the reader and pads out the book with brainy essays.

I see I have been writing about *Middlemarch* as though it was a piece of engineering. What about the life, the humour, the pleasure? There are failures: Dorothea and Ladislaw do not escape the fate of so many Victorian heroes and heroines who are frozen by their creator's high-mindedness. Has George Eliot forgotten how much these two difficult, sensitive and proud people will annoy each other by the stupidity which so frequently afflicts the intellectual? Such scruples, such play-acting! But Lydgate and Rosamond quarrelling about money; Rosamond quietly thwarting her husband's decisions, passing

without conscience to love affairs with his friends and ending as
a case-hardened widow who efficiently finds a second father for
her family – these things are perfect. Mary Garth defying the
old miser is admirable. But the most moving thing in the book
– and I always think this is the real test of a novelist – is
given to the least likeable people. Bulstrode's moral ruin
and his inability to confess to his dull wife are portrayed in a
picture of dumb human despondency which recalls a painting
by Sickert. One hears the clock tick in the silence that attends
the wearing down of two lives that can cling together but dare
not speak.

The humour of George Eliot gains rather than loses by its
mingling with her intellect. Here we feel the sound influence
of her girlish reading of the eighteenth-century novelists who
were above all men of education. This humour is seen at its
best in scenes like the one where the relations of the miser come
to his house, waiting to hear news of his will; and again in the
sardonic description of the spreading of the scandal about
Bulstrode and Lydgate. George Eliot followed causes down to
their most scurrilous effects. She is good in scandal and public
rumour. Her slow tempo is an advantage, and it becomes
exciting to know that she will make her point in the minor
scenes as surely as she will make it in the great ones. Mrs Dollop
of The Tankard has her short paragraph of immortality:

[She had] often to resist the shallow pragmatism of customers
disposed to think their reports from the outer world were of equal
force with what had 'come up' in her mind.

Mr Trumbull, the auctioneer, is another portrait, a longer
one, smelling of the bar and the saleroom. Dickens would have
caricatured this gift from heaven. George Eliot observes and
savours. Characteristically she catches his intellectual pretensions and his offensive superiority. We see him scent the coming
sale and walk over to Mary Garth's desk to read her copy of
Scott's *Anne of Geierstein*, just to show that he knows a book
when he sees one:

'The course of four centuries', he reads out unexpectedly, 'has well enough elapsed since the series of events which are related in the following chapters took place on the continent.'

That moment is one of the funniest in the English novel, one of those mad touches like the insertion of a dog stealing a bone, which Hogarth put into his pictures.

There is no real madness in George Eliot. Both heavy feet are on the ground. Outside of *Wuthering Heights* there is no madness in Victorian fiction. The Victorians were a histrionic people who measured themselves by the Elizabethans; and George Eliot, like Browning and Tennyson, was compared to Shakespeare by her contemporaries. The comparison failed, if only because madness is lacking. Hysteria, the effect of the exorbitant straining of their wills, the Victorians did, alas, too often achieve. George Eliot somehow escapes it. She is too level-headed. One pictures her, in life, moralising instead of making a scene. There is no hysteria in *Middlemarch*; perhaps there is no abyss because there is so much determination. But there is a humane breadth and resolution in this novel which offers neither hope nor despair to mankind but simply the necessity of fashioning the moral life. George Eliot's last words on her deathbed might, one irreverently feels, be placed on the title-page of her collected works: 'Tell them', she is reported to have said, 'the pain is on the left side.' Informative to the last and knowing better than the doctor, the self-made positivist dies.

(from *The Living Novel*, 1947)

BARBARA HARDY: 'Possibilities'
George Eliot has a simple and not very varied moral scheme but her novels are never schematic or rigid in their generalizations about human beings. The human examples are always variations of the theme rather than examples which fit it perfectly. The result is an impression of expansiveness which gives new life to the old cliché of the novelist's imagined 'world': this is like a world because of its flux and its size.

This sense of expansion and movement – life going on beyond this particular selection of life, implied in all the characters, in their convincing shadows which establish them all as human centres – this depends to some extent on actuality blurring into unacted possibility.

A simple example of this pressure of possibility is found in the relations of Dorothea and Lydgate. Some readers – encouraged no doubt by the serial habit of guessing what is to follow – found some hint of a lovers' ending for these two. The reviewer in the *Edinburgh Review* for January, 1873, expected the 'real hero' to marry the 'real heroine'. The guess may have been encouraged by the initial pointed exclusion of Dorothea from Lydgate's desires:

'She is a good creature – that fine girl – but a little too earnest,' he thought. 'It is troublesome to talk to such women. They are always wanting reasons, yet they are too ignorant to understand the merits of any question, and usually fall back on their own moral sense to settle things after their own taste.'   (chap. 10)

This possibility, if it is felt at all, is there as a faint stirring of irony asserting itself whenever Lydgate is made to reassess his first intellectual rejection of Dorothea or to make the contrast between the woman he wanted and the woman he did not want. It is certainly not felt at all on Dorothea's side. Both Dorothea and Lydgate are committed by their disastrous desires before they meet, but Dorothea plays a larger part in his reflections than he does in hers.

The romantic possibility for Dorothea might be expected to arise in her early relation with Will, but in fact there is instead a marked and sometimes irritatingly innocent absence of the kind of speculative fantasy which might well mark such a relationship. Will, it is true, has 'dreamy visions of possibilities' but these are left vague, and George Eliot emphasizes that the precise fantasy about the future is Casaubon's, while Will takes a romantic delight in the very hopelessness of his love:

It may seem strange, but it is the fact, that the ordinary vulgar vision of which Mr Casaubon suspected him – namely, that Dorothea might become a widow, and that the interest he had established in her mind might turn to acceptance of him as a husband – had no tempting, arresting power over him; he did not live in the scenery of such an event, and follow it out, as we all do with that imagined 'otherwise' which is our practical heaven. (chap. 47)

Dorothea, in spite of her short-sighted abstraction from the present in dreams of 'things as they had been and were going to be', has 'no visions of their ever coming into closer union'. The innocence of this relation may be exaggerated by the sexless glamour George Eliot often casts over love, but it is presented in striking contrast to Rosamond's vulgar little dreams of uncommitted adultery. Will has certainly no room in his dreamy visions for Rosamond, but the reader's knowledge of her fantasy-life supplies an ironical supplement to their relationship.

And when he is cut off from Dorothea Will moves into a curious imagined relation with Rosamond. It is perhaps one of the best examples of what George Eliot said she wanted to show in *Middlemarch* as the slow movement of ordinary causes.

She often shows temptation as a casual almost undesired drift towards the strongest current. Fred's drift back to gambling is like this, and so in a sense, though it is also characteristic of the man, is Lydgate's drift towards the engulfing Rosamond. At one stage in *Middlemarch* both Lydgate and Ladislaw are held in moral suspense, and it is then that they come for the first time into formally emphatic relation. Lydgate is poised between two ways, the way of redemption which means staying in Middlemarch, and the other way of capitulation, which means Rosamond's victory and departure from Middlemarch. Ladislaw, though with less prominent urgency, since his presence in the book is considerably less concentrated and sustained than Lydgate's, is also torn between staying and going. His departure is brought into direct contact with Lydgate's.

This pressure of possibility begins in the scene with Rosamond, after Dorothea's departure, when for the first time her

egoism is bitten into by Will's 'I would rather touch her hand
if it were dead, than I would touch any other woman's living'.
Then Will's anger goes beyond his fear of what may have
happened to Dorothea's faith in him, and this is where the
vision of possibility comes in:

The vindictive fire was still burning in him, and he could utter no
word of retraction; but it was still in his mind that having come
back to this hearth where he had enjoyed a caressing friendship he
had found calamity seated there – he had had suddenly revealed to
him a trouble that lay outside the home as well as within it. And
what seemed a foreboding was pressing upon him with slow pincers:[1]
– that his life might come to be enslaved by this helpless woman
who had thrown herself upon him in the dreary sadness of her
heart. But he was in gloomy rebellion against the fact that his
quick apprehensiveness foreshadowed to him. . . .   (chap. 78)

This crisis is complicated because it is Lydgate's crisis too.
In an earlier scene with Rosamond he has failed in his effort to
'bring her to feel with some solemnity that here was a slander
which must be met and not run away from' and he has also
said to Dorothea 'I have not taken a bribe yet. But there is a
pale shade of bribery which is sometimes called prosperity.'
And there is the additional irony that Dorothea's discovery of
Will and Rosamond is brought about by her promise to help
Lydgate.

The next step brings the possibility of a linked future for the
two men:

When Lydgate spoke with desperate resignation of going to settle
in London, and said with a faint smile, 'We shall have you again,
old fellow,' Will felt inexpressibly mournful, and said nothing.
Rosamond had that morning entreated him to urge this step on
Lydgate; and it seemed to Will as if he were beholding in a magic
panorama a future where he himself was sliding into that pleasureless
yielding to the small solicitations of circumstance, which is a com-
moner history of perdition than any single momentous bargain.

We are on a perilous margin when we begin to look passively at
our future selves, and see our own figures led with dull consent into

insipid misdoing and shabby achievement. Poor Lydgate was inwardly groaning on that margin, and Will was arriving at it.

(chap. 79)

The possibilities cross. But it is only Lydgate who is led into the shabby achievement. The crisis gives Will's character a measure of realistic toughening which counteracts the glamour and innocence with which the imagery endows him. Once more fate is seen as fragile, success as variable. The rigid moral process is there, but so is the precariousness of chance. The elaborate pattern of reflecting mirrors is given a further recession. The real event is not only mirrored and modified in other real events but in the flickering reflection of possibilities.

These converging possibilities are present in other situations in *Middlemarch*, and with the same kind of expansive suggestiveness. There is the 'imagined otherwise' of that other set of characters, Mary, Fred, and Mr Farebrother. The happy success, both romantic and moral, which Fred and Mary achieve, is preserved from glibness by Farebrother's wry vision of possibility. As Mrs Garth says, 'she might have had a man who is worth twenty Fred Vincys', and that possibility has its brief presence in Mary's vision of the future.

'Fred has lost all his other expectations; he must keep this,' Mary said to herself, with a smile curling her lips. It was impossible to help fleeting visions of another kind – new dignities and an acknowledged value of which she had often felt the absence. But these things with Fred outside them, Fred forsaken and looking sad for the want of her, could never tempt her deliberate thought. (chap. 57)

The possibility is strengthened when Fred begins to slide back into his old ways. Farebrother's warning words have a double irony in the context of our knowledge of Mary's fleeting visions:

'But relations of this sort, even when they are of long standing, are always liable to change. I can easily conceive that you might act in a way to loosen the tie she feels towards you – it must be remembered that she is only conditionally bound to you – and that in that case, another man, who may flatter himself that he has a hold on her

regard, might succeed in winning that firm place in her love as well
as respect which you had let slip. I can easily conceive such a result,'
repeated Mr Farebrother, emphatically. 'There is a companionship
of ready sympathy, which might get the advantage even over the
longest associations.'   (chap. 66)

The unplayed possibilities emerge everywhere in *Middlemarch*.
There are the possibilities which Featherstone dangled before
his prospective heirs, which certainly played a large part in
Fred's life. There is Dorothea's decision to accept Casaubon's
blank cheque for the future – it is cancelled only because she
finds Casaubon is dead before she can accept. And there is the
backward glance cast by Bulstrode, whose 'imagined otherwise'
was having his time again – 'And yet – if he could be back in
that far-off spot with his youthful poverty – why, then he would
choose to be a missionary' (chap. 61). This persistent vision of
possibilities plays an extensive part because it becomes part of
the theme. Like the image of the mirror, it is one of George
Eliot's ways of showing the nature of illusion and the colliding
multiplicity of human points of view. . . .

(from *The Novels of George Eliot*, 1959)

NOTE
  1. Another echo in imagery: the 'pincers' are used of Rosamond's
power over Lydgate (chaps. 65, 78).

DAVID DAICHES: 'An Important Moral Centre'
. . . The Garth family provide an important moral centre in the
novel and, though we may not fully realise it at the time, Lydgate is failing a moral test when in chap. 17 he dismisses Mary
Garth when her name is introduced by Mr Farebrother with
'I have hardly noticed her'. We are told specifically that he
does not care 'to know more about the Garths'. Fred's love for
Mary is an important point in his favour. Throughout the
novel, attitude to the Garths provides a moral test; Fred is the
only member of his family who passes it. Lydgate's failure here
is bound up with a certain lack of imagination which in turn is
linked with his kind of pride. 'He had always known in a general

way that he was not rich, but he had never felt poor, and he had no power of imagining the part which the want of money plays in determining the actions of men.' Rosamond takes for granted that Lydgate will keep her in the style to which she aspires; she 'never thought of money except as something necessary which other people would always provide'. In this she is curiously like her husband, who takes for granted that he will continue to live elegantly until the pressure of tradesmen's bills forces him into an awareness of the important part played by money in maintaining the style of a gentleman. This is part of his 'commonness' – George Eliot is interestingly original in seeing a refusal to understand the economic realities that underlie class distinctions as a sort of vulgarity. This seems to reverse the usual view, but it does not so much reverse it as go behind and beyond it to trace the links between imagination, understanding and distinction of character. Dorothea is affectionately mocked by the author for her disappointment in finding that her husband's parishioners are comfortably housed and do not need her good works; this is another kind of sentimentalising of economic reality. Mr Brooke, who preaches reform but allows his own tenants to go ill-housed at inflated rents, provides yet another variety.

Attitudes to money are important in the novel. Fred feels that the world owes him a living (a milder version of his sister's fault) and lowers his character by joining the group of potential legatees awaiting Featherstone's death, and in her magnificently drawn picture of the grasping relations besieging the dying man George Eliot rubs in the importance of the *idea* of money, rather than the money itself, to so many people. Rosamond, by contrast, was not 'sordid or mercenary', nor was Lydgate. But to take money for granted is a kind of selfishness just as corroding to the character as to pursue it obsessively. Bulstrode has made his money by devious ways for the greater glory of God; Will refuses Bulstrode's money when the latter wishes to make financial amends to him; Dorothea thinks that her husband should give Will that part of his fortune deriving from Will's grandmother (who was Casaubon's aunt) having been

disinherited; Lydgate is helped out of his financial difficulties
by Bulstrode's lending him the sum he had offered to Will and
Dorothea relieves Lydgate from the danger to his reputation
resulting from this by letting him have the money to repay
Bulstrode – money is clearly a potent force in the novel. Good
characters often feel the need of it – Farebrother, for example,
who lives on £400 a year until he gets the Lowick living. Fred's
involving the relatively poor Garths in financial loss reveals
some central aspects of his own and the Garths' character.
Behind all this lies something like Marx's labour theory of value.
Caleb Garth supplies the clue: we are told in chap. 23 that 'he
could not manage finance' although 'he knew values well' and
in chap. 56 that 'by "business" Caleb never meant money
transactions but the skilful application of labour'. The moral
implications of money are tested by its sources and its use: its
proper source is good and happy labour (one thinks of Ruskin
and William Morris here) and its proper use is social good. . . .

Fred Vincy's expectations from life are not dissimilar to those
of the unmarried Lydgate. . . . But it was not pride or 'commonness' that produced them; it was his optimism, his easy confidence that with his bearing and education life was bound to
do something to help him. 'That he should ever fall into a
thoroughly unpleasant position – wear trousers shrunk with
washing, eat cold mutton, have to walk for want of a horse, or
to "duck under" in any sort of way – was an absurdity irrecon-
cilable with those cheerful intuitions implanted in him by
nature.' Fred is educated by circumstances into self-reliance –
the circumstances being mainly the Garth family. Caleb Garth's
position with respect to money and labour has already been
noted. Caleb is used also to emphasise George Eliot's insistence
that practical virtues rather than doctrinal orthodoxy are what
really matter. This is a recurring theme in all her novels, and
is important also in her portrait of Farebrother. Though Caleb
'never regarded himself as other than an orthodox Christian,
and would argue on prevenient grace if the subject were
proposed to him, I think his virtual divinities were good practical schemes, accurate work, and the faithful completion of

undertakings: his prince of darkness was a slack workman'.

While there is certainly an element of idealisation in the portrait of Caleb Garth (George Eliot was thinking partly of her father) and occasionally a false note is sounded, as in the parenthetical 'pardon these details for once – you would have learned to love them if you had known Caleb Garth' in chap. 23, this element does not significantly diminish the effectiveness with which he and his family work into the pattern of the novel. Their accurate social placing helps to give them concreteness. 'Mrs Vincy had never been at her ease with Mrs Garth, and frequently spoke of her as a woman who had had to work for her bread – meaning that Mrs Garth had been a teacher before her marriage; in which case an intimacy with Lindley Murray [the standard school grammar] and Mangnall's Questions was something like a draper's discrimination of calico trade-marks, or a courier's acquaintance with foreign countries: no woman who was better off needed that sort of thing.' The slight tenseness in the relations between the Vincys and the Garths, so precisely realised in the scene between Mary and Rosamond in chap. 12, gives a moral as well as a psychological meaning to Fred's love for Mary, for it is an assertion of genuine affection in the face of class prejudice and of apparent self-interest. Yet Fred's moral position is for a long time very dubious, and it is precisely his juxtaposition with Mary and her family which reveals this. When his foolish optimism and bad judgment have lost him the money with which he was to repay the bulk of the money he had borrowed on Mr Garth's guarantee, his immediate reaction is to consider himself unfortunate and ill-used. It was Mrs Garth's brisk, uncomplaining, practical way of meeting the disastrous loss which this involved for the Garths which first makes him see the situation from another view than his own. (Again, we think of the parallel with Rosamond and the one occasion – of a very different kind – when she was forced to *feel* another's view. Fred is always shown as more educable in sympathy than his sister: the potentiality is there from the beginning.)

But she had made Fred feel for the first time something like the tooth of remorse. Curiously enough, his pain in the affair beforehand had consisted almost entirely in the sense that he must seem dishonourable, and sink in the opinion of the Garths: he had not occupied himself with the inconvenience and possible injury that his breach might occasion them, for this exercise of the imagination on other people's needs is not common with hopeful young gentlemen.

The reproach to Fred is somewhat mitigated by his lack of imagination with respect to others' needs being ascribed to 'hopeful young gentlemen' in general. The implication is that this is a fault of his age and class, not deep-seated in his character. The change of his own view of himself in response to Mrs Garth's reaction is immediate and drastic: 'he suddenly saw himself as a pitiful rascal who was robbing two women of their savings'. This is an important sign of grace. True, his egotism rises again soon afterwards, only to receive an even more severe blow from Mary.

'I wouldn't have hurt you so for the world, Mary,' he said at last. 'You can never forgive me.'

'What does it matter whether I forgive you?' said Mary, passionately. 'Would that make it any better for my mother to lose the money she has been earning by lessons for four years, that she might send Alfred to Mr Hanmer's? Should you think all that pleasant enough if I forgave you?'

The repeated rising of Fred's egotism and its as repeated rebuff by Mary is half-comic, but the underlying seriousness – indeed, the absolute centrality – of the episode cannot be missed.

'I am so miserable, Mary—if you knew how miserable I am you would be sorry for me.'

'There are other things to be more sorry for than that. But selfish people always think their own discomfort of more importance than anything else in the world: I see enough of that every day.'

'It is hardly fair to call me selfish. If you knew what things other young men do, you would think me a good way off the worst.'

'I know that people who spend a great deal of money on themselves without knowing how they shall pay, must be selfish. They are always thinking of what they can get for themselves, and not of what other people may lose.'

Here, spelt out in the simplest and most direct language, is a moral problem with which every major character in the novel is, in one way or another, involved.

The Garth family are the most fully realised as a *family* of all the characters in *Middlemarch*, and it is this fullness of realisation that makes their moral centrality in the novel acceptable. Mrs Garth testing her younger children in English grammar or Roman history as she attends to the cooking in the kitchen is one of those thoroughly established domestic scenes in which the Victorian novel excels. George Eliot could do this, as other Victorian novelists could, but with her it is not domestic comedy for its own sake, not merely an appeal to the reader's recognition or sympathy or moral approval or cosiness of feeling; it plays its part in establishing the moral pattern of the novel, and everything else that happens to all the other characters can, in one way or another, be related to the moral centre provided here. The point is worth repeating and emphasising, because so many critics, following the misleading Prelude, take Dorothea as the moral centre of the novel. The Garth family are the only major characters in *Middlemarch* (apart from the ineducable Rosamond) who are not educated by experience; they do not change. This is because they are already in possession of the moral education that matters by the time the novel opens. This is a significant clue. The Dorothea–Casaubon story and its aftermath, and the Lydgate–Rosamond story, are of course more important in the pattern of the novel's action than the Mary–Fred story or than anything which involves the Garth family, but the Garth family establishes the criteria to which most other actions are referred.

An important part of virtue, according to the view that emerges in the novel, consists in not making extravagant or vain claims upon life, yet at the same time in not lowering one's moral sights when one restricts any claim. This is most explicitly suggested in a remark about Mary:

Mary was fond of her own thoughts, and could amuse herself well sitting in twilight with her hands in her lap; for, having early had strong reason to believe that things were not likely to be arranged for her peculiar satisfaction, she wasted no time in astonishment and annoyance at that fact. And she had already come to take life very much as a comedy in which she had a proud, nay a generous resolution not to act the mean or treacherous part. Mary might have become cynical if she had not had parents whom she honoured, and a well of affectionate gratitude within her, which was all the fuller because she had learned to make no unreasonable claims.

This is a very carefully balanced attitude and that the author's approval lies behind it there can be no doubt. In the light of it, what becomes of the Saint Theresa concept with which the novel opened? Surely it is now seen as a form of unreasonable claim on life, which it is the part of moral maturity to forego. Idealism is precious and valuable, but boundless idealism is a kind of folly, based on self-delusion. To set bounds to moral as to other expectations without becoming cynical is the part of wisdom, and it is the ties of personal relationships (love *and* honour) that enable us to achieve this balance. The whole novel can be read in the light of such insights, for the whole novel contributes to establishing them. . . .

(from *George Eliot: 'Middlemarch'*, 1963)

W. J. HARVEY: Lydgate's Engagement
The moral enlargement of many of George Eliot's characters is essentially a recognition of the complex relations of things, that life is rarely a matter of simple categories; similarly the moral effect of the novels is accomplished for the reader if his vision is enlarged in the same way. To this end all aspects of George Eliot's technique are subordinated; hence, for example, her usual method of interweaving concurrent stories within one narrative framework, hence all the devices of gradually

enlarging perspectives. . . . It is only necessary here to notice the intricacy of pattern in the usual George Eliot novel, the careful marshalling of all the many kinds of relationships which go to make up her picture of life. There are the interaction of private and public within one character, of past and present, of the small society and the great world outside, of one character and another, of all the various interactions between character and society. All of these build up that 'solidity of specification' so much desired by Henry James and it is a solidity we never feel to be theoretic. It is remarkable, for example, how much social analysis George Eliot can pack into a novel without ever swamping the individuality of her characters and without ever allowing the novel to degenerate into a sociological treatise. As she wrote in her essay on *The Natural History of German Life*:

The tendency created by the splendid conquests of modern generalization, to believe that all questions are merged in economical science, and that the relations of men to their neighbours may be settled by algebraic equations . . . none of these diverging mistakes can coexist with a real knowledge of the people, with a thorough study of their habits, their ideas, their motives.

It is a lesson she never forgot in her novels. Perhaps the best way of discovering how vital to a right appreciation of her work is a full understanding of the various and complex modes of connection, both social and aesthetic, is to examine in some detail one incident from one novel. This should help to show the local density and richness, the packed-without-being-clotted quality of her prose and also how firmly and subtly local detail is related both to its immediate context and to the book as a whole. For these purposes I have chosen a passage from the end of chap. 31 of *Middlemarch*, the scene describing Lydgate's engagement to Rosamond; although it is a fairly lengthy passage I print it here for convenience.

Miss Vincy was alone, and blushed so deeply when Lydgate came in that he felt a corresponding embarrassment, and instead of any playfulness, he began to speak at once of his reason for calling, and to beg her, almost formally, to deliver the message to her father. Rosamond, who at the first moment felt as if her happiness were returning, was keenly hurt by Lydgate's manner; her blush had departed, and she assented coldly, without adding an unnecessary word, some trivial chainwork which she had in her hands enabling her to avoid looking at Lydgate higher than his chin. In all failures, the beginning is certainly the half of the whole. After sitting two long moments while he moved his whip and could say nothing, Lydgate rose to go, and Rosamond, made nervous by her struggle between mortification and the wish not to betray it, dropped her chain as if startled, and rose too, mechanically. Lydgate instantaneously stooped to pick up the chain. When he rose he was very near to a lovely little face set on a fair long neck which he had been used to see turning about under the most perfect management of self-contented grace. But as he raised his eyes now he saw a certain helpless quivering which touched him quite newly, and made him look at Rosamond with a questioning flash. At this moment she was as natural as she had ever been when she was five years old; she felt that her tears had risen, and it was no use to try to do anything else than let them stay like water on a blue flower or let them fall over her cheeks, even as they would.

That moment of naturalness was the crystallizing feather-touch; it shook flirtation into love. Remember that the ambitious man who was looking at those Forget-me-nots under the water was very warm-hearted and rash. He did not know where the chain went; an idea had thrilled through the recesses within him which had a miraculous effect in raising the power of passionate love lying buried there in no sealed sepulchre, but under the lightest, easily pierced mould. His words were quite abrupt and awkward, but the tone made them seem like an ardent, appealing avowal.

'What is the matter? You are distressed. Tell me, pray.'

Rosamond had never been spoken to in such tones before. I am not sure that she knew what the words were: but she looked at Lydgate and the tears fell over her cheeks. There could have been no more complete answer than that silence, and Lydgate, forgetting everything else, completely mastered by the outrush of tenderness at the sudden belief that this sweet young creature depended on him for her joy, actually put his arms round her, folding her gently and protectingly – he was used to being gentle with the weak and the suffering – and kissed each of the two large tears. This was a strange way of arriving at an understanding, but it was a short way. Rosamond was not angry, but she moved backward a little in timid happiness, and Lydgate could now sit near her and speak less incompletely. Rosamond had to make her little confession, and he poured out words of gratitude and tenderness with impulsive lavishment. In half an hour he left the house an engaged man, whose soul was not his own, but the woman's to whom he had bound himself.

I will start by briefly sketching in the context of this passage. It is Lydgate's profession that first brings him into contact with the Vincy family. In chap. 26 Fred falls ill and Lydgate is called in to replace Dr Wrench: 'the event was a subject of general conversation in Middlemarch'. The function of gossip as a connecting and relating agent in the novel is extremely important; it is a kind of crude social oil which soon clings to Lydgate and Rosamond. Not without cause, for Rosamond admirably acts the part of a sister concerned for her brother's health (we may contrast this with Dorothea's anxiety for Casaubon) and Lydgate's professional duties soon entangle him in a personal relationship. 'Her presence of mind and adroitness in carrying out his hints were admirable and it is not wonderful that the idea of Rosamond began to mingle itself with his interest in the case.' A flirtation soon springs up which of course does not escape the attention of the Middlemarchers since 'it was not more possible to find social isolation in that town than elsewhere'. Mrs Bulstrode gossips about it with Mrs Plymdale (a masterly piece of cattish dialogue), catechizes Rosamond and hints to Lydgate through her husband that his attentions are not desired. The irony of this is a very common one in George Eliot, the irony of a character acting to produce one result and actually producing the reverse of his intentions. Gossip and social pressure as represented here by Mrs Bulstrode combine to force the flirtation to such a degree of explicitness that some irreversible decision has to be taken. (In a minor way Farebrother unwittingly abets Mrs Bulstrode in this.) Lydgate decides to end the flirtation and does not visit her for ten days – hence Rosamond's distress and hence Lydgate's downfall. On the eleventh day he does go to the Vincys' house, ostensibly for professional reasons, though 'It must be confessed, also, that momentary speculations as to all the possible grounds for Mrs Bulstrode's hints had managed to get woven like slight clinging hairs into the more substantial web of his thoughts.' (A very characteristic and revealing image.) Thus the scene we are about to examine takes place in a wide social context; George Eliot sharpens her focus to concentrate on the two individuals, but once the scene is over and the engagement made, she broadens her vision again; the chapter ends with a social occasion, with Lydgate visiting Mr Vincy to gain his approval and being welcomed into the family circle.

George Eliot does not in this scene attempt to portray directly the developing emotional relationship between Lydgate and Rosamond; the reason for this we shall discuss later. The scene is conveyed to us mainly by description and comment, yet at the same time it does achieve a peculiar kind of concreteness and immediacy. On analysis we find, I think, that this is due to the sharply visualized nature of the passage, the way in which emotions are expressed by physical postures or gestures. Rosamond refusing to look at Lydgate, her dropping the chainwork, his stooping, looking up at her, his embrace; these are all the physical correlatives of their developing relationship. This is a common and recurring technique in George Eliot's novels; the peaks of *Middlemarch* are nearly always conveyed at least in part by sharply defined stances – we remember Casaubon in the posture of death, Bulstrode in the posture of despair, Dorothea and Will in the stance of love. In this passage the sense of physical presence is the unobtrusive but necessary condition for the other effects George Eliot wishes to achieve. It defines, for instance, the quality of Rosamond at this moment. Rosamond, the pathetic product of Mrs Lemon's academy for young ladies, is analysed throughout the novel in terms of artifice; her egoism expresses itself largely through dramatic stance and imagery. (Drama, as we shall see later with *Daniel Deronda*, is nearly always in George Eliot's novels a metaphor for the self-deluding, dream-spinning, narcissistic type of egoism of which Rosamond is an example.) Earlier in this chapter Rosamond has withstood Mrs Bulstrode's questions 'with a great sense of being a romantic heroine, and playing the part prettily'; later, when she thinks Lydgate has broken off the flirtation she 'felt as forlorn as Ariadne – a charming stage Ariadne left behind with all her boxes full of costumes and no hope of a coach'. But at this moment – and only for the moment – the self-control wavers, the artifice drops away and it is, ironically, the unusual naturalness of the girl that captivates Lydgate, which traps him into marriage and so ruins both their lives. The moment of naturalness which here does the damage is balanced by the one other moment in the novel when Rosamond transcends her egoism and breaks through the mask of artifice to do good; if here she ruins herself and Lydgate, later she saves Will and Dorothea. I am thinking, of course, of chap. 81, the great scene – again marked by a keen sense of physical presence, in which Rosamond tells Dorothea the truth about her relationship with Will. In the one case, things go wrong, in the other things are put right.

Of course, the ironic effectiveness of Rosamond's moment of naturalness in this scene depends vitally upon the character of Lydgate. Lydgate, we know, has his 'spots of commonness', and one of them is to regard women as a relaxation and an adornment to life – hardly an attitude likely to lead to a successful marriage. (It is an attitude not far removed from Casaubon's to Dorothea.) But Lydgate is also, as George Eliot tells us, 'warm-hearted and rash' (we have the previous evidence of his affair with the French actress), and these qualities betray him. Moreover, even here he is a doctor as well as a man; one notices the revealing force of the parenthesis, 'he was used to being gentle with the weak and the suffering'; indeed, in many ways the whole interview has the incongruous flavour of a doctor's visit – 'In half an hour he left the house. . . .' Love dwindles down to an emotional therapy.

I have said that George Eliot evades any direct expression of a complicated human relationship and indeed, at first glance, this whole passage might be taken as evidence of her failure to deal adequately with that area of life which involves mature sexual relationships. Such a criticism has its point elsewhere, but it does not apply here. For the whole passage is precisely concerned to show the failure of such a relationship, without which marriage will almost certainly come to disaster. In fact, it is not love in any full sense of the word which binds Lydgate to Rosamond; it is affection, tenderness, compassion, the consciousness of having hurt her, the sense that she depends on him for her joy – admirable qualities but insufficient as a basis for marriage. (This is clearly paralleled by the relationship of Dorothea and Casaubon; that Dorothea can regard Casaubon as a father as much as a husband bodes no good for their union.) This genuine, but fatally limited, relationship is expressed most clearly when Lydgate embraces Rosamond, 'folding her gently and protectingly – he was used to being gentle with the weak and the suffering'.

As Lydgate begins, so he must go on; he will be disillusioned – at best his marriage will never amount to much more than what is implied in this passage; the beginning foreshadows the end. Excluding the Epilogue, the Lydgate–Rosamond story in *Middlemarch* finishes thus:

Poor Rosamond's vagrant fancy had come back terribly scourged – meek enough to nestle under the old despised shelter. And the shelter was still there; Lydgate had accepted his narrowed lot with sad resignation. He had chosen this fragile creature, and had taken the burthen of her life upon his arms. He must walk as he could, carrying that burthen pitifully.

The tone of the two passages, with its basic image of nestling, folding, sheltering, is strikingly similar. The wheel has come full circle; the working out of the whole of this part of the novel has given substance to George Eliot's touch of omniscient generalization in this passage – 'In all failures, the beginning is certainly the half of the whole.'

There is one other important way in which this pa[ ] relates to its context. Lydgate's aroused emotion is described a striking, rather odd image:

An idea had thrilled through the recesses within him which had a miraculous effect in raising the power of passionate love lying buried there in no sealed sepulchre, but under the lightest, easily pierced mould.

This image, which risks blasphemy, gains in power and relevance if we see it in relation to the pattern of tombs, closets, sealed rooms which cluster around Casaubon. Casaubon is 'a sealed sepulchre'; that is one reason why his marriage comes to grief. Lydgate's will come to grief for exactly the opposite reasons. Thus language itself is an important mode of connection in the novel. One might possibly notice another instance of the same sort of thing in this passage though I hesitate to press the point since I am not sure that it is genuinely there to be pressed. At any rate, it will serve as a good index of the difficulties and delicacies involved in discussing language as creatively used. Rosamond, at the beginning of the scene, is doing some 'trivial chainwork', later 'she dropped the chain . . . Lydgate instantaneously stooped to pick up the chain . . . he did not know where the chain went. . . . In half an hour he left the house an engaged man, whose soul was not his own, but the woman's to whom he had bound himself.'

We may not be justified in seeing any symbolic significance in the insistently repeated chain motif; but we should give full weight to the note of Lydgate binding himself. Imagery of entanglement, of bonds, yokes, fetters, bridles is . . . a dominant though unobtrusive pattern in the book.

To sum up; the modes of connection revealed by this passage are many and complex. Within the subject matter, the actual life portrayed, they include the relation of private life to public society, with particular reference to gossip as a social force, and also the relation of private to public within the individual – Lydgate the man cannot be separated from Lydgate the doctor.

.volves and in part betrays him. Aesthetically,
.ructural contrasts and parallels, anticipations
.ns, and various patterns of language. The result
istic density and solidity which is an important
.1 in George Eliot's realism and in her moral

(from *The Art of George Eliot*, 1961)

W. J. HARVEY: A Critique of Henry James on *Middlemarch*
. . . Let us return for a moment to James's review of *Middlemarch*.
This, like most of his criticism of George Eliot, reflects . . . mixed
feelings. . . . On the one hand he tries once again to shape the
formal structure of the book around one central figure, faulting
it because naturally it refuses to conform to this pattern. 'And
yet, nominally,' he writes, '*Middlemarch* has a definite subject –
the subject indicated in the eloquent preface. . . . Dorothea's
career is, however, but an episode, and though doubtless in
intention, not distinctly enough in fact, the central one.'

What we know of the history of *Middlemarch*'s creation is
evidence enough for supporting that James has mistaken George
Eliot's intention. But even taking the novel in isolation, we
should surely not allow the impression of the preface (in itself
unfortunate) to overrule or to predetermine the impression
derived from the novel as a whole.

'It is not compact, doubtless, but when was a panorama
compact?' James's ambivalent attitude, his mixture of admiration and exasperation, comes out in this question. But the
question itself conceals a view of the novel which is at best only
half true. Certainly *Middlemarch* is, in one sense, panoramic;
that is to say, if one wants to find a unifying centre, one does
better to locate it in a society, in Middlemarch itself, rather
than in any one individual. And yet, one must insist in the face
of James, the novel *is* extraordinarily compact; it is remarkable
how little one can cut out or reduce in scale without vitally
impairing its essential achievement – certainly much less than
in *Adam Bede* or *The Mill on the Floss*. Fortunately James has
given us an idea of what, he thinks, could have been excised.

The greatest minds have the defects of their qualities, and as George Eliot's mind is preeminently contemplative and analytic, nothing is more natural than that her manner should be discursive and expansive. 'Concentration' would doubtless have deprived us of many of the best things in the book – of Peter Featherstone's grotesquely expectant legatees, of Lydgate's medical rivals, and of Mary Garth's delightful family. . . . Mr Farebrother and his 'delightful womankind' belong to a large group of figures begotten of the superabundance of the author's creative instinct. At times they seem to encumber the stage and to produce a rather ponderous mass of dialogue; but they add to the reader's impression of having walked in the Middlemarch lanes and listened to the Middlemarch accent. To but one of these accessory episodes – that of Mr Bulstrode, with its multiplex ramifications, do we take exception. It has a slightly artificial cast, a melodramatic tinge, unfriendly to the richly natural colouring of the whole. Bulstrode himself – with the history of whose troubled conscience the author has taken great pains – is, to our sense, too diffusely treated; he never grasps the reader's attention.

James, in part, answers his own objection. The minor characters do cumulatively create that sense of social density from which the protagonists derive so much of their strength, without which they would be unimaginable. Granted that a large part of Lydgate's solidity of specification lies in his professional life and granted that his tragedy lies in the corrosion of his ambition by social forces, how could we do without a picture of his medical colleagues? Confronted with James's criticism of Bulstrode, one can only assert the contrary; he is, surely, one of the book's great successes, with a certain grasp of 'the reader's attention'. He is one of the book's finest end-products; with his equals he provides us with the best possible reason for reading the novel. We may grant that the 'multiplex ramifications' of his story can be criticized. Not so much, I think, the Raffles–Rigg part of the plot mechanism; George Eliot persuades us of the paradoxical naturalness of chance and coincidence in a quite remarkable way. The weak point, rather, is the linking of Bulstrode's past history with that of Ladislaw; this is the wrong kind of coincidence and it does have 'a slightly artificial cast, a melodramatic tinge'.

What of the centres of interest represented in the novel by Featherstone and the Garth family? That the Featherstone episodes provide locally a good deal of grotesque comedy is true but is not a sufficient reason for their presence in the novel. We may also discount the fact that Featherstone's death starts in motion the Rigg–Raffles chain of events which leads to Bulstrode's downfall – some other device of plot could easily have been made to produce the same results. But, of course, Featherstone relates also to Casaubon and to Bulstrode. The novel does not – must not – make the relationship overt, but we are surely led to connect the effect of Featherstone's will on Fred and Mary with the effect of Casaubon's will on Dorothea and Ladislaw. The connecting element is just strong enough, the results sufficiently diverse, for us to feel that effect of unity in variety which is so important a part of George Eliot's sense of the quality of life. And if we assimilate these two instances, seeing them as particular examples of the dead hand of the past controlling the living present, then we can contrast these two cases with Bulstrode. The dead hand of Featherstone or Casaubon paradoxically liberates and re-vivifies those whom it was meant to govern or thwart; Bulstrode's past, which he thought dead and buried, springs to life and destroys him. Bulstrode is in many ways close to Featherstone; for both of them – for Featherstone crudely, for Bulstrode subtly – money is power. This is Featherstone:

He loved money, but he also loved to spend it in gratifying his peculiar tastes, and perhaps he loved it best of all as a means of making others feel his power more or less uncomfortably. (chap. 34)

Set him beside Bulstrode:

His private minor loans were numerous, but he would inquire strictly into the circumstances both before and after. In this way a man gathers a domain in his neighbours' hope and fear as well as gratitude; and power, when once it has got into that subtle region,

propagates itself, spreading out of all proportion to its
means.   (chap

It is no wonder that Featherstone, in one of those anticipatory
hints we discussed earlier, sees so clearly into Bulstrode's heart,
diagnosing so acutely the tangled strands of money and religion:

And what's he? – he's got no land hereabout that ever I heard tell
of. A speckilating fellow! He may come down any day, when the
devil leaves off backing him. And that's what his religion means:
he wants God A'mighty to come in.   (chap. 12)

It is entirely appropriate that Stone Court should pass from
Featherstone to Bulstrode. If Featherstone were removed from
the novel, two of its main centres (although, for James, Bulstrode
himself is only accessory) would be considerably weakened.

The role of the Garth family is more complex. Again, I
discount their own intrinsic interest, their function in the plot
and their role in composing part of the social strata of Middlemarch – though these, in themselves, might be thought sufficient
reasons for their presence in the novel. We must examine their
other structural functions. Caleb Garth is an embodiment –
like Farebrother – of a moral norm, of the good life; as such
he is much more successful than George Eliot's similar attempts
in her other novels. His integrity is clear when, having heard
the truth from Raffles about Bulstrode, he refuses to work for
him any longer,

'I would injure no man if I could help it,' said Caleb; 'even if I
thought God winked at it.'   (chap. 69)

In the one sentence he puts straight all that is perverted in
Bulstrode himself, for Bulstrode lives under the special Providence of a God who conveniently looks the other way. In his
integrity, his refusal to be involved or compromised, Garth
contrasts in this and succeeding chapters with Lydgate. (Incidentally, Garth's real poverty throws Lydgate's financial
worries into relief.)

G.E.M.—E

...e one solidly happy family in the book
...e a standard whereby the failings of the
...n be measured. Apart from the devious con-
...saubons and the Lydgates, the Garths relate
...use of Fred – to the Vincy household. The
...onships of parents to children is especially well
...chap. 25 while the different reactions of Mrs
Ga... ...rs Vincy to the news of Fred's decision to work for
Caleb ill... ...ate George Eliot's mature control over that difficult
and complex area of human experience where likeness and
unlikeness merge into each other. Comparison and contrast
always involve a fine sense of psychological and moral discrimination.

Mary Garth most obviously throws Rosamond into relief;
chap. 12 is a fine illustration of this. Mary is at this stage a kind
of deputy for Dorothea so far as this particular relationship is
concerned. She is used here so that the direct contrast of Rosamond and Dorothea – they have already been linked in Lydgate's mind – need not be introduced too early in the novel but
can be reserved for later climactic moments. But Mary is in
many ways a minor analogue to Dorothea; she is very much to
Fred (and Featherstone) what Dorothea is to Will (and Casaubon). Her refusal to burn Featherstone's will is very like
Dorothea's delay in agreeing to Casaubon's final request.

Of course, Mary cannot be treated adequately without
reference to Fred. I will notice here only two minor points.
Just as Fred serves to illuminate more important characters
– generally Will and Lydgate – so he in turn is illuminated by
an even lesser character, by the visit to the Garth home of this
favourite and successful son, Christy. The smallest roles, the
most fragmentary appearances have their function. Secondly
the novel ends not with any great climax, but quietly, in the
Garth family. This casts further doubt on James's views of
George Eliot's intention concerning Dorothea. George Eliot
does allow Dorothea her climactic moment and she prepares
for it by a device which she also used in *The Mill on The Floss*
(and of which James also was very fond); the mounting series

of interviews – Dorothea and Lydgate, Dorothea and Rosamond, Dorothea and Will. But the quiet close reminds us that
the story is not Dorothea's alone; it contributes to that peculiarly
open effect in George Eliot's novels, that sense of life spreading
out and continuing in time. It is for this reason primarily that
we can accept the Epilogue as something more than an awkward
convention.

Mary Garth leads us to Fred Vincy and Fred, if we had
time to deal with him properly, would lead us to larger and still
larger characters and issues until we had encompassed the
whole novel. It is in this sense of connection, of relationship,
that the true form and unity of *Middlemarch* is to be discovered. . . .

(from *The Art of George Eliot*, 1961)

FRANK KERMODE: *Middlemarch* and Apocalypse
Middlemarch is [a] novel of . . . crisis. It was begun in 1867.
The Sixties were thought then, and are thought now, to have
been critical, a transition between two worlds. They opened
with the American Civil War and ended with the Franco-
Prussian War. *Essays and Reviews* comes at the beginning,
Culture and Anarchy, the First Vatican Council and the dogma of
Papal Infallibility, at the end. The Education Act, which did
as much as any single statute could to alter the whole character
of society, became law in 1870. The source of the Nile was
discovered in 1860, the Suez Canal opened in 1869. Various
post-Gutenbergian techniques were taking hold: the telephone
was invented, and ironclad warships, and the dynamo, and
dynamite. For the first time you could telegraph to India and
travel by tube. In the very year of dynamite and the telephone
– 1867 – Marx published the first volume of *Das Kapital*, a
genuinely revolutionary event to which hardly anybody in
England paid the slightest attention, and Disraeli got through
his Reform Bill, an event thought by a great many people to
be as fraught with revolutionary possibilities as the passage of
its predecessor thirty-five years earlier. It seems not only that a
world we know well was struggling to be born, but that people
felt strongly, as they often do, that there was a crisis in their

vicinity, even if they did not always agree with us as to where, exactly, it was.

In the year of the Second Reform Act, the telephone and *Das Kapital*, George Eliot began to plan *Middlemarch*. Writing began in 1869, 'simmered' for a long time, and got properly under way in 1871. Then the story formed a union with an independently conceived story called 'Miss Brooke', and was published in eight parts between December 1871 and December 1872. Throughout these vicissitudes two factors remained constant. One was that this novel was to deal with 'contemporary moral history' (to steal a phrase used by the Goncourts of their own *Germinie Lacerteux* published in 1864). The other, which seems to indicate a programme different from that of the French realists, was that from the earliest stages George Eliot set her story very firmly not in the decade that was ending but at the beginning of the Thirties. Her notebook lists political and private events, which were to be cross-referenced in the narrative, and modern scholarship has illuminated this oblique historical accuracy. The author not only copied out lists of events from the *Annual Register* but also got up medicine, hospital management, scientific research. Bible scholarship, which is equally important to her design, she did not have to get up. She was particularly careful about medicine, as the notebook shows; and we must guess that this was not only because her principal male character was a doctor, but because 1832 is the date not only of the first Reform Bill, but of a catastrophic event, the arrival in England for the first time of the Indian cholera. It is a reasonable guess that, in the early stages of planning, she meant to have a cholera epidemic as well as an election in *Middlemarch*. It would be a great test not only for her doctor, but for the well-disposed gentry with their interest in sanitary dwellings.

Cholera was a disease unknown in England before this time, though there were of course later Victorian epidemics. This first onslaught of the disease must have seemed a new plague for a new age, much as syphilis had been for the period of her previous novel *Romola*, and it coincided exactly with the omin-

ous political upheavals of the months preceding the passage
the Bill. She made a note to the effect that the preamble to a
bill in Parliament spoke of the disease as an infliction of Providence, and that six members of the Commons voted for the
exclusion of this phrase. The coincidence of these events is a
sufficient explanation of her fixing upon the years preceding the
Reform Bill's passing, and her choosing an advanced young
doctor as her principal character in the 'Middlemarch' part of
the book. Other details fell into place; in the Thirties but not
in the Sixties she could have a serious biblical scholar who yet
remained ignorant of the advances of the New Criticism. After
all she herself had translated Strauss in the Forties.

So she turned to earlier crisis-years, the years when the
civilisation she knew, and which seemed in its turn to be on the
brink of radical change, was being born out of great political
and scientific events. Of all English novelists she came closest
to accepting the Goncourt programme for using novels as
means of prosecuting *les études et les devoirs de la science*, though
in making one crisis the model or type of another for the
purposes of the study, she was, though with a new scientific
seriousness, adopting a device not uncommon in English fiction
she knew, and which is, of course, a characteristic of all narrative
explanation. George Eliot was in any case not interested in
radical formal innovation; her attempt is rather to explore and
modify the existing novel schemata. Thus she maintained, despite a conviction early on in the writing that the novel had 'too
many *momenti*', the several continuous, elaborate and inter-
related plots to which readers had become accustomed.

Middlemarch has nothing in it quite like the famous intrusive
chapter in *Adam Bede* ('in which the story pauses a little') but it
is not without authorial interpolation, and there is one passage,
uneasily facetious as George Eliot sometimes was when she felt
she was being self-indulgent, which must cause pain to post-
Jamesian purists. Yet it tells us something useful about the
book. Mr Standish has just been reading old Featherstone's
will, and we have heard how vexed the family is at Joshua
Rigg's inheriting. The conclusion is that no one in the neigh-

d be happy at this turn of events; nobody could
long-term effects of Rigg's arrival. Whereupon
ds:

naturally led to reflect on the means of elevating a
low subject. Historical parallels are remarkably efficient in this way.
The chief objection to them is, that the diligent narrator may lack
space, or (what is often the same thing) may not be able to think of
them with any degree of particularity, though he may have a
philosophical confidence that if known they would be illustrative.
It seems an easier and a shorter way to dignity to observe that –
since there never was a true story which could not be told in parables
where you might put a monkey for a margrave, and *vice versa* –
whatever has been or is to be narrated by me about low people,
may be ennobled by being considered a parable. . . . Thus while I
tell the truth about my loobies, my reader's imagination need not
be entirely excluded from an occupation with lords. . . . As to any
provincial history in which the agents are all of high moral rank,
that must be of a date long posterior to the first Reform Bill, and
Peter Featherstone, you perceive, was dead and buried some months
before Lord Grey came into office.

That this is facetious, muddled and evasive does not entirely
destroy its value. It is one of the few places in which the novelist
openly adverts to a matter which, on other evidence, she had
incessantly in mind as she planned and wrote *Middlemarch*. She
is merely pretending to be sarcastic on a well-worn issue, the
right of novelists to concern themselves with low characters –
the sort of thing she did in *Adam Bede* when she remarked correctly, though with an evil emphasis, that 'things may be lovable
that are not altogether handsome, I hope'. It is the attitude
controverted by Ruskin in his observations on *The Mill on the
Floss* ('the sweepings of the Pentonville omnibus'). Perhaps the
question had not entirely lost importance – certainly George
Eliot herself had not entirely solved it, as we shall see; but it is
very unlikely that she here states it with any real seriousness.
For in *Middlemarch* the problem is not so much to justify one's
rendering of a provincial society for its own sake as to make

that society serve to illustrate a great historical crisis. The point is not that you can read lord for looby, or George IV for Featherstone, as she ironically proposes, but that if the novelist has got the detail right you can find in the book a 'parable' concerning these events in the mind and the conscience of society which, at a particular historical crisis, signal the birth of a modern age, that great theme of the modern novel.

And that is what the paragraph is trying to say. It tells us to relate the events of the novel to Lord Grey's Act and the other great changes of that time. The period of the novel is precisely the years and months before the Act. The notebook contains not only lists from the *Annual Register*, but precisely dated events for the unwritten novel. Thus the marriage of Lydgate is timed to coincide with the dissolution of July 1830, and the height of the cholera in Paris; Mr Casaubon's death coincides with the last days of the Parliament whose dissolution in 1831 led to the General Election in May of that year, the election at which Mr Brooke failed to win a seat in what was to be the Reform Parliament. Not all these dates eventually coincided, but the book retains, as Mr Jerome Beaty has shown, a good many delicate cross-references to political events, to the vicissitudes of Peel and Wellington, the death of Huskisson, and so on. The final illness of George IV, mentioned in relation to that of Featherstone, was enough, if you coupled it with the dissolution of parliament on the Reform issue, and a general election, to make Mr Vincy ask whether all these were not signs that the world was coming to an end. But this overt though facetious allusion to the apocalyptic archetype of crisis is not repeated; the author is content with unspoken allusions and parallels. Lydgate's efforts at medical reform are specifically related to the political struggle after the dissolution of 1831; chap. 84, of which the main business is the family's opposition to Dorothea's re-marriage, begins with an allusion to the rejection of the Bill by the Lords. And many other events are sketched in thus. The book ends a few weeks before the final enactment of the Bill. In the narrative there are a few major crises – those of the two marriages, and the attendant crises in the reformist activities of

Lydgate and Dorothea; there are also minor ones, relating to
religion and business – Fred Vincy's attitude to Holy Orders
and Bulstrode's disgrace. But these personal crises are shadows
of the historical crises, of the 'new life' struggling to be born in
1832; they are parables, to use George Eliot's word, of that
crisis which is in its turn a model for the modern crisis of 1867,
the leap in the dark, the end of another world. For in some ways
we are all, even learned historians, Vincys. A crisis date gives
history structure, and provides ways of talking about it.

This is the larger issue – crisis as a mode of historical explanation. The present point is that *Middlemarch* is a novel concerned
with the end of a world. But it was expressly intended to in-
culcate 'a religious and moral sympathy with the *historical life
of man*', and it issued from the hands of an author who was done
with all manner of explanations requiring a mythology of
transcendence. Such divinity as may occur in *Middlemarch* must
be humanised in the manner of Feuerbach; the history must be
human also, Comtian not Christian. Thus the types of Dorothea
are Antigone, Theresa, even the Virgin Mary (an extravagant
observation of Lydgate which the author partly endorses), but
they are systematically Feuerbachised, qualified as human.
Rosamond's 'confession' is another instance; it is sacramental
only as to efficacy, not as to mystery. The Joachite elements in
George Eliot's history belong, like those of Comte, to an age in
which apocalypse has been positivised. This humanised apocalypse is what we are all familiar with, for we habitually allude
to it when we consider our own historical crisis.

The type of apocalypse, however transformed, is still operative
in *Middlemarch*. The word may seem very strong; it only means
apocalypse of the kind Feuerbach might have contemplated had
he given his attention to eschatology – a 'Copernican' apocalypse, brought down to its true level, the human crisis. It is a
good many years since Mark Schorer[1] discovered in the novel
what he calls 'metaphors of . . . "muted" apocalypse', mention-
ing the figures of light, fire, transfiguration, epiphany, fulfilment
and the deliberate antithesis between *Middlemarch* and the New

Jerusalem. He found prophecy and pseudo-prophecy, vision and growth. This is a muted apocalypse, certainly: the jewels of St John's Revelation are mentioned early, but the context seems to make them serve only as a way of noting Dorothea's priggish attitude to Celia. Schorer quotes a passage from chap. 10 in which Dorothea's hopes of revelation from Casaubon's learning are given a strong though of course ironical apocalyptic tone. Above all, the historical events mentioned in the novel – again in a muted way – serve to emphasise the fulfilment of a time, and a renewal; though that, since the novel is set in the past, can be left to retrospective prophecy, the kind we, as historians, are best at. These are the last days; humanly speaking, the last days of an epoch, which is a Feuerbachian equivalent of the mythical apocalypse. The myth abandoned, this is still part of the structure of our historical thinking. And one reason why we relish *Middlemarch* still is that we understand the muted eschatology of its design.

For example, the crisis in bible criticism seemed at the time catastrophic in its implications. Casaubon, firmly planted on the wrong, mythological side of it, is typed in the same way as other characters – his name relates him ironically to the great Casaubon; he is a Milton, he is a Locke – all great men associated with major crises in the history of thought; but Casaubon's relation to them is ironically qualified, as Dorothea's is to hers, or as Lydgate's to Vesalius and the other great medical men whose names and dates George Eliot copies out so carefully into her notebook. They stand for virtues or certainties thought to be in decadence at this turn of time; though they also, by implying the meliorist scientific achievements of the succeeding age, suggest also renovation, always in apocalyptic thought the obverse side of decadence. Middlemarch itself, as Schorer says, silently proposes its antitype, the New Jerusalem.

If Casaubon's biblical methodology illuminated the historical crisis, so did Lydgate's medicine. The opposition between Lydgate and the older provincial doctors is not the whole story: the parable is incomplete if it does not include allusions to modern differentiations between typhus and typhoid, the new treatment for delirium tremens (which becomes the material of an important narrative crisis), the general theory of fever, and indeed modern developments in 'cell-theory'. Of course part of the point is that to know about all these things is not enough; that in the new dispensation as well as in any older one the virtues, under whatever demythologised form one knows them, must be preserved. A spot of commonness, a failure to apply the proper kind of attention to another person, a neglect of duty, a cheapening of love, will bring disaster. Lydgate's 'commonness', as it happens, is associated with his caste – it proceeds from an inability to treat as true persons his sexual, social and intellectual inferiors – and so derives from a system that was beginning, with the Reform Acts (and perhaps more with the Education Act of 1870), slowly to collapse. In much the same way the dryness and sexual impotence of Casaubon reflect the sterility of a world-view that lingers on in survivors of the older ruined order.

The historical antitheses of *Middlemarch* go beyond scholarship and medicine, and are far from simple. It is not only, we see, a matter of one age, characterised by myth and ignorance, yielding to a new, of history and science, or of a supernatural giving way to a natural religion. Religious beliefs of many kinds – Farebrother's, Fred Vincy's, Tyke's, and especially Bulstrode's – are ironically exposed at this historical crisis, but their forms survive that crisis, as fiction survives religious belief. Bulstrode's error is to suppose too exact a relationship between plot (providence) and the random actuality on which it is imposed. He takes his prosperity as a figure of his justification, as arising from divine but mechanical plotting; his God knows nothing of contingency; the logic of his plots is the logic of myth, not of everyday life. The tide of plausible human events is not in accordance with his Calvinist prediction, and his discomfiture is proof of the obsolescence of another mythology, one that was still in favour among some of the novelist's contemporaries. George Eliot has her own Feuerbachian version of predestination, worked out many times and most explicitly in Tito Melema; this and the erroneous old version play against each other in the Bulstrode crisis. That which works through Raffles is not, any longer, God; but neither is it mocked.

Many incidents are invented to strengthen the sense of an historical transition. There is the talk of new building and improvement, the tone of political dispute, Brooke's inability to command the respect of the labourer Dagley, even – great Victorian symbol of the division of time – the railway; and Garth, that wondrous necessary instrument of capital, suppressing resentment at its progress through midland meadows. This critical balance is characteristic of even the minor crises of the book. Casaubon's scholarship hangs posthumously over Dorothea in her decision to marry Ladislaw. Lydgate voting for Tyke is voting, he thinks, in the interests of progress, but they turn out to be the interests of Bulstrode; he accepts Bulstrode's saving loan, and Raffles is given medical treatment acceptable in current obsolete medical opinion, but to Lydgate's new knowledge dangerous. A good deal of the corruption, impotence and ineffectiveness of characters in *Middlemarch* is imposed upon them by a dying but stubborn past, and they are part of the price one pays for living in 'an age of transition'. This is what Dorothea means, really, when she says she will 'find out what everything costs'. She takes on the new world. Lydgate finds himself cursed by the old; he must take Bulstrode on his arm; he is not one of the élite in any new world, even in a new world of which the millennialist ideal is so severely chastened by contact with a powerful sense of reality. The scientific figures which, as has often been observed, penetrate the texture of this novel are not arbitrary reflections of the author's own interests: they establish the modernity of the problem, and they also, by indicating the tone of the future, judge the moral effectiveness of the characters who faced it then as we must now, and suggest the consequences of a failure such as Lydgate's. The eschatology is humanised, but the old judgment remains, as to type, applicable: 'I know thy works, that thou art neither cold nor hot . . . so then because thou art lukewarm and neither cold nor hot, I will spew thee out of my mouth.'

Thus *Middlemarch* arranges itself as an image of crisis, and a study of the moral obligations of men in transition. Its typology relates it to the archetypes of crisis, and this is one of the ways in which we understand human history. As I said at the outset, such terms as *crisis* and *revolution* describe to our satisfaction what it is in the utter particularity, the randomness and disparateness of events, that we can recognise and understand; indeed, people concerned in the making of history have often shaped it in conformity with such types, just as novelists do. Real events comply with archetypes of this kind; why should not fictional events? At the centre of this novel is a great and typical historical event. But it is only the nucleus. Round it accrete all these other images of crisis. The manner in which the basic apocalyptic figure permeates the texture is strikingly demonstrated in one of the greatest passages of the novel: the frustrated Dorothea contemplates Rome, the eternal city a wreck, a marble confusion, St Peter's and its statues disfigured by red drapery, as if seen by a diseased eye: the vision of the *urbs aeterna* blighted. 'Images are the brood of desire', says the novelist at the opening of the fourth chapter (in which Lydgate is on the point of marrying a woman he has presented with a whip). The image of Rome is the brood of desire that fails. To balance the scene, there is the wonderful moment of Dorothea's return to Lowick and the blanched winter landscape, when the fire glows incongruously and she, seeking confirmation in the glass for her sense of deathly defeat, finds an image of health and vitality, the human and perhaps specifically female strength that comes through these crises. Lawrence – who saw so clearly that the novel must make *this* kind of sense and not fob us off with papers stuck into brandy-flasks, meticulously rendered lawsuits – Lawrence not only learned from the good and the bad in Eliot's figures, but . . . remembered and reproduced this one at the climax of *Women in Love*. He meant that Crich, like Casaubon, belonged to death, to an old order.

However the relation between story and apocalyptic type is visualised, it presupposes an imaginative feat and a large degree of intellectual control. Occasionally this fails. There are lapses: for instance in the climactic interview between Dorothea and Rosamond, by which George Eliot set so much store. This was to be a flow of Feuerbachian feeling, confession and all, and so warm and spontaneous that she claimed to have refrained from thinking about it till it happened, and then to have written it entire, without revision, a claim which the manuscripts show to be untrue. However, it has virtual truth: it suggests a deliberate letting-go, a kind of moral failure (nothing in Dorothea gives her the right to be even a Feuerbachian confessor to Rosamond) and is redeemed only at its end, when Lydgate, dismissed from the elect, takes up his meaner burden. This is a failure of spiritual pride, like Bulstrode's.

There are more serious faults proper to be mentioned here. One is, if one may so put it, that George Eliot runs out of love; or we could say, she too has her élite. I mean that she cannot sustain that special love by which a novelist knows and preserves the identity of characters. The indications of this are her slipping away into caricature or humour-characterisation when she moves out of the sociological middle area. At the extreme edge is Mrs Dollop, in the pub, but Trumbull the auctioneer is only good for a laugh and as a handy pneumonia patient. The Garths, even, are honourable pastoral prigs about whom one wants to know no more. As one moves out from the central figures, the two married couples, towards the periphery, the figures are increasingly distorted. In a certain sense, she is interested most in the good bourgeoisie and a little above it, the Vincys to the Brookes. The others she more or less deprives of moral reality much as Lydgate deprives Rosamond, and with similar results. What happens is that an authentic relation of type to history is distorted by adherence to novel conventions which are meaningless except as reflections of a caste system. Possibly the degree of distortion is as little as could be managed in the England of the time. But one sees why Arnold Kettle can attribute the failures of *Middlemarch* – a novel about change – to a view of society and morality 'somewhat static', not incorporating 'a dialectical sense of contradiction and motion'. This is overstated, but does locate, in this novel of crisis, a spot of commonness. . . .

Another fault of *Middlemarch* is in the plotting: or so it must seem to us. We are not, for various reasons too complicated to enter into now, so interested nowadays in what Beckett, praising Proust, called 'the vulgarities of a plausible concatenation' as our great-grandfathers, or even our grandfathers, but we cannot excuse George Eliot so simply, because in this respect she was obviously on our side, and admired narrative with a strong thematic aspect. Yet she wrote a good deal of unnecessary plot, not so much of it in *Middlemarch* as in *Felix Holt* and *Daniel Deronda*, but still too much. The Bulstrode affair is an instance. In its elements this is impeccable 'thinking with the story' – Lydgate's association with the banker contaminates him with an odious pre-scientific religion, and the climax turns upon an issue between old and new medical practice. The conduct of Mrs Bulstrode is a grace, one of those favours that drop upon a writer because he has worked hard for something else, and not been a slave of the types. Yet in order to get to the point of Bulstrode she invented all the perfunctory business of Rigg and Raffles, the note stuffed in the brandy-flask, the unnecessary relationship with Ladislaw. In the notebook she laboured over the elaboration of all this in such unusual detail that, as Mr Beaty very credibly suggests, it looks as if she was not interested enough to carry such essentially extraneous material in her head. And this plotting damages the modernity of the novel. It is regressive, it takes us back to a more naïve kind of novel, in which it is assumed that the mere delights of concatenation are enough, in which serious thematic or typical interest is largely a matter of luck. Such plots are anti-historical, destructive of the crisis-'set'. Of course we have many later books to be wise by; yet there is no reason why we should not say that this kind of thing diminishes the critical force of the book, given its historical theme. . . .

(from Continuities, 1968)

NOTE

1. For Schorer on apocalypse and metaphor in *Middlemarch*, see 'Fiction and the "Matrix of Analogy"', *Kenyon Review*, XI (autumn 1949), and 'The Structure of the Novel: Method, Metaphor and Mind', in Barbara Hardy (ed.), *Middlemarch: Critical Approaches* (1967). [Ed.]

PART THREE

Recent Studies

Arnold Kettle

MIDDLEMARCH (1951)

This is so large a novel, spacious, unhurried, broad in scope and attitude, that to insist that it is the same *kind* of novel as *Emma* may seem at first a little perverse. The range of interest, obviously, is far greater. A concern which includes such issues as the relation of art to life, the progress of the biological sciences, the social consequences of the Reform Bill of 1832, the problems of the scholar's vocation, the psychology of martyrdom, such a concern would not appear superficially to be usefully comparable with the interests of Jane Austen. Yet the range of interest, wonderfully impressive as it is, does not reveal any basically new attitude to the art of fiction. George Eliot extends the method of Jane Austen but does not substantially alter it.

The world of Middlemarch is bigger and more various than that of Highbury, the interests of its inhabitants take different forms and lead us to issues which can justly be called wider; but *Middlemarch*, though it is in some respects the most impressive novel in our language, and one which it is not ridiculous to compare with the novels of Tolstoy, is not in any sense a revolutionary work.

The comparison with Jane Austen is worth developing. In the very first chapter of the novel we come upon the description of Mr Brooke:

A man nearly sixty, of acquiescent temper, miscellaneous opinions, and uncertain vote. He had travelled in his younger years, and was held in this part of the country to have contracted a too rambling habit of mind. Mr Brooke's conclusions were as difficult to predict as the weather: it was only safe to say that he would act with benevolent intentions, and he would spend as little money as possible in carrying them out.

Apart perhaps from an already apparent interest in her characters' 'opinions', an interest which on this level Jane Austen anyway shares, there is nothing whatever to distinguish this passage, even in its diction, from similar descriptions in *Emma*. The same quality of wit is there, dependent on a poise which in its turn depends on a precise and highly conscious set of social values which emanate from full participation in the life of a particular community. The next sentence, however, marks a change:

For the most glutinously indefinite minds enclose some hard grains of habit; and a man has been seen lax about all his own interests except the retention of his snuff-box, concerning which he was watchful, suspicious, and greedy of clutch.

It is not merely that with the introduction of the word 'glutinously' we sense a lack of 'elegance' which in *Emma* would never do; the whole sentence has a heaviness, almost a clumsiness, which corresponds to a habit of mind in George Eliot quite distinct from that of the earlier novelist. A certain forcing of the issue, one might call it, a tendency to illustrate a shade too often the moral generalisation. From a description, witty and certainly not morally uncritical, of Mr Brooke, a description in which *his* vitality as a character and *our* view of him are developed together, we pass immediately to the generalisation which has the effect of putting Mr Brooke away at a distance again. Almost imperceptibly, with the 'has been seen', we have passed from Mr Brooke's 'mind' (such as it is) to 'minds' in general. The transition is not offensive and it marks one of the great strengths of George Eliot as a novelist, her insistence that we should continuously relate her fiction to our lives, that we should not lose ourselves in the fantastic world of the novel; but it illustrates the direction of the modification she brings to Jane Austen's method. When Jane Austen in *Emma* offers us a generalised comment, such as her remarks about dancing and the holding of dances, we feel no temptation to apply her irony as a thought on the meaning of Life; with George Eliot the more presumptuous claim implicit in the capital letter is for ever being made.

That the claim is not fatuous is ensured by the breadth of her interest and the inclusiveness of her prodigious intelligence. Let us turn to another of her minor characters, Mrs Cadwallader:

Her life was rurally simple, quite free from secrets either foul, dangerous, or otherwise important, and not consciously affected by the great affairs of the world. All the more did the affairs of the great world interest her when communicated in the letters of high-born relations: the way in which fascinating younger sons had gone to the dogs by marrying their mistresses, the fine old-blooded idiocy of young Lord Tapir, and the furious gouty humours of old Lord Megatherium; the exact crossing of genealogies which had brought a coronet into a new branch and widened the relations of scandal, – these were topics of which she retained details with the utmost accuracy, and reproduced them in an excellent pickle of epigrams, which she herself enjoyed the more because she believed as un-questioningly in birth and no-birth as she did in game and vermin. She would never have disowned any one on the ground of poverty: a De Bracy reduced to take his dinner in a basin would have seemed to her an example of pathos worth exaggerating, and I fear his aristocratic vices would not have horrified her. But her feeling towards the vulgar rich was a sort of religious hatred; they had probably made all their money out of high retail prices, and Mrs Cadwallader detested high prices for everything that was not paid in kind at the Rectory: such people were no part of God's design in making the world; and their accent was an affliction to the ears. A town where such monsters abounded was hardly more than a sort of low comedy, which could not be taken account of in a well-bred scheme of the universe. Let any lady who is inclined to be hard on Mrs Cadwallader inquire into the comprehensiveness of her own beautiful views, and be quite sure that they afford accommodation for all the lives which have the honour to coexist with hers.

With such a mind, active as phosphorus, biting everything that came near into the form that suited it, how could Mrs Cadwallader feel that the Miss Brookes and their matrimonial prospects were alien to her? (chap. 6)

George Eliot is sometimes regarded as a worthy but essentially forbidding writer; her Puritanism is too easily associated with a moral narrowness. It is a very unfair criticism. The vivacity of the passage just quoted has nothing narrow about it. The wit is 'deeper' than Jane Austen's wit only in the sense that a more variously stocked consciousness is involved. 'Rurally simple' places the parish of Tipton in a world larger than anyone in *Emma* contemplates. The play on 'the great affairs of the world' and 'the affairs of the great world', involves a knowledge of 'affairs' to which Jane Austen would make no claim – and it is not a bogus knowledge. On the contrary George Eliot's urbanity is quite without the shallowness of a superficial sophistication and it gives a wonderful breadth and solidity to her criticism. 'Fine old-blooded idiocy': the phrase might easily be shrill, the criticism crude, but in fact it adequately encompasses a whole stratum of society. Mrs Cadwallader's 'excellent pickle of epigrams' is backed by her creator's own wit, just as the force of 'active as phosphorus' is backed by George Eliot's awareness of scientific processes. The point is not, of course, that George Eliot is more intelligent than Jane Austen but that her intelligence has encompassed a larger field.

In the passage on Mrs Cadwallader, as in that on Mr Brooke, a tell-tale sentence intrudes. 'Let any lady who is inclined to be hard on Mrs Cadwallader inquire into the comprehensiveness of her own beautiful views, and be quite sure that they afford accommodation for all the lives which have the honour to coexist with hers.' Again we have the direct thrust at the reader's conscience, not offensive in itself, yet less than fully incorporated in George Eliot's overall purposes. The adjective 'beautiful' is clumsy and inadequate, the irony implicit in it crude, not on the level of the use of previous adjectives. And the phrase 'all the lives which have the honour, etc.' is an uncertain one. In what sense is 'honour' to be read? Against what is the irony detected? The ambiguity betrays a weakness. Why is the sentence there at all?

Can we, perhaps, in these sentences in which George Eliot turns her moral gaze direct upon the reader and beckons to his personal conscience, isolate a weakness in her method and put our finger on a note in *Middlemarch* which may justly be described as a shade flat? It is a complicated question to which we shall have to return.

Meanwhile let us turn to another description in *Middlemarch*, that scene when Dorothea, six weeks after her marriage, is disclosed weeping in her apartment in Rome.

To those who have looked at Rome with the quickening power of a knowledge which breathes a growing soul into all historic shapes, and traces out the suppressed transitions which unite all contrasts, Rome may still be the spiritual centre and interpreter of the world. But let them conceive one more historical contrast: the gigantic broken revelations of that Imperial and Papal city thrust abruptly on the notions of a girl who had been brought up in English and Swiss Puritanism, fed on meagre Protestant histories and an art chiefly of the hand-screen sort; a girl whose ardent nature turned all her small allowance of knowledge into principles, fusing her actions into their mould, and whose quick emotions gave the most abstract things the quality of pleasure or pain, a girl who had lately become a wife, and from the enthusiastic acceptance of untried duty found herself plunged in tumultuous preoccupation with her personal lot. The weight of unintelligible Rome might lie easily on bright nymphs to whom it formed a background for the brilliant picnic of Anglo-Foreign society: but Dorothea had no such defence against deep impressions. Ruins and basilicas, palaces and colossi, set in the midst of a sordid present, where all that was living and warm-blooded seemed sunk in the deep degeneracy of a superstition divorced from reverence; the dimmer but yet eager Titanic life gazing and struggling on walls and ceilings; the long vistas of white forms whose marble eyes seemed to hold the monotonous light of an alien world: all this vast wreck of ambitious ideals, sensuous and spiritual, mixed confusedly with the signs of breathing forgetfulness and degradation, at first jarred her as with an electric shock, and then urged themselves on her with that ache belonging to a glut of confused ideas which check the flow of emotion. Forms both pale and glowing took possession of her young sense, and fixed themselves in her memory even when she was not thinking of them, preparing strange associations which remained through her after-years. Our moods are apt to bring with them images which succeed each other like the magic-lantern pictures of a doze; and in certain states of dull forlornness Dorothea all her life continued to see the vastness of St Peter's, the huge bronze canopy, the excited intention in the attitudes and garments of the prophets and evangelists in the mosaics above, and the red drapery which was being hung for Christmas spreading itself everywhere like a disease of the retina.

Not that this inward amazement of Dorothea's was anything very exceptional: many souls in their young nudity are tumbled out among incongruities and left to 'find their feet' among them, while their elders go about their business. Nor can I suppose that when Mrs Casaubon is discovered in a fit of weeping six weeks after her wedding, the situation will be regarded as tragic. Some discouragement, some faintness of heart at the new real future which replaces the imaginary, is not unusual and we do not expect people to be deeply moved by what is not unusual. That element of tragedy which lies in the very fact of frequency, has not yet wrought itself into the coarse emotion of mankind; and perhaps our frames could hardly bear much of it. If we had a keen vision and feeling of all ordinary human life, it would be like hearing the grass grow and the squirrel's heart beat, and we should die of that roar which lies on the other side of silence. As it is, the quickest of us walk about well wadded with stupidity.

(chap. 20)

It is a passage which shows George Eliot, if not quite at her best, as the great novelist she is; and it shows very clearly the direction of her extension of Jane Austen's method. It is, for a piece of writing describing and analysing a peculiarly intimate personal emotion, a remarkably impersonal passage. Dorothea's own feelings, though we are persuasively made to understand them, are revealed as embedded within a generalised situation. George Eliot begins by recalling the Roman scene, not through anyone's sense-impressions, but in its historical, highly intellectualised context. The clash of Catholic and Protestant, pagan and Puritan, are evoked at first objectively and then made gradually to illuminate Dorothea's mental state.

Only very occasionally are we brought into contact with her actual feelings. We do not feel *closer* to her as we read on, but we understand her better and the understanding is not a purely objective one. George Eliot has here herself the power to give 'the most abstract things the quality of a pleasure or a pain' because under her contemplation of the particular, concrete situation (Dorothea's state of mind at this moment) the generalised experience and abstract thought cease to be abstract and become symbolic – the squirrel's heart-beat and the roar which lies on the other side of silence.

The achievement of the symbolic moment, the instant in which through our gained insight into the particular situation a new apprehension of the processes of life is reached, is not frequent in *Middlemarch*. By and large the novel is no more symbolic than *Emma*. It works on our consciousness through the presentation of very real, rounded characters in a very real, solidly constructed social situation.

George Eliot takes a great deal of pains with her 'background' and the question arises as to whether background is the right word to use. What, we have to ask ourselves, is the central theme, the unifying subject of this *Study of Provincial Life*?

From the Prelude one gathers that this is to be a novel about latter-day Saint Theresas, about those whose flames, 'fed from within, soared after some illimitable satisfaction, some object which would never justify weariness, which would reconcile self-despair with the rapturous consciousness of life beyond self'; and we are given the hint that the problem of such modern saints is that they are 'helped by no coherent social faith and order which could perform the function of knowledge for the ardently willing soul'.

This expectation is immediately justified by the introduction of Dorothea Brooke, the mention of the Blessed Virgin in the second sentence of the first chapter confirming all our anticipation. And the first movement of the novel, the whole of the first book up to the introduction of Lydgate, continues the development of the theme. Dorothea is the centre of it and Dorothea is presented to us wonderfully, her limitations, her immaturity, her 'theoretic' mind no less than her ardour, her yearning for a life more deeply satisfying than Tipton and Middlemarch can give.

Up to this point Middlemarch may be said to be to the novel

what Highbury is to *Emma*, the world in which Dorothea and Casaubon and the surrounding characters live, and very subtly does George Eliot convey how Middlemarch has made them what they are. We feel no temptation to abstract these characters from the society that contains them. Dorothea is not Saint Theresa. She is an intelligent and sensitive girl born into the English landed ruling class of the early nineteenth century, full of half-formulated dissatisfactions with the fatuous, genteel life of the women of her class, seeking something beyond the narrow 'selfishness' of her acquaintances and turning towards a religious Puritanism and a high-minded philanthropy (cottages for the farm-labourers) to satisfy her unfulfilled potentialities, finally and disastrously imagining that in marriage to Casaubon she will find the fulfilment of her aspirations.

It is with the introduction of Lydgate, quickly followed by the Vincys and Bulstrode, that the basic structure of the novel changes. We know now that George Eliot in fact joined together in *Middlemarch* two novels originally planned separately – the story of 'Miss Brooke' and the story of Lydgate. But even without this knowledge we should find, before the end of the first book, a change coming over *Middlemarch*. George Eliot forces the problem on our attention in chap. 11, just after the introduction of Lydgate and Rosamond.

Certainly nothing at present could seem much less important to Lydgate than the turn of Miss Brooke's mind, or to Miss Brooke than the qualities of the woman who had attracted this young surgeon. But any one watching keenly the stealthy convergence of human lots, sees a slow preparation of effects from one life on another, which tells like a calculated irony on the indifference or the frozen stare with which we look at our unintroduced neighbour. Destiny stands by sarcastic with our *dramatis personæ* folded in her hand.

Old provincial society had its share of this kind of subtle movement: had not only its striking downfalls, its brilliant young professional dandies who ended by living up an entry with a drab and six children for their establishment, but also those less marked vicissitudes which are constantly shifting the boundaries of social intercourse and begetting new consciousness of inter-dependence.

Some slipped a little downward, some got higher footing; people denied aspirates, gained wealth, and fastidious gentlemen stood for boroughs; some were caught in political currents, some in ecclesiastical, and perhaps found themselves surprisingly grouped in consequence; while a few personages or families that stood with rocky firmness amid all this fluctuation, were slowly presenting new aspects in spite of solidity, and altering with the double change of self and beholder. Municipal town and rural parish gradually made fresh threads of connection – gradually, as the old stocking gave way to the savings bank, and the worship of the solar guinea became extinct; while squires and baronets, and even lords who had once lived blamelessly afar from the civic mind, gathered the faultiness of closer acquaintanceship. Settlers, too, came from distant counties, some with an alarming novelty of skill, others with an offensive advantage in cunning. In fact, much the same sort of movement and mixture went on in old England as we find in older Herodotus, who also, in telling what had been, thought it well to take a woman's lot for his starting point.

It is a clumsy passage and its clumsiness comes from its function as a bridge between what the novel started as and what it is becoming; but it is also a passage full of interest to an analysis of the book. 'Destiny stands by sarcastic with our *dramatis personæ* folded in her hand': it is a pretentious, unhelpful sentence, calling up a significance it does not satisfy. Who, one feels tempted to ask, is this Destiny, a character previously unmentioned by the author? And, as a matter of fact, the figure of a sarcastic fate does not preside over *Middlemarch*. On the contrary George Eliot is at pains to dissociate herself from any such concept. Throughout the novel with an almost remorseless insistence, each moral crisis, each necessary decision is presented to the participants and to us with the minimum of suggestion of an all-powerful Destiny. It is the very core of George Eliot's morality and of the peculiar moral force of the book that her characters, despite most powerful pressures, and above all the prevailing pressure of the Middlemarch way of life, are not impelled to meet each particular choice in the way they do. Lydgate *need* not have married Rosamond, though we understand well enough why he did. Neither need Fred Vincy have reformed; it is George Eliot's particular achievement here that she convinces us of a transformation against which all the cards of 'Destiny' have been stacked.

My point here is that the appearance of this concept in chap. 11 is not justified by the total organisation of the book and that it betrays a weakness, a lack of control, which is intimately connected with the transformation of the novel from the story of Dorothea to something else.

The something else is indicated in the sentence beginning 'Old provincial society . . .'. We realise as we read on that the centre of attention of the novel is indeed being shifted, so that the story of Miss Brooke is now not an end in itself but a starting-point. What we are to contemplate is nothing less than the whole subtle movement of old provincial society. The background has become the subject.

That it was bound to do so has already been hinted. So firmly is the story of Dorothea in those early chapters 'set' in the society of which she is a part, that it seems almost inevitable that an adequate examination of Dorothea must involve an examination of the Middlemarch world more thorough than that so far contemplated, and there is no doubt that it was under a sense of this compulsion that George Eliot altered the plan of the book and called it *Middlemarch*. And the central question in our estimate of the novel is how far she succeeds in this great, ambitious attempt thus to capture and reveal the relation of each individual story, the stories of Dorothea, of Lydgate, of Bulstrode, to the whole picture, the Middlemarch world.

Dr Leavis, in his extremely interesting section on George Eliot in *The Great Tradition*, writes:

George Eliot had said in *Felix Holt*, by way of apology for the space she devoted to 'social changes' and 'public matters': 'there is no private life which has not been determined by a wider public life.' The aim implicit in this remark is magnificently achieved in *Middlemarch*, and it is achieved by a novelist whose genius manifests itself in a profound analysis of the individual.   (p. 61)

With the last statement – the emphasis on the profound analysis – one must assuredly agree and one could not hope valuably to add to Dr Leavis's remarks on Casaubon, Lydgate, Rosamond and Bulstrode; nor is one disposed to quarrel with his estimate of the treatment of Ladislaw and Dorothea.

Middlemarch is a wonderfully rich and intelligent book and its richness lies in a consideration of individual characters firmly placed in an actual social situation (it is because Ladislaw is never thus placed but remains a romantic dream-figure that he is a failure). But there seems to me a contradiction at the heart of *Middlemarch*, a contradiction between the success of the parts and the relative failure of the whole.

Middlemarch as a whole is not a deeply moving book. The total effect is immensely impressive but not immensely compelling. Our consciousness is modified and enriched but not much changed. We are moved by particular things in the book: by the revelation of Casaubon's incapacity; by the hideous quality of the Lydgate–Rosamond impasse (certainly upon our pulses this), he unable to find a chink in her smooth blonde armour and she incapable of understanding the kind of man he could have been; by Dorothea's disillusionment in Rome; by the scene in which Mrs Bulstrode accepts her share in her husband's downfall. Mrs Bulstrode, conventional, unprofound, more than a little smug, a pillar of the church and the Middlemarch bourgeoisie, learns of the black disgrace of her husband through the revelation of his totally discreditable past:

'But you must bear up as well as you can, Harriet. People don't blame you. And I'll stand by you whatever you make up your mind to do,' said the brother, with rough but well-meaning affectionateness.

'Give me your arm to the carriage, Walter,' said Mrs Bulstrode, 'I feel very weak.'

And when she got home she was obliged to say to her daughter, 'I am not well, my dear; I must go and lie down. Attend to your papa. Leave me in quiet. I shall take no dinner.'

She locked herself in her room. She needed time to get used to her maimed consciousness, her poor lopped life, before she could walk steadily to the place allotted her. A new searching light had fallen on her husband's character, and she could not judge him leniently: the twenty years in which she had believed in him and venerated him by virtue of his concealments came back with particulars that made them seem an odious deceit. He had married her with that bad past life hidden behind him and she had no faith left to protest his innocence of the worst that was imputed to him. Her honest ostentatious nature made the sharing of a merited dishonour as bitter as it could be to any mortal.

But this imperfectly-taught woman, whose phrases and habits were an odd patch-work, had a loyal spirit within her. The man whose prosperity she had shared through nearly half a life, and who had unvaryingly cherished her – now that punishment had befallen him it was not possible to her in any sense to forsake him. There is a forsaking which still sits at the same board and lies on the same couch with the forsaken soul, withering it the more by unloving proximity. She knew, when she locked her door, that she should unlock it ready to go down to her unhappy husband and espouse his sorrow, and say of his guilt, I will mourn and not reproach. But she needed time to gather up her strength; she needed to sob out her farewell to all the gladness and pride of her life. When she had resolved to go down, she prepared herself by some little acts which might seem mere folly to a hard onlooker; they were her way of expressing to all spectators visible or invisible that she had begun a new life in which she embraced humiliation. She took off all her ornaments and put on a plain black gown, and instead of wearing her much-adorned cap and large bows of hair, she brushed her hair down and put on a plain bonnet-cap, which made her look suddenly like an early Methodist.

Bulstrode, who knew that his wife had been out and had come in saying that she was not well, had spent the time in an agitation equal to hers. He had looked forward to her learning the truth from others, and had acquiesced in that probability, as something easier to him than any confession. But now that he imagined the moment of her knowledge come, he awaited the result in anguish. His daughters had been obliged to consent to leave him, and though he had allowed some food to be brought to him, he had not touched it. He felt himself perishing slowly in unpitied misery. Perhaps he should never see his wife's face with affection in it again. And if he turned to God there seemed to be no answer but the pressure of retribution.

It was eight o'clock in the evening before the door opened and his wife entered. He dared not look up at her. He sat with his eyes bent down, and as she went towards him she thought he looked smaller – he seemed so withered and shrunken. A movement of new compassion and old tenderness went through her like a great wave, and putting one hand on his which rested on the arm of the chair, and the other on his shoulder, she said, solemnly but kindly –

'Look up, Nicholas.'

He raised his eyes with a little start and looked at her half amazed for a moment: her pale face, her changed mourning dress, the trembling about her mouth, all said 'I know': and her hands and eyes rested gently on him. He burst out crying and they cried together, she sitting at his side. They could not yet speak to each other of the shame which she was bearing with him, or of the facts which had brought it down on them. His confession was silent, and her promise of faithfulness was silent. Open-minded as she was, she nevertheless shrank from the words which would have expressed their mutal consciousness as she would have shrunk from flakes of fire. She could not say, 'How much is only slander and false suspicion?' and he did not say, 'I am innocent.' (chap. 74)

In such an episode as this the moral and emotional basis of a personal relationship is explored with an insight and a sympathy wholly admirable. And we are moved not simply because George Eliot's moral concern is so profound and sure but because the scene, with its many ramifications (including the implicit comparison with the attitude of Rosamond), is presented with so deep a sense of the social interpenetration that makes up life. And yet – it is the paradox of the novel – this sense of social interpenetration, so remarkably revealed in the exploration of the individual dilemma and so consistently and consciously sought after by George Eliot throughout the novel, does not in fact infuse the book as a whole.

Middlemarch taken in its completeness has almost everything except what is ultimately the most important thing of all, that final vibrant intensity of the living organism. Despite its superb achievements, despite the formidable intelligence which controls the whole book and rewards us, each time we return to it, with new insights, new richness of analysis and observation, there is something missing. We do not care about these people in the way in which, given the sum of human life and wisdom involved, we ought to care. What is lacking is not understanding, not sympathy, not warmth, certainly not seriousness.

George Eliot is the most intelligent of novelists; she always knows what she ought to do and she never shirks any issue. But she seems to lack what one might call a sense of the vital motion of things: she feels after this sense, but does not capture it. For all her intellect, all her human sympathy, all her nobility and generosity of mind, there is something of life that eludes her, that sense of the contradictions within every action and situation which is the motive-force of artistic energy and which perhaps Keats was seeking to express when he referred to Shakespeare's 'negative capability'.

George Eliot possesses this negative capability when she explores a particular situation, a concrete problem; *then* the conflicts within the essence are perforce accepted and in fighting themselves out breathe the breath of life into the scene. But it is as though in her philosophy, her consciously formulated outlook, there is no place for the inner contradiction. The word 'determined' in the sentence from *Felix Holt* quoted by Dr Leavis is, I think, significant.

I believe that most of the weaknesses of *Middlemarch* spring from this. It is behind the failure to impose an organic unity on the novel. The intention is, clearly, that Middlemarch itself should be the unifying factor, but in fact it is not. The 'subtle movement' of society which George Eliot herself refers to is not, in the achieved novel, caught. On the contrary the view of society presented is a static one. Nor is this simply because provincial society in the Midlands about 1832 was indeed comparatively unchanging (no society is really static when an artist looks at it), though it is perhaps significant that George Eliot, writing in the 1870s, should have set her novel forty years back. What is more important is the failure of the attempts to give 'historical colour' (like the surveying of the railroad and the election scenes) which are conscientious but not – on the artistic level – convincing, not integral to the novel's pattern.

More vital still is the fact that the various stories within the novel, though linked by the loose plot, have no organic unity. Many of the chief characters are related by blood, but their artistic relationship within the pattern of the novel is not fully realised. Between the story of Dorothea and that of Lydgate there is, it is true, an essential link. Lydgate's career (it is not by accident that he is a man) is the other side of the Saint Theresa theme. 'Lydgate and Dorothea together are the vehicle for the main theme in *Middlemarch*. The compromise each ultimately makes between the life to which they aspired and the life the conditions permit symbolises the conception at the heart of the book!'[1] Mrs Bennett's remark is to the point; and the phrase 'the life the conditions permit' is, I think, most significant.

For in such a phrase the limitation of the view of society implicit in *Middlemarch* is revealed and the reason for George Eliot's ultimate failure to capture its movement indicated. Society in this novel is presented to us as 'there'; that it is a part of a historical process is suggested intellectually only. And because the Middlemarch world is the given, static reality, the characters of the novel must be seen as at its mercy. They are free to make certain moral decisions within the bounds of the Middlemarch world, yet they are held captive by that world.

Hence the temptation of George Eliot, once she accepts the social implications of her story, to introduce an unconvincing, unrealised 'Destiny'. The artist in her does not believe in this Destiny and therefore when her imagination is fully engaged in the exploration of a concrete problem of individual relationships the concept of an impregnable social destiny disappears. But it is always lurking in the background and it eats into the overall vitality of the novel. In a sense it is a product of George Eliot's strength, her recognition of the complex social basis of morality. Had she not felt compelled to make Middlemarch the chief character of her book (a compulsion springing from her own honesty of analysis) she would not have needed the further social understanding which her later conception of the novel involved. She would not have attempted that advance

on the art of Jane Austen which makes her at once a more
impressive novelist and a less satisfactory one.

George Eliot's view of society is in the last analysis a mechanistic and determinist one. She has an absorbing sense of the
power of society but very little sense of the way it changes.
Hence her moral attitudes, like her social vision, tend to be
static. 'We are all of us born in moral stupidity, taking the
world as an udder to feed our supreme selves' (chap. 21). The
image, more than half ironical as it seems to be in the particular
context, is significant, hinting as it does at a fully mechanistic
outlook (not unlike Locke's conception of the mind as a blank
sheet of white paper) in which the individual is essentially
passive, a recipient of impressions, changed by the outside world
but scarcely able to change it.

It is not by chance that human aspirations fare poorly in
Middlemarch. All of the main characters, save Dorothea and
Ladislaw and Mary and Fred, are defeated by Middlemarch,
and Mary and Fred are undefeated only because they have
never fought a thorough-going battle with the values of
Middlemarch society. Mary and the Garths, it is true, reject the
more distasteful aspects of nineteenth-century morality – the
money-grabbing of old Featherstone, the hypocritical dis-
honesty of Bulstrode – but they accept as proper and inevitable
the fundamental set-up of Middlemarch. Integrity and hard
work within the framework of the *status quo* is the ideal of conduct
that Mary demands of Fred, decent enough standards as far
as they go but scarcely adequate (as one immediately realises
if one applies them to Lydgate's dilemma) as an answer to
the profound moral problems raised by the book as a whole or
its central theme, and it is observable that the tensions of the
book in the Garth–Vincy passages are considerably lower than
in the Dorothea, Lydgate or Bulstrode sections.

It is George Eliot's mechanistic philosophy, too, which is at
the root of the weakness, noted at the beginning of this essay, in
her method of posing to us the moral issues at stake in the novel.
The point here, it is worth insisting, is not that her moral
concern should be consistent and explicit, not that she should

continuously refer us back to our own consciences, but that she should do so in a way which weakens the tension of the scene she is describing and places her characters at a distance which makes an intimate conveying of their feelings difficult. Dr Leavis is, I am sure, quite right to stress as inadequate the view of George Eliot expressed in Henry James's words:

We feel in her, always, that she proceeds from the abstract to the concrete; that her figures and situations are evolved, as the phrase is, from her moral consciousness, and are only indirectly the products of observation.[2]

I do not think that the continuous moral concern in *Middlemarch* is abstract or that George Eliot is trying to impose abstract concepts on a recalcitrant chunk of life. For all the deep moral preoccupation the novel has little of the moral fable about it.

On the contrary her method is to present most concretely a particular situation and then draw to our attention the moral issues involved in the choices which have to be made. The method is perhaps a little heavy-going; as we pass in the novel from moral crisis to moral crisis we feel a shade oppressed by the remorselessness of the performance. But what is oppressive is not any abstract plan lurking behind the screen but the very nature of George Eliot's moral judgments; there is too often a kind of flatness about them, which actually weakens the conflicts within the scene she is presenting. And the flatness comes, I think, from the assumptions implicit in her moral view of the world as an udder.

To put it in another way, her standards of right and wrong (perhaps her emphasis on Law and her sympathy for Judaism – not revealed in this particular book – are significant) are not quite adequate to the complexity of her social vision. Henry James's criticism that her figures and situations are not *seen* in the irresponsible plastic way is unfortunately expressed and invites the drubbing Dr Leavis rightly gives it, but it nevertheless hints at a genuine weakness. George Eliot's high-minded moral seriousness (which might in fact be described as Utilitarianism modified by John Stuart Mill, Comte and her early evangelical Christianity) does have an unfortunate effect on the novel, not because it is moral or serious, but because it is mechanistic and undialectical.

And like all mechanistic thinkers George Eliot ends by escaping into idealism. In this study of bourgeois society there are three rebels – Dorothea, Ladislaw and Lydgate – whose aspirations lead them to a profound dissatisfaction with the Middlemarch world. All three stand for, and wish to live by, values higher than the values of that world. They are the 'ardent spirits' who seek to serve humanity through science and art and common sympathy. Lydgate is defeated by Middlemarch through his marriage with Rosamond and the bitter story of his defeat is the finest and most moving thing in the novel. But it is significant that Lydgate, like all the other failures of the novel, fails not through his strength but through his weakness.

There is no heroism in *Middlemarch* (leaving aside for the moment Dorothea and Ladislaw), no tragic conflict and there cannot be, for the dialectics of tragedy, the struggle in which the hero is destroyed through his own strength, is outside George Eliot's scheme of things. Because her outlook is mechanistic and not revolutionary no one can fight Middlemarch or change it. The most that they can do is to improve it a little (as Farebrother does and perhaps Dorothea) by being a little 'better' than their neighbours. But the best that most can rise to – like Mary Garth and Mrs Bulstrode – is a sincere and unsentimental submission to its will. And therefore even the 'sympathetic' characters must either be passive or else be brought to their knees through their own faults. For though George Eliot hates Middlemarch she believes in its inevitability; it is the world and our udder.

Yet because she hates the values of the society she depicts and has a faith in men and women which her mechanistic philosophy cannot destroy, George Eliot has to find a way out of her dilemma. She, whose noble humanity informs the whole novel, even its weaknesses, cannot submit emotionally to a philosophy that binds her people for ever to the Middlemarch world.

Hence the significance of the Saint Theresa theme, both as to its place in the novel and as to the rather breathless, uncontrolled, even embarrassing emotional quality which it exudes. Hence, too, the whole problem of Dorothea and Ladislaw. Dr Leavis has brilliantly indicated the nature of the unsatisfactoriness of Dorothea, the aspect of what he calls self-indulgence inherent in her conception.

Dorothea . . . is a product of George Eliot's own 'soul-hunger' – another day-dream ideal self. This persistence, in the midst of so much that is so other, of an unreduced enclave of the old immaturity is disconcerting in the extreme. We have an alternation between the poised impersonal insight of a finely tempered wisdom and something like the emotional confusions and self-importances of adolescence.

(p. 75)

And yet, for all the penetration of Dr Leavis's analysis, it is hard to agree entirely with his conclusion that 'the weakness of the book . . . is in Dorothea'. For although there is this weakness (which increases as the book goes on) it is also true that the strength of the book is in Dorothea. In spite of all our reservations it is Dorothea who, of all the characters of the novel, most deeply captures our imagination. It is her aspiration to a life nobler than the Middlemarch way of life that is the great positive force within the novel and the force which, above all, counteracts the tendency to present society as a static, invincible force outside the characters themselves. It is Dorothea alone who, with Ladislaw, successfully rebels against the Middlemarch values.

The word 'successfully' needs qualification. For one thing Dorothea herself has more of the Lady Bountiful about her than George Eliot seems prepared to admit, and there is always (though let us not overestimate the point) seven hundred a year between her and the full implications of her attitude. More important, the success of her rebellion is limited by the degree of artistic conviction which it carries. The 'day-dream' aspect of Dorothea which Dr Leavis has emphasised is a very basic limitation. But this quality, this sense we have of idealisation, of something incompletely realised, is due, I would suggest, not so much to any subjective cause, some emotional immaturity in George Eliot herself (it is hard to see how she could combine her remarkable total achievement in the novel with such immaturity) as to the limitations of her philosophy, her social understanding.

Dorothea represents that element in human experience for which in the determinist universe of mechanistic materialism there is no place – the need of man to change the world that he inherits. Dorothea is the force that she is in the novel precisely because she encompasses this vital motive-force in human life; and she fails ultimately to convince us because in George Eliot's conscious philosophy she has no place. The 'unreduced enclave' represented by the degree of George Eliot's failure here is the unreduced enclave of idealism in her world-outlook.

As for Ladislaw, he is far less successfully realised than Dorothea, far more than she a mere dream-figure, a romantic idealisation of the kind of man she deserves. Indeed it is only when she becomes involved with Ladislaw that we become seriously uneasy about Dorothea. And Ladislaw, interestingly enough, is an aesthete, a respectable dilettante, a Bohemian minus the sordid reality of Bohemianism. He is in fact almost everything into which the ineffectual rebels of the late Victorian era escaped, and he is saved from the degeneracy implicit in his way of life only by the convenient financial support of Casaubon, Mr Brooke and finally Dorothea herself. The artistic failure of George Eliot with Ladislaw, her failure to make him a figure realised on the artistic level of the other characters of the novel, is inseparable from the social unrealism in his conception. Artistically he is not 'there', not concrete, because socially he is not concrete, but idealised.

It is important, I think, to recognise the link between the weaknesses of *Middlemarch* and the limitations of George Eliot's philosophy. For there are two sorts of weakness in the novel which at first appear unrelated and even antithetical. In the first place there is the tendency towards a certain flatness or heaviness, a tendency which we have seen to be associated with her somewhat static view of society and mortality. In the second place there is the element of unresolved emotionalism involved in the Dorothea–Ladislaw relationship. The two weaknesses are not, in fact, contradictory; but rather two sides of the same coin. It is the very inadequacy of her mechanistic philosophy, its failure to incorporate a dialectical sense of contradiction and motion, that drives George Eliot to treat the aspirations of Dorothea idealistically.

Just as *War and Peace* – despite Tolstoy's enormous, penetrating sense of the dialectics of life, of birth, growth and development – is weakened by his mechanistic, determinist view of history, so in *Middlemarch* does George Eliot's undialectical philosophy weaken the total impact at which she aimed. And yet no novelist before her had so consciously and conscientiously tried to convey the inter-relatedness of social life or the changing nature of individuals and their relationships. She is a great, sincere and humane writer and it may well be that – despite the ultimate weaknesses within her work – the novelists of the future will turn to *Middlemarch* more often than to any other English novel.

NOTES

1. See Joan Bennett, *George Eliot* (1948) p. 167.

2. See *Partial Portraits*, p. 51 (quoted by F. R. Leavis in *The Great Tradition*, p. 33).

Quentin Anderson

GEORGE ELIOT IN
MIDDLEMARCH (1958)

In *The Prelude* Wordsworth notes that while he was taken up
with Godwinian rationalism he had discovered that rationalism
had a special danger: it denied the existence of the passions
which actually informed it. The briefest possible answer to
the question, What is the greatness of George Eliot? is to say
that she knew and could show that every idea is attended by a
passion; that thought is a passional act. Of course it is on the
showing, the accomplishment of the artist, that the emphasis
must finally rest, but it seems politic to begin this account by
suggesting to a somewhat unreceptive age how much she has
to tell her readers. Widely read and highly respected during
the last four decades of her century, George Eliot (1819–80)
became schoolroom fare in ours; but the assumption that she
is once more coming into the light is current, it may be the
misleading consequence of the appearance of Professor Gordon
Haight's monumental edition of her *Letters* and F. R. Leavis's
fine chapters on her in *The Great Tradition*. There is a seeming
paradox in the fact that, although admired, she is not much
read, because no novelist in English has come closer to answer-
ing a question which is very important to us: How can a social
world be felt and understood? It appears probable that there
is some resistance in us against the terms in which George Eliot
answers this question; we may well want a chance for vicarious
or imagined mastery over the social order – a chance to judge
and discriminate with sureness – but most of us find something
remote, something truly 'Victorian', in a world so fully humanized as the world of *Middlemarch*; perhaps this is because it

requires more love than we can give, more assurance than we can muster. Before we inquire just what *Middlemarch* does demand of us, a brief introduction is necessary.

George Eliot's Midland birth and lasting absorption in Midland scenes and manners largely defined her first efforts in fiction. The earnest, plain girl who kept house for her father, Robert Evans (her own given name was Mary Anne), was awkwardly and heavily pious in the way that girls who have no other way to express intense emotions are pious. Friendship with two families, the Brays and Hennells, who might be described as provincial intellectuals, widened her horizon immensely. She soon outstripped her friends, though she remained characteristically loyal to them, and became an enormous reader. Her first sustained literary endeavour was the translation of Strauss's *Das Leben Jesu* (1846), a work to which she was drawn by her earnest concern with the human meaning of the Christian legend, for legend it had now come to be for her. She made the leap from provincial society to the world of literature and ideas in London as assistant editor of the *Westminster Review*, which John Chapman was trying to put on its feet. She did some further translating (including Spinoza's *Ethics*), and, as a reviewer, formulated her requirements for fiction with prophetic precision. She did not undertake fiction herself until after she had made the great passional commitment of her life – to live as wife to George Henry Lewes, the gifted biographer, translator, and historian of philosophy. Since Lewes's wife was still living, the couple was socially stigmatized until the novelist won them a partial acceptance. Lewes's unremitting devotion and faith in her powers were essential to George Eliot. Their union covered the span of her productive life in fiction, which began with *Scenes of Clerical Life* in *Blackwood's* (1857).

Her second venture was *Adam Bede* (1859). This was followed by *The Mill on the Floss* (1860), *Silas Marner* (1861), *Romola* (in the *Cornhill*, 1862–3), *Felix Holt, the Radical* (1866), a dramatic poem, *The Spanish Gypsy* (1868), *Middlemarch* (which appeared in eight parts, 1871–2), and *Daniel Deronda* (1876). The works

she published before *Romola*, an historical novel about Savon-
arola's Florence, all depend for their matter on her memories
of childhood and young womanhood in Warwickshire, where
eighteenth-century ways were still common in her day. *Adam
Bede* and *The Mill on the Floss* remain delightful for their
provincial humours and their affectionate rendering of a
provincial scene; there are passages in both which are masterly,
yet both at crucial moments demand that uncritical assent to
affirmed rather than established motivations which the Victorian reader was so often ready to supply, partly because they
were (or were supposed to be) his own, but more often perhaps
simply because they were the condition of further vicarious
participation in the feelings of an Adam Bede or a Maggie
Tulliver. To find George Eliot at her best one turns to the three
books which follow *Romola*. Among these, *Felix Holt, the Radical*
is much the weakest, though it contains superlative passages.
Daniel Deronda is about the most splendid failure among English
novels, and the reader who responds to *Middlemarch* may be
assured that it is well worth his time. But *Middlemarch* is
unquestionably the best of the three.

This novel is subtitled 'A Study of Provincial Life', and the
climax in the national life which it partly chronicles, the period
in which the Reform Bill of 1832 was moving towards adoption,
was selected with the apparent intention of giving the novel
the representative quality which we associate with Flaubert's
Sentimental Education and Tolstoy's *War and Peace*. But one of
the first things we must note about the novel is that this particular intention masks a more general one. Flaubert's choice
of the revolution of 1848 or Tolstoy's of Napoleon's invasion
of Russia as events which bring together various strands of the
national experience was motivated in part by a desire to put
that experience before us. George Eliot's notebook for the novel
shows that she looked up such matters as the stages in the
passage of the Reform Bill, the medical horizons of the 1830s,
the industrial uses of manganese, and various other details.
But the uses to which she puts these things are not terminal;
she is not concerned as Flaubert is to lodge firmly in the reader's

sensibility a mass of impressions deliberately selected to inform us of the political, industrial, and social life of the time. She is, in fact, incapable of suggesting the tone of a given period or historical moment. In the Middlemarch world, as in George Eliot generally, change is something intrusive, an irruption from without. The more general intention of which I have spoken is the attempt to render in a novel her sense of the 'primitive tissue' of a community.

This term is employed by Tertius Lydgate, a surgeon with excellent training, who buys a Middlemarch practice and hopes to combine medical work with research in physiology. His studies in Paris have persuaded him that a promising line of inquiry lies in the attempt to find the primal tissue which is the basis of all those adapted to special bodily functions. The master image of the book precisely parallels Lydgate's physiological inquiry: this is the image of human relationships as a web. Each of us stands at what seems to us a centre, our own consciousness, though it is in fact but one of numerous nodes or junction points. This is further illustrated in George Eliot's figure of the metal mirror bearing many scratches, which when illuminated at any given point produces the illusion of concentric circles ranged about that point. This figure enriches the suggestion of the recurrent web image and those associated with it by enforcing the fact that in dealing with a particular person we must consider: his appearance in the eyes of each of the other persons whom he encounters; the way he appears among various social groups to which he is known or which know of him; and his own complex of feelings which leads him to offer the world a version (or various versions) of himself. This does not at first seem an epoch-making kind of viewpoint for a novelist, since all novelists must somehow convey the quality of each character's self-regard and the opinions that others have of him. But George Eliot's special success in *Middlemarch* is the consequence of making the reciprocal workings of self-regard and opinion primary – in effect an extraordinary economy of means, and not simply of means, for it appears when we look closely that the matter of the book is people's opinions about one another, and that its particular method consists in contriving scenes in which the disparity between the intentions of agents and the opinions of observers is dramatically exhibited. This consistency of method accounts for our sense of the unity of a book which embraces a whole social order and four, or by another reckoning, five principal stories.

Of course these stories are intertwined by the plot as well as by our developing sense of Middlemarch as a community. The first of these stories is that of Dorothea Brooke, which was begun as an independent tale and later worked into the plan of the larger novel. Dorothea is somewhat externally characterized in a brief 'Prelude'. She belongs to a group of great spirits who remain unknown and unsung: 'with dim lights and tangled circumstance they tried to shape their thought and deed in noble agreement; but, after all, to common eyes their struggles seemed mere inconsistency and formlessness; for these later-born Theresas were helped by no coherent social faith and order which could perform the function of knowledge for the ardently willing soul.' The account concludes: 'Here and there is born a Saint Theresa, foundress of nothing, whose loving heart-beats and sobs after an unattained goodness tremble off and are dispersed among hindrances, instead of centring in some long-recognizable deed.' F. R. Leavis discerns a tendency on the part of George Eliot to make rather too personal invest- ments in her heroines, and the tone of this 'Prelude' bears him out. The reader ought to be assured that the Dorothea he meets in the opening scenes of the novel is not this portentous figure, but a young lady whose foible in marrying an elderly pedant has the consequences – comic, pathetic, and even, in a minor and domestic key, tragic – that we might expect it to have in life. As the novel goes forward, however, Dorothea's demand that the world afford chances for heroic achievement does begin to seem much too categorical. We must return to the question of her role in the imaginative economy of the novel at a later point.

Lydgate, the principal figure of the second intrigue, is closer to the working centre of the book than Dorothea, since his fate turns not simply on his marriage to Rosamond Vincy, but upon the sum of his actions and reactions in response to Middlemarch. His story is linked with the third in the group of four, the story of Bulstrode, the banker guilty of moral defalcations, whose self-arraignment is one of the finest episodes in the book (although the whole Bulstrode strand in the novel is less impressive than the others because his past is somewhat stagily rendered and the agents out of that past who hunt him down seem melodramatic conveniences). The fourth strand, closer in tone to the earlier Midland novels, functions in part to provide a standard by which the others may be placed and judged. It involves the Garth family, Mary, her father, Caleb, her successful suitor Fred Vincy, and the Reverend Farebrother, who also aspires to Mary. Here also belong the provincial humours of the book, which centre about old Peter Featherstone's disposition of his property.

Middlemarch is carefully (contemporary readers tend to say exhaustively) plotted. One or more of the characters in each of the four stories plays an important part in each of the other three. The Victorian reader was offered a multiplicity of occasions for sympathetic concern. One of the things about George Eliot and her readers which it is hardest for us to recapture is the artless and unashamed emotionalism of the latter over the fate of her characters, and the benign acceptance of this situation on the part of the writer. The century which wrenched Hamlet out of *Hamlet* had not the least scruple about lobbying for its favourite character while the novel was in the course of publication in parts – while it was in fact still being written. One may imagine that if the modern objection to such innocence about the fashion in which a work is made an artistic whole had been stated it would have been met with the response that the whole was really constituted by the assurance of moral conformity – George Eliot could be trusted. Blackwood, George Eliot's publisher, wrote her in this vein while *Middlemarch* was appearing; he sets down his hopes and fears for the characters, and tells her in effect that her interposition in their lives has been both touching and morally impeccable. The novelist and her fellows were of course affected by this atmosphere: they wrote with a consciousness of the awakened and palpitant sensibilities of the readers who were speculating about what would happen in the next part; they watched the sale of each part with anxiety, and made anxious inquiry about a falling-off. Some of the occasions for sympathetic concern in this novel may be listed: How will Dorothea awake to a consciousness of the meaning of her marriage to the pedant, Casaubon? Will Fred Vincy inherit old Featherstone's money? Failing that, will he reclaim himself and marry Mary Garth, or will Farebrother cut him out? Will Rosamond's 'torpedo contact' paralyse her vigorous husband, Lydgate? Can he succeed in medical practice in the face of the bigotry of Middlemarch? Can he extricate himself from his debts? How will Bulstrode be found out, and what will thereupon happen to him and his devoted wife? There is a cognate familiarity about many of the motifs of the story: the idealism of Dorothea, the earnest and rather wry Christianity of Farebrother, the weakling reclaimed in Fred Vincy, the dryness, harsh fun, and moral beauty of the plain Mary Garth. Neither plot nor traits of character taken alone are sufficiently distinctive to set this novel apart from others. I have found that youthful readers nowadays are restive when confronted by such careful plotting and such familiar traits of character; they shy away and quite miss the light which illumines all these things in their mutual relations, the voice of the wise woman. That voice is often heard speaking directly with an authority which makes use of the Victorian reader's involvement with the characters to make him look up and look about, to see how human relations are established with the world of the story – to see the whole of what the wise woman surveys.

What she surveys may be called a landscape of opinion, for it is not the natural landscape that is dominant here. In fact, there are only two fully realized natural landscapes, Lowick Manor and Stone Court, and in these cases the landscape is realized by an individual whose situation and interests make him aware of an external world at that particular moment. For the most part we may characterize the book's use of the physical world by referring to George Eliot's own sense of Warwickshire as a physical locale which has been wholly humanized, and to the Reverend Cadwallader's half-serious remark that it is a very good quality in a man to have a trout stream. This transposition of the natural into the moral and psychological is further illustrated by the novelist's use of snatches of poetry – Dorothea Brooke's hope for social betterment 'haunted her like a passion' – and we may say that the affectionate sense of nature and the objects that man makes and handles which suffuses *Adam Bede* has been deliberately subdued here. Nothing comparable to the description of Hetty Sorrel in Mrs Poyser's diary can enter into *Middlemarch*, not because it is a more 'intellectual' book, but because its immediacies are not things seen but things felt and believed. It is striking that we know almost nothing of the appearance of Middlemarch itself, although our sense of the life of the town as a community is very full indeed, ranging as it does from a pot-house to the Green Dragon, the town's best inn, from horse-dealers, auctioneers, and grocers to the lawyers, physicians, merchants, clergymen, and landowners who stand at the head of the scale. Although we see little of the activities of all these people we hear their voices, each pitched to the tone of its own desire, each capable of dropping suggestively or rising assertively on grounds which George Eliot shows to be wholy inadequate when related to the facts of the particular case. Chap. 45 is a good instance of the masterly way in which she can demonstrate the drifts and swirls of opinion through the town. In this account of various responses to Lydgate's principled refusal to dispense drugs himself, each of the voices establishes a character so fully and with such economy that it is hard to believe that Mawmsey, the grocer, and Mrs Dollop of the Tankard have not always been known to us. Yet this single chapter does much more. In it we learn that the clouds of misapprehension and selfishness gathering about Lydgate cannot possibly be dispelled, that he is more than likely to get into debt, and that his wife's awful insularity will resist his earnest and even his desperate attempts to penetrate it. George Eliot had much earlier (chap. 15) used her author's privilege to warn the reader of all these possibilities. 'For surely all must admit that a man may be puffed and belauded, envied, ridiculed, counted upon as a tool and fallen in love with, or at least selected as a future husband, and yet remain virtually unknown – known merely as a cluster of signs for his neighbours' false suppositions.' The novelist, writing of *Middlemarch*, says: 'I wanted to give a panoramic view of provincial life . . .'; but what she does give is something far more active, far more in accord with the image of the web – or perhaps a vast switchboard in which every signal is interpreted differently by each receiver, and each receiver is in its turn capable of propagating in response a signal of its own with equally dissonant consequences. Yet in the end, roughly but surely, the dissonances die out and a consensus of sorts emerges, for as George Eliot remarks at one point, not everyone is an originator, and there is a limit to the varieties of error people can fall into.

The characters move in a landscape of opinion, but those who concern us have an inner life; they can look within as well as without, and measure their sense of themselves against the world's demands and expectations. The economy of means and materials I have referred to consists in the use of the landscape of opinion as the scene of action. It does not exclude, it rather informs and gives depth to the conventional motifs and the conventional attributes of character mentioned above. A long quotation extracted from the description of Casaubon illustrates the method:

If to Dorothea Mr Casaubon had been the mere occasion which had set alight the fine inflammable material of her youthful illusions, does it follow that he was fairly represented in the minds of those less impassioned personages who have hitherto delivered their judgements concerning him? I protest against any absolute conclusion, any prejudice derived from Mrs Cadwallader's contempt for a neighbouring clergyman's alleged greatness of soul, or Sir James Chettam's poor opinion of his rival's legs, from Mr Brooke's failure to elicit a companion's ideas, or from Celia's criticism of a middle-aged scholar's personal appearance. I am not sure that the greatest man of his age, if ever that solitary superlative existed, could escape these unfavourable reflections of himself in various small mirrors; and even Milton, looking for his portrait in a spoon, must submit to have the facial angle of a bumpkin. Moreover, if Mr Casaubon, speaking for himself, has a rather chilling rhetoric, it is not therefore certain that there is no good work or fine feeling in him. Did not an immortal physicist and interpreter of hieroglyphics write detestable verse? Has the theory of the solar system been advanced by graceful manners and conversational tact? Suppose we turn from outside estimates of a man, to wonder, with keener interest, what is the report of his own consciousness about his doings or capacity; with what hindrances he is carrying on his daily labours; what fading of hopes, or what deeper fixity of self-delusion the years are marking off within him; and with what spirit he wrestles against universal pressure, which will one day be too heavy for him, and bring his heart to its final pause. Doubtless his lot is important in his own eyes; and the chief reason that we think he asks too large a place in our consideration must be our want of room for him, since we refer him to the Divine regard with perfect confidence; nay it is even held sublime for our neighbour to expect the utmost there, however little he may have got from us. Mr Casaubon, too, was the centre of his own world; if he was liable to think others were providentially made for him, and especially to consider them in the light of their fitness for the author of a 'Key to all Mythologies', this trait is not quite alien to us, and, like the other mendicant hopes of mortals, claims some of our pity.

Certain aspects of this passage invite attention. George Eliot is here gathering up a series of notations about Casaubon which have been established in dialogue. In doing so she becomes a sharply marked present voice. We have come a long way from Fielding's interposed addresses to the reader in *Tom Jones*, a long way from Dickens and Thackeray as well – Thackeray cannot step on his stage without shaking it or dwarfing it; the effect is always of diminution, a voice which condescends to or coos about the pettiness or charm of the creatures displayed, while Dickens's effects in this kind involve facing about, leaving the characters to fend for themselves while he carries on his special pleading. George Eliot, however, speaks to the issues of her own work, and addresses the reader in terms which set her above it but never to one side. In her 'I protest against any absolute conclusion . . .' we find a gentle schoolmistress's irony which places her between the book and our apprehension of it. In this instance she is saying that we are guilty, not because we are all egocentrics by definition, but because these notations about Casaubon have indeed composed our picture of him. She goes on to indicate what she is about to do with the figure: we shall end by finding him pathetic; we are to be converted – to be forced to abandon the stereotyped social gesture which leads us to 'refer him [Casaubon] to the Divine regard' and refer him instead to our own failures to get the world to concede our majesty. Her own rhetoric, the somewhat heavy verbal play of 'solitary superlative', the clinical remoteness and buried scientific analogy of 'what deeper fixity of self-delusion the years are marking off within him', the carefully indicated central image of the mutually mirroring selves, the fact that she is playing prologue to her own action – for each of her generalities is a forecast of a part of Casaubon's fate – are all elements of that voice which frames the whole book.

Within this frame the dialogue presents dramatically the same interplay between opinion and self-regard, mirror and mirrored self. In the chapter from which the long quotation above is drawn, Lydgate encounters Dorothea for the first time. What he sees and fails to see is indicative of his angle of vision and of part of the truth about the elder Miss Brooke:

'She is a good creature – that – fine girl – but a little too earnest,' he thought. 'It is troublesome to talk to such women. They are always wanting reasons, yet they are too ignorant to understand the merits of any question, and usually fall back on their moral sense to settle things after their own taste.'

Each leading character has a serious delusion: Dorothea's belief that she can do good through learning; Lydgate's that the demands of science are compatible with those that Middlemarch makes of its physicians; Mr Casaubon's idea that marriage with a beautiful and passionate young girl will bring him pleasure and repose; Bulstrode's belief that he can make an inward moral restitution for the act of misappropriating his original fortune. As Farebrother (who, along with Mary Garth, sometimes functions as a surrogate for the novelist's voice) says to Lydgate (who has been preaching his medical ideals):

Your scheme is a good deal more difficult to carry out than the Pythagorean community though. You have not only got the old Adam in yourself against you, but you have got all those descendants of the original Adam who form the society around you.

Some of George Eliot's devices to enforce her view of the landscape of opinion are transparently such. Young Fred Vincy has long held expectations based on old Peter Featherstone's will. Peter, who lives to torment his relatives, teases him about a story that he has been trying to borrow money on post-obits. Fred is instructed to get a letter from the stiff-necked Bulstrode to the effect that this is not true.

'You must be joking, sir. Mr Bulstrode, like other men, believes scores of things that are not true, and he has a prejudice against me. I could easily get him to write that he knew no facts in proof of the report you speak of, though it might lead to unpleasantness. But I could hardly ask him to write down what he believes or does not believe about me.'

Old Featherstone is here made to demand of Fred Vincy more than Bulstrode's testimony as to the *facts*; had he limited himself to this Fred would be less uncomfortable – but what has actually been demanded is an account of the way in which Fred is envisioned by another man – an account of one facet of his social being. The imaginative coherence of *Middlemarch* is observable on many levels; in this instance old Featherstone's demand is the counterpart of what chiefly obsesses his last months: the effect that another document, his will, will have on those who survive him. *His* opinion will emerge when his last will is read, and it will comfort no one on the *Middlemarch* scene.

Fred, meanwhile, is buoyed up by an opinion generally held that he will inherit from old Featherstone: 'In fact, tacit expectations of what would be done for him by Uncle Featherstone determined the angle at which most people viewed Fred Vincy in Middlemarch; and in his own consciousness, what Uncle Featherstone would do for him in an emergency, or what he would do simply as an incorporated luck, formed always an immeasurable depth of aerial perspective.'

Fred is the son of a ruddy, genial merchant who is shortly to become mayor of the town, and it is part of the pattern that the elder Vincy's sense of self is more completely dependent on the views that others hold of him than that of any other character. When Bulstrode, his brother-in-law, scolds him for training Fred for the Church on simply worldly grounds, his inward reaction is described in this way: 'When a man has the immediate prospect of being mayor, and is ready, in the interests of commerce, to take up a firm attitude on politics generally, he has naturally a sense of his importance to the framework of things which seems to throw questions of private conduct into the background.' When Wrench, the family doctor, fails to diagnose Fred's typhoid fever Mr Vincy feels indignant: 'What Mr Vincy thought confusedly was, that the fever might somehow have been hindered if Wrench had shown the proper solicitude about his – the Mayor's – family.'

When men and affairs do not conspire to supply his self-love, the elder Vincy very quickly loses his head. Old Featherstone's latest will brings Fred nothing, and the father's view of the son changes instantly: 'He's an uncommonly unfortunate lad, is Fred. He'd need have some luck by-and-by to make up for all this – else I don't know who'd have an eldest son.'

Fred's own sense of the way in which the world ought to respond to the desires of a young man in his position in life has been fostered by the father who rejects him. He has long been fond of Mary Garth; this affection and the more effectual fatherhood of Caleb Garth rescue him from the family delusion that the world will cater to their handsome children. Caleb Garth is strongly reminiscent of the novelist's father, Robert Evans. He is wholly committed to the religion of 'business', by which he means the actual performance of work. In Middlemarch he stands very much alone. It is not the least important of George Eliot's observations about this community that it lacks the instinct of workmanship and the pleasure in a job well done. We hear of shoddy cloth, inferior dyestuffs, oppressed weavers, ill-housed tenants, and all these things are comments on the adequacy of the landscape of opinion; it is very badly and weakly rooted in nature.

Moreover, it can show few explicit principles. Most of those who advance moral or political convictions are shown to be riding a hobby or exhibiting a personal foible. Mrs Cadwallader is exceedingly well-born and – of necessity – very close-fisted. As the wife of a country parson, she functions admirably. But prick her to generalization and you will get either pride of birth or stinginess exemplified. So it goes in and about Middlemarch. Old Peter Featherstone has made it out that God is on the side of those who want land and cattle, though the devil backs (for a time) such 'speckilating' fellows as Bulstrode. The labourers at Frick who are incited to chase away a party of railroad surveyors, and Dagley, Mr Brooke's tenant, who defies his bad landlord in the name of 'rinform', have no more comprehension of railroads or of Brooke than Brooke has of those who stand below him in the Middlemarch scale. Politics share the same obscurity. Middlemarch knows how to manipulate the Middlemarch voter; how to discomfit the bumbling Brooke on the occasion of the nominations for Parliament, but it has no sense of the national meaning of the Reform Bill. There is shrewdness on many levels, but respect for accuracy, dispassionate judgement, are confined to the Garths and Farebrother, persons who are of little consequence on the Middlemarch scene. The other character whose judgement and information are offered as authoritative is Casaubon's cousin, Will Ladislaw, who marries Dorothea after her husband's death. He, however, is so alien to Middlemarch that he cannot act on it directly: the principles, ideas, and standards which prevail in the wider world outside Middlemarch cannot be articulated within it.

The medium is too dense; it is not permeable from without.

Joan Bennett, in her sensible little book on the novelist, emphasizes George Eliot's observation about the medium in which her characters move: 'It is the habit of my imagination to strive after as full a vision of the medium in which character moves as of the character itself' (Cross, *Letters and Journals*, II 10). *Middlemarch* authorizes an extension of this principle; George Eliot has created a common medium which completely immerses most of the characters. It is hard to conceive how an individual can on this scene really originate anything. Dorothea's wide charity finds no direct expression; Lydgate's scientific interest in the town's health meets blank incomprehension and effectual resistance, not only from all ranks in the medical hierarchy but from almost every element in the town. Indeed, the reader may by now feel (partly because I have played down the humour of the book) that Middlemarch is as oppressive as that provincial town inhabited by Emma Bovary in another study of the *mœurs de province*. In Flaubert's book there are at least the passionate impulses of Emma to combat her stifling world. What is there here?

Professor Haight, in his introduction to a recent edition of *Middlemarch*, repudiates the figure of the Wise Woman, which he finds rampant in John Walter Cross's biography. It seems to him too heavy, too statuesque, to refer to George Eliot. However, George Eliot herself is partly responsible for the dissemination of this image (she aided the compiler of a book of wise and tender sayings from her work), and the Wise Woman, or whatever we wish to call her, is an indispensable figure in discussing her work. In fact, the only thing which can possibly balance, can possibly support *Middlemarch*, is this image of the writer which the novel creates in the reader. Were she not there we should not be attending.

George Eliot is present as the only fully realized individual in her book. This sounds like a harsh saying, but it may not be quite so harsh as it sounds. When one is reading *Middlemarch* there are many moments when one looks up and says, 'How intelligent, how penetrating this woman is!' And, of course, one is speaking of George Eliot. In reading the fine chapter of analysis which has to do with Lydgate's character and the situation in which he finds himself in Middlemarch, we come upon this passage:

He was at a starting-point which makes many a man's career a fine subject for betting, if there were any gentlemen given to that amusement who could appreciate the complicated probabilities of an arduous purpose, with all the possible thwartings and furtherings of circumstance, all the niceties of inward balance, by which a man swims and makes his point or else is carried headlong. The risk would remain, even with close knowledge of Lydgate's character; for character too is a process and an unfolding.

Those who like *Middlemarch* take pleasure in the writer's judiciousness. They are far more tempted to invest themselves with her sensibility than they are to identify themselves with that of any of her characters. It is notable that analytic passages like the one just quoted predominate among those chosen for quotation from Leslie Stephen's day to our own. The description of Caleb Garth, of Rosamond Vincy's terrible self-absorption, of Dorothea's aspirations and her blindness to her sister Celia's world, of Bulstrode's casuistical inner life, of Casaubon's tortured consciousness of inadequacy – all these are analytic though all are matched by passages of dialogue in which their substance is exemplified. Certain dramatic scenes – that between Dorothea and Rosamond in particular – are also favourites, but again the most familiar passage about Rosamond seems to be that which describes her reaction to the awful, the inconceivable fact that there is another self in the world, one which Ladislaw cherishes far more than hers. These fine and satisfying analytic passages are not additions or decorations, nor do they represent a division within George Eliot, rather they exhibit her sense of process at work within the frame of actuality; it is her life *in* the novel which lies at its heart; this is what we rejoice in. Admittedly this means that no character is freed to exist as Don Quixote or Julien Sorel are enfranchised; the very firmness and clarity of George Eliot's vision, extending to the edges of her canvas, quite preclude her granting to any one of her creatures the authority of existence. Like a goddess, she suffers them to exist in so far as they may be known through sympathy and comprehension. No more life than this can emerge – any further measure would make her characters novelists. Those who are her surrogates, her delegated voices, are in a sense independent of her, but they are wholly caught up within a system of morally and aesthetically statable responses – as is Mary Garth – and correspond rather to Mary Anne Evans, who had once lived within a provincial society, than to George Eliot, the novelist.

Those who live completely within the shelter of a community never apprehend it as an entity. In a sense, the very notion of 'society' came to imaginative fulfilment for the first time in nineteenth-century romanticism; the assumption of one of the roles of the romantic involved a reciprocal identification: here am I, a discriminable self, there is the world, the other to which I stand opposed. Of course such opposition was never total; the romantic was forced to call on some aspect of existence for support and sanction – on nature, on the philosophic status of the imagination, on libertarian politics, on the wider experience of the remote and exotic – whatever might give poetic actuality to the insights of the self. To George Eliot, a member of a succeeding generation, all these options were familiar, but none of them was acceptable. The experience which gave society objectivity for her was the loss of her religious faith. And the striking thing is that she did not thereupon become a rationalist, a scientific blue-stocking, or a lecturer on the rights of women. Only a few months after she had informed her father that she could not in conscience accompany him to church she realized that her fresh point of view towards the meaning of religion made such gestures unnecessary and foolish. She had made a massive discovery.

This discovery was very simple, but its effects were profound. Miss Evans repossessed the world imaginatively when she came to the conclusion that the creeds, formulae, practices, and institutions in which people shrouded themselves were no less significant if one saw that they were not absolute. With a feminine directness she now accepted everything she had momentarily rejected. But human behaviour was now seen as a set of symbolic gestures expressive of individual needs and desires. The positivism of Auguste Comte undoubtedly played a role in this, but it did not teach her to interpret human actions; it is clear that this was a spontaneous gift which was hers before she began to write fiction. She was able to see the emotional concomitants of churchgoing; able to make out what Diderot calls the 'professional idioms' of behaviour. Each of us is like the marine animal which borrows a shell: we borrow our shells for social purposes, but our feelers wave no less expressively for that. George Eliot found that she could translate the psychic gestures involved in our religion, our politics, our superstitions, our local traditions, and discover, as she had in herself, a common root of action and reaction. She wrote to the American novelist, Harriet Beecher Stowe, that her novel, *Oldtown Folks*, showed a comprehension of the 'mixed moral influence shed on society by dogmatic systems', which was 'rare even among writers'. She saw, in other words, that the interplay between creeds, ideas, and desires was the novelist's business. But we must still ask what binds the novelist's world together? What sanction remains after the absoluteness of creeds and institutions has been denied?

A curious inversion in a sentence from the 'Prelude' to *Middlemarch* which has been quoted above supplies an answer. In speaking of those whose career resembles Dorothea's, George Eliot remarks that the 'later-born Theresas were helped by no coherent social faith and order which could perform the function of knowledge for the ardently willing soul'. There is a suggestion here that if you find fulfilment through knowledge you do not need the pressure of an unquestioned social order and religious faith to sustain you. This brave assumption was written into George Eliot's work and acted out in her life. Her role as novelist involved finding and telling the truth. It was not a matter of occasional didactic interjections, but of a continuously present intelligence speaking in the declarative.

There is a famous sentence descriptive of Lydgate's character which will serve as a leading instance:

Lydgate's spots of commonness lay in the complexion of his prejudices, which in spite of noble intention and sympathy, were half of them such as are found in ordinary men of the world: that distinction of mind which belonged to his intellectual ardour, did not penetrate his feeling and judgement about furniture, or women, or the desirability of its being known (without his telling) that he was better born than other country surgeons.

The scenes in which Lydgate's character is rendered in dialogue do not have the power of this passage of commentary. The dialogue cannot render as much as George Eliot can see. I do not mean that we are not persuaded by her statement or that we feel that dialogue and statement are not in accord; it is simply the fact that she scores most heavily as commentator that we must recognize. The very best things in George Eliot are no doubt her account of Lydgate, Rosamond, and their marriage, in *Middlemarch*, the encounters between Mrs Transome and her former lover, Matthew Jermyn, in *Felix Holt*, and the story of Gwendolen Harleth's struggle with Grandcourt in *Daniel Deronda*. In each case it is the voice of George Eliot the writer which is finally persuasive. It is absurd to say, as a good many people have, that her insight is intrusive or an aesthetic impropriety; it is her genius made manifest.

Middlemarch, the scene of this novel, is wholly dominated by the finely tempered mind which envisions it. But how is this scene framed and judged from without? What are the effectual boundaries of the landscape of opinion? The town – though it is a middling place from the point of view of one considering a group of provincial towns – lies on the marches, it is on the periphery of the great world, not simply the world of London or even Rome, but the world of science, the arts, and of history; realized human greatness does not enter it. We must inquire how the writer who herself moved in the great world acknowledged that world in *Middlemarch*.

There is a finely scaled scene in *Daniel Deronda* in which

Gwendolen Harleth asks the musician, Klesmer, to help her to launch a musical career on nothing more than a feeble talent and her social pretensions. Klesmer confronts Gwendolen with the audacity and the ignorance of her claim. The scene has a wonderfully tonic effect – it is as if George Eliot had managed a dramatic confrontation of the austerities of art with the blind abundant energies of youth and beauty. Klesmer's treatment of Gwendolen is exquisitely modulated; it is at once a denunciation and a tribute to her as a woman. But she must be told that social lies and politeness have nothing to do with being an artist. In the world of art you must tell the truth; self-regard and the world's opinion must give way before realized mastery. There is an analogous scene in *Middlemarch*, though the standard invoked is not impersonal. Rosamond's flirtation with Ladislaw is abruptly ended when she discovers that Dorothea is all-important to him. She had found in Ladislaw a representative of the world outside Middlemarch to which she had ignorantly aspired, and Ladislaw thinks her of no account. She is momentarily awed into a generosity which brings Ladislaw and Dorothea together. Throughout the book Ladislaw speaks authoritatively about the world outside the town's awareness. It is he who tells Dorothea that Casaubon's work is useless because he has not read the German scholars; it is he who demands fidelity to a standard of artistic accomplishment; he alone has some sense of national politics.

Yet Ladislaw does not have the authority of Klesmer; he is the weakest of the major characters, not merely because he is made to behave like a dilettante, but because George Eliot's judiciousness does not extend to him; he is not understood. In fact, he is rather like a character in an ordinary novel. F. R. Leavis sees this as a consequence of the weakness of the figure of Dorothea. Since she is in part a self-indulgent fantasy of George Eliot's and not wholly disciplined by the demands of the novel, we may think of Ladislaw as an accessory required by the fantasy. Certainly the scenes they share are full of high-flown nonsense. But there is a good deal of evidence that Dorothea and Ladislaw represent something more than the

unresolved longings of Mary Anne Evans. The leading characters in *Romola, Felix Holt, Middlemarch,* and *Daniel Deronda* all
escape the circle of the author's judgement. It is claimed for
each of them that they aspire to or escape into the great world.
Dorothea is the partial exception. When confronted by her
uncle, Casaubon, her sister Celia, or the Chettams, she is fully
controlled, fully understood. But Romola, Felix Holt, and
Deronda are all extravagantly moral or extravagantly spiritual
or both. And Dorothea and Ladislaw in their scenes together
have the same defect.

Instead of thinking of *Middlemarch* as showing two strains, an
artistically responsible element and a neurotically compelled
one, we must, I believe, adopt a fresh version of the traditional
assertion that George Eliot's conception of her fiction is inter-
nally divided. Leavis has pointed to the meaninglessness of the
form this assertion of a split took in the criticism of Henry
James and Leslie Stephen. The disjunction between an 'intellectual' George Eliot and a George Eliot who has the novelist's
sympathetic comprehension of human beings is, as we have
seen, a clear-cut contradiction. It is the voice heard within the
frame of her best fiction which has high intellectual distinction.

But there is an internal division in her conception of *Middle-*
march which corresponds to the far more serious split in *Daniel*
Deronda, in which Deronda's mystical religiosity is given pre-
cedence over the fictionally superior story of Gwendolen
Harleth. (The argument may also be applied to *Romola* and
Felix Holt.) This split in the writer's conception of fiction
appears to have a biographical root. The novels of George
Eliot's maturity re-enact her own emancipation; the values
which the Garths and Farebrother assert within the little
world of Middlemarch are reasserted from the viewpoint of
liberated intelligence by the voice of the narrator; her loss of
faith, her translation to the metropolis, her defiance of propriety
in living with Lewes, are all justified by the activity of the
novelist who surveys Middlemarch. The right opinion of the
Garths and Farebrother gives way before the knowledge of the
novelist. But for George Eliot the re-enactment brought with

it an irresistible impulse to include a character who could function as knower, an *embodied* voice.

She was unable, even in the years of her maturest art, to conceive of fiction as a truly independent form. It would seem to have been enough to bring that fine intelligence to bear on the enclosed world of Middlemarch, but she is never content with this. She must bring forward some instance of principled nonconformity, as if to feed an appetite for self-justification. We must conclude, I think, that the fairy-tale triumph of Romola over the physical and moral ills of a fever-stricken village, and the fantastic errand which takes Deronda to Jerusalem – he is, in effect, to build a culture! – are not merely tributes to a Victorian taste for moral exaltation. They are attempts on the part of the writer to give herself a recognizable moral status.

The English novel is so much the richer for George Eliot's contribution that one may be tempted into scolding her for not doing what no English novelist of the century did: for not taking possession of the great world. Her sense of community, her finely modulated articulation of passion and idea, the clarity and firmness of her characterization – these things alone justify Virginia Woolf's remark that *Middlemarch* was one of the few English novels written for grown-up people. Since the grown-up perspective includes Flaubert and Tolstoy, we are of course conscious that George Eliot did not share their power to incarnate the great world in the lesser one, to make the novel an instrument which can register the fate of a society in the perspective of history and heroic achievement. To exercise this power she would have had to take her own splendid powers for granted, and this she could not do.

W. J. Harvey

'INTRODUCTION' TO
MIDDLEMARCH (1966)

I

For Virginia Woolf, *Middlemarch* was 'the magnificent book which for all its imperfections is one of the few English novels written for grown-up people'. She was, no doubt, thinking of George Eliot's unblinking but compassionate delineation of her characters, of the subtlety of psychological analysis and the maturity of moral comment which underlie this complex and varied novel of English provincial life in the early nineteenth century. These qualities were emphasized by contemporary critics of George Eliot when they related her to Scott, Jane Austen, and Thackeray. Like Scott she has a sure historical grasp of diverse and slowly changing cultures; like Jane Austen she has a delicate sense of social comedy; like Thackeray she subjects her characters to a steady flow of ironic and moral comment. What also lies behind Virginia Woolf's judgement is a new infusion of intellectual power into the art of fiction; of all English novelists, George Eliot has the best mind. This intellectual power, combined with her other gifts, links her more to an artist like Thomas Mann than to any other English writer. But we never feel, as we sometimes do with Mann's novels, that her work is overweighted with ideas, that it lapses into the merely cerebral. Her basic humanity, her lively Tolstoyan sense of individuals enmeshed in their society, transmute her philosophic view of life into a richly rewarding art.

From the manuscript of *Middlemarch*, from the notebook or 'Quarry' she compiled while writing it, and from her letters and journals, we can learn a great deal about her art and about the genesis and growth of this particular novel. Early in 1869 she began a story, having Lydgate as its central character and concerned entirely with the fictional town which gives the novel its title; this went slowly and painfully and looked like petering out. In December 1870 she started a separate work, originally designed to be quite short, called 'Miss Brooke'. Like many of her works this grew in complexity and she must soon have recognized the many similarities of theme and setting which it shared with the Middlemarch tale; at any rate, by the spring of 1871 the two stories had been fused. From an early stage the resulting profusion of material threatened to grow too large even for a three-volume novel and George Eliot knew, from *The Mill on the Floss,* how so spacious a structure could become cramped at the end by an over-leisurely beginning. Her consort, G. H. Lewes, suggested that it should be published in bimonthly parts, and so it first appeared, from December 1871 until December 1872, the last three parts being issued at monthly intervals. The actual writing of the novel was not completed until October 1872.

Granted the complex origins and slow growth of the novel, it is astonishing how complete and successful is the unity of the final work. This achievement is magnified when one thinks of the prodigality and diversity of George Eliot's material. At the heart of the book we have the stories of Dorothea and Lydgate, twin studies in defeated aspiration. Dorothea is the innocent idealist, anxious to do great good in a world which cramps and confines her ardour so that she dwindles into marriage with the pedantic and sterile Casaubon. After his death she struggles towards the love and relative freedom of Will Ladislaw, the vaguely artistic and somewhat idealized outsider whose presence in Middlemarch impinges on so many aspects of this insulated society. Lydgate, who aims to combine the reform of medical practice with basic research, is also trapped into a stultifying union with the shallowly egoistic Rosamond Vincy, his ambitions withering under the pressure of provincial narrowness. Interwoven with these central studies we have the story of Bulstrode, banker and religious hypocrite, whose dishonest

past betrays him; Fred Vincy, amiable but aimless, who is saved
by his love for Mary Garth and the example of her father,
Caleb; and beyond these a host of lesser characters who serve
to give range and depth to the world of the novel. Urban society
interacts with rural life; the provincial scene is densely populated with a profusion of vividly imagined characters.

Victorian novelists in general delight in the abundance and
plenitude of life, in a teeming world of human idiosyncrasy.
Yet often – as sometimes with Dickens – the results are near
anarchic. The vitality of the individual characters breaks away
from the limits of a frequently conventional and melodramatic
plot, threatening to overwhelm and destroy the novel's central
themes. But with George Eliot, thanks largely to her philosophic
power, all is disciplined to the demands of the whole. Certainly
we enjoy the liveliness of individual characters – Casaubon, Mr
Brooke, Mrs Cadwallader, Featherstone are all vivid creations –
but they are only strands in a total pattern. Henry James was
certainly right when he called *Middlemarch* a 'treasure-house
of detail'; certainly wrong when he judged it 'an indifferent
whole'. The novel's greatness lies in its overall design; in discussing this I shall break it down into what may be called the
unities of narration, theme, society, and vision. But these categories, though convenient, must do less than justice to so well
integrated a novel; George Eliot's philosophic vision is expressed
through the fineness and sureness of her artistic powers.

II

By narrative unity I mean in general the mechanics of connecting the various plots of the novel, and in particular the fusion
of the two original tales, with the consequent technique of interweaving many roughly concurrent stories and of constantly
switching the reader's attention from one character, or set of
characters, to another.

This technique was demanded by the method of publishing
Middlemarch in bi-monthly parts; the original reader, encoun-
tering the novel at large intervals of time, could not be allowed
to forget any of the main characters. Most of these thus appear

in most of the separate part issues and so enforce on George Eliot the necessity of closely and constantly interweaving the chief interests of the novel. With such a method, the most crucial transition from one story to another is likely to be the first one – in this case, the switch from Dorothea, Casaubon, and the world of county gentry to Lydgate, Rosamond, and the world of the urban bourgeoisie. George Eliot's technique here is an example of triumphant economy; she solves the problem by the simple device of having Brooke give a dinner party, at which representatives of town and county mingle, to celebrate the impending marriage of Dorothea and Casaubon. Social barriers are thus for once broken down. Moreover, at the party the men, conventionally but naturally, talk about women, thus introducing the name of Rosamond and the contrast between her and Dorothea. The women, equally conventionally, talk about ailments and remedies, thus introducing the name of Lydgate, who is present at the party though not directly introduced to the reader. We are thus prepared for the switch to the world of Middlemarch made in the next chapter and once we have been manœuvred into accepting *this* transition we are likely to accept all subsequent changes.

The nature of her raw material also helped George Eliot in her quest for unity. Thus, though her vision expands to include a whole society, it is still the relatively narrow and cramped society of provincial England just before the Reform Bill of 1832. Again, since she is so concerned with the social lives of her characters, their professional activities often provide connecting links; it is not unnatural that Lydgate, as a doctor, should be drawn into contact with many of the other characters. The same holds true for Bulstrode as a banker, Farebrother as a cleric, and Caleb Garth as an estate-manager. The political theme of the novel also serves to break down barriers and bring together, if only briefly and tangentially, the destinies of otherwise disparate individuals.

But the nature of her raw material also poses great problems of plot construction. One of George Eliot's main concerns is the way in which the past moulds the present and the attempts of various characters – Featherstone and Casaubon even from their graves – to shape and control the future. Indeed, it is one of the great achievements of the novel to immerse its characters at a particular moment in their history so deeply and firmly in the large, overflowing continuum of time, stretching before and after. Thus the whole body of the novel gives point and substance to George Eliot's assertion in her Finale, that:

Every limit is a beginning as well as an ending. Who can quit young lives after being long in company with them, and not desire to know what befell them in their after-years? For the fragment of a life, however typical, is not the sample of an even web: promises may not be kept, and an ardent outset may be followed by a long declension; latent powers may find their long-waited opportunity; a past error may urge a grand retrieval.

But even in so long a novel as *Middlemarch*, the past histories of so many characters must be heavily compressed and bluntly stated, and such bald remembrance of things past can never have the force or vividness of dramatically imagined experience. When the past is used too much to explain and create connexions of plot in the dramatic present, then the reader may well feel uneasy. The crucial instant is that of Bulstrode. This fine example of a warped Protestant ethic, who rationalizes his worldly success as an example of divine providence, is familiar enough as a type for the reader to suspect that his present eminence is founded upon some shady episode in his past which will ultimately prove his downfall. Sure enough, the corrupt past incarnates itself in the figure of Raffles, who appears on the scene as an indirect consequence of Featherstone's death. The way in which this is done involves a series of coincidences to which George Eliot herself draws attention (in chap. 41); to these as such we do not greatly object. But when, through Raffles, the ugly secret of Bulstrode's past is linked with the history of Ladislaw and the Casaubon family, we discern too clearly the mechanical and contriving hand of the author; we may well agree with James that this part of the plot 'has a slightly artificial cast, a melodramatic tinge, unfriendly to the richly natural colouring of the whole'.

Yet even here we may see George Eliot discovering strength in weakness. The actual encounter of Bulstrode and Raffles is a masterpiece of bitter irony, which Raffles himself underlines when he insists that it is 'what you may call a providential thing' (chap. 53). This one phrase corrodes Bulstrode's belief in a divinity shaping his particular ends; for the reader the notion of a special providence clashes headlong with the blind operation of mere coincidence. In this encounter George Eliot dramatizes something essential to the meaning of the whole novel; namely, man's various attempts, often fumbling and frustrated, to chart his destiny in a world so deeply swayed by the random tides of chance and contingency. The accumulation and interaction of countless small choices, of insignificant actions of minute and subtle pressures, of invisible motives and unforeseen consequences – all these create a highly complex field of force which acts, now with and now against, the individual will. This force may be, misleadingly perhaps, personified; but when George Eliot writes that 'Destiny stands by sarcastic with our *dramatis personæ* folded in her hand' (chap. 11), she is not invoking a crudely deterministic notion of Fate or Nemesis. Rather she is simply summing up what the novel as a whole evokes: the infinitely complicated shape and motion of the world as we know it to be.

III

Thus one particular aspect of the novel's narrative structure may lead us close to its thematic heart. Once we accept the interweaving of concurrent stories, the advantages of this technique become obvious. By means of it George Eliot can refract her meanings into the individual colours of different characters and settings, can create a network of parallels and contrasts which expresses her vision of life while at the same time paying homage to the variegated qualities and plenitude of the human scene.

It is not difficult to discern the pattern of this network. The contrast between Rosamond and Mary Garth, or between Rosa-

mond and Dorothea; the combined parallel and contrast between the researches of Casaubon and Lydgate (both of them
searching for a 'key'); the way in which Brooke's butterfly mind
and cluttered pigeon-holes become a comic analogue to their
scholarly endeavours; the varying and unpredictable results of
Casaubon's and Featherstone's wills – these are just a few of the
strands in the total web. Sometimes these effects are emphatic:
thus Casaubon and Lydgate have an attitude towards women –
the one wanting a secretary, the other an ornament – which
bodes no good for their marriages. Sometimes the effects are
subtle and oblique: thus Dorothea's changing attitude to Casaubon – the growth from disillusionment to understanding and
tenderness – is cut short by Casaubon's death. But this so
abruptly concluded relationship is extended in the novel by
Lydgate's parallel attitude to Rosamond; the theme is, so to
speak, unconsciously passed from one character to another.

Indeed, the danger is not that we shall fail to recognize this
pattern or the moral intention which dictates it, but rather that
we shall come to think of the pattern as over-schematic and of
the moral vision as too heavily insistent. Many critics have felt
that in her later novels George Eliot, to use her own words,
'lapses ... from the picture to the diagram'. The frequent charge
that the stern philosopher in her subdues the artist is best
expressed by Henry James:

We feel in her, always, that she proceeds from the abstract to the
concrete; that her figures and situations are evolved, as the phrase
is, from the moral consciousness, and are only indirectly the products
of observation.

The question, then, is one of how far George Eliot successfully
submerges her moral vision into the texture of life, vividly
imagined and dramatically presented. In attempting this, she is
greatly helped by her narrative technique of interweaving concurrent stories and by the consequent proliferation of a great
number of widely varying characters.

Let us consider one theme as it ramifies and mutates through-

out the novel. The search for one's true vocation, and the ways
in which this may be warped or frustrated by one's environment, are most clearly exemplified in the stories of Dorothea
and Lydgate. But one comes to feel that the theme is not so
much exemplified as incarnated in these characters; they are
not mere illustrations of some moral point George Eliot wishes
to drive home. One reason for this response is the fact that
Lydgate and Dorothea are but two of the many variations on
the theme; they take their place in a host of lesser characters
who collectively create a spectrum of human possibilities in
their differing reactions to society. Thus one thinks of Casaubon,
whose arid pedantry is the shrivelled husk of intellectual endeavour; his failure throws light on the way in which Lydgate's
scientific aspirations dwindle into a fashionable practice and a
treatise on Gout. One recalls the scientific hobbies of Farebrother; these, too, are evidence of a misdirected talent. But
unlike Casaubon and Lydgate, Farebrother represents at worst
a partial failure, at best a decent success; if, as he admits, he has
chosen a wrong vocation in the church, then he has at least
achieved a reasonably honest compromise with the world and
quietly makes the best of a bad job. A good shepherd, he contrasts with the doctrinal barrenness of Tyke and the pastoral
indifference of Cadwallader. He leads on to Fred Vincy, tempted by circumstance and the social ambitions of his family, to
repeat Farebrother's mistake but finally taking the modest but
happy, limited but right course. Fred is saved, in part, by Caleb
Garth, the exemplar in the novel of the fulfilled man, proud of
his work, happy in his family (in a novel full of unhappy
families), undismayed by bad fortune, steady in good fortune,
and at peace with the world.

All of these characters enrich the theme of vocation with
their individual characteristics; between them they diversify
and enliven what might otherwise remain a moral abstraction.
They provide a crowded and ample human context in which
Lydgate and Dorothea are firmly rooted and from which they
derive a depth and resonance, so that we can agree with James
when he remarks of their stories:

Each is a tale of matrimonial infelicity, but the conditions in each one are so different and the circumstances so broadly opposed that the mind passes from one to the other with that supreme sense of the vastness and variety of human life, under aspects apparently similar, which it belongs only to the greatest novels to produce.

The theme of vocation, though important, is still subsidiary: many other equally apt illustrations could be produced of the way George Eliot reconciles moral interests with her creation of a densely populated and interesting human scene. The tap-root of her vision, that which nourishes the whole fabric, is her concern with what we may call the transcendence of self. The typical psychological and spiritual development of her pro-tagonists is the painful struggle to break free from the prison of egoism into a life of sympathy with their fellow men. Her most acute studies are often of the reverse process, the spiritual degeneration and petrifaction of the corrupted soul as it creates its own private hell. In *Middlemarch* we have Bulstrode, for example, who chokes his conscience in the padding of doctrinal justification. Above all, there is Casaubon; chill, impotent, a creature of shadows who walks an interior labyrinth and says of himself, with unconscious irony: 'I feed too much on the inward sources; I live too much with the dead'. In Rosamond we have the naïve but deadly egoism of the spoilt child; on one occasion only – in chap. 81 – does she rise above her cold neutrality, only to lapse again into her habitual self. Fred Vincy, too, displays an equally childish selfishness, though treated more lightly here, since unlike his sister he is capable of reform; he is no match for the sturdy good sense of Mary Garth. But the most complex exemplars of moral self-education are, of course, Lydgate and, above all, Dorothea.

Dorothea's nature is 'altogether ardent, theoretic, and intel-lectually consequent' and it is 'hemmed in by a social life which seemed nothing but a labyrinth of petty causes, in a maze of small paths that led no whither'. Provincial society seems to her a prison from which she longs to escape by doing great good or by espousing a noble cause; with this we can sympathize and we pity her when she equates freedom with Casaubon's claustrophobic world. For as the word *theoretic* suggests, Dorothea is innocent, ignorant of her self and the world; she is morally, as well as literally, myopic. It is in her marriage that her painful self-education must begin, and George Eliot makes explicit the lesson to be learnt:

It had been easier to her to imagine how she would devote herself to Mr Casaubon, and become wise and strong in his strength and wisdom, than to conceive with that distinctness which is no longer reflection but feeling – an idea wrought back to the directness of sense, like the solidity of objects – that he had an equivalent centre of self, whence the lights and shadows must always fall with a certain difference. (chap. 21)

The recognition of 'an equivalent centre of self' in another person is the beginning of self-transcendence. For Dorothea true charity must begin at home; only then can any real social good be accomplished. George Eliot is always careful to stress how philanthropic actions may disguise perverted motives; thus Bulstrode's public zeal is really an extension of his personal power and a substitute for genuine atonement. Similarly, though in a lighter vein, Brooke's liberalism is that of a bad landlord; the hostile journalist scores a palpable hit when he cites 'the wag's definition of a philanthropist is a man whose charity increases directly as the square of the distance'. Dorothea is a subtler variation on the same theme. We feel, at the outset, that the objects of her reforming passion are disproportionate to the intensity of her ardour. That is not necessarily a criticism of her; it is also a comment on the narrowness of society. But we also feel that her reforming passion is streaked with egoism, that there is an element of play-acting about her schemes. When Casaubon's curate assures her that all is well in his parish, 'she felt some disappointment, of which she was yet ashamed, that there was nothing for her to do in Lowick; and in the next few minutes her mind had glanced over the possibility, which she would have preferred, of finding that her home would be in a parish which had a larger share of the world's misery, so that she might have had more actual duties before her'. George Eliot never divorces the individual from the social; Dorothea's attitude to the great world outside changes as she learns more about herself and her personal relationships. It is a private crisis that inspires the deeply moving passage which – far more than her marriage to Ladislaw – forms the culmination of Dorothea's story:

> She opened her curtains, and looked out towards the bit of road that lay in view, with fields beyond, outside the entrance-gates. On the road there was a man with a bundle on his back and a woman carrying her baby; in the field she could see figures moving – perhaps the shepherd with his dog. Far off in the bending sky was the pearly light; and she felt the largeness of the world and the manifold wakings of men to labour and endurance. She was a part of that involuntary, palpitating life, and could neither look out on it from her luxurious shelter as a mere spectator, nor hide her eyes in selfish complaining.   (chap. 80)

IV

Before we consider the social unity of *Middlemarch*, there are several interesting but minor problems to be cleared out of the way. How far George Eliot drew on historical originals for her characters is not really relevant to a sensitive reading of her fiction. Sometimes it may affect the way in which a character is drawn; for example, the slightly idealized portrait of Caleb Garth may be due to George Eliot's memories of her own father. But while it may be academically amusing to debate whether Casaubon was based on Mark Pattison, Dr Brabant, or some other actual person, it is much more important to recognize that the very name of Casaubon creates a calculated ironic discrepancy between the great Renaissance scholar and the fictional pedant. Nor should we interpret the novel too strictly as a historical study. George Eliot's preliminary research does, as a matter of fact, result in a historically accurate picture of her chosen period; there are a few minor mistakes and anachronisms – some of which are mentioned in the notes to this [1966

Penguin English Classics] edition – but it would be quite pedantic to quibble about them. As we shall see, a certain knowledge of social history does do much to illuminate certain aspects of her creative achievement, but the important criterion in our use of such extrinsic information is its relevance. For example, while it is obvious from several details in the novel that Middlemarch is based on Coventry, this is of little importance to our general recognition of George Eliot's success in creating a dense, coherent, and credible social world.

Rather more interesting is the question raised by Professor Asa Briggs,[1] when he asserts that 'the problem [George Eliot] sets Lydgate and Dorothea is in its essence a mid-Victorian problem. Their vision and their struggle are the same as her own.' How far did George Eliot project into the past of her childhood the issues facing her as an adult? In what ways does *Middlemarch* represent an essentially mid-Victorian world? If George Eliot did this at all, it was certainly not in the sharply topical manner of Dickens, for example, with his attack on the Circumlocution Office in *Little Dorrit*. Professor Briggs is right in the sense that many aspects of the Middlemarch world persisted into, or had their analogues in, later Victorian decades. Thus it is no accident that *Felix Holt* (1866) and *Middlemarch* (1871–2) – both concerned with the politics of the first Reform Bill of 1832 – span in their publication the politics of the second Reform Act of 1867. Again, cholera figures briefly in the novel (and there is some evidence that George Eliot originally intended to make it more central), so it is useful to remember that there was a major outbreak of the disease in England as late as 1866. Will Ladislaw is as close in some respects to the Pre-Raphaelites as to the later Romantics. Yet again, the feminist aspects of the novel, though certainly appropriate to the chosen historical period, would be equally relevant to the society for which *Middlemarch* was written. In these general terms, then, the novel is a historical document not only of the 1830s, but also of the 1860s and 1870s; but beyond this I do not think we can safely go.

If George Eliot's creation of a social scene is impressive for

what James called 'solidity of specification', is it surely not
simply because she is historically accurate and detailed. The
strength of this aspect of *Middlemarch* derives from two sources,
firstly, the way in which individuals mesh so realistically with
their environment. Dorothea's destiny is the result, not just of
the narrowness of her provincial world, but also of her ardent,
theoretic nature; Lydgate fails, not just because of circumstances, but also because of intrinsic flaws, those 'spots of commonness' in his nature. In this way George Eliot avoids any
crude kind of social determinism; her characters are both agents
and patients in the human scene, just as we all are. Secondly,
George Eliot's strength derives from her ability to analyse and
to set dramatically into motion those forces and pressures which
we feel to be the sinew and bloodstream not just of Middlemarch but of *any* reasonably sophisticated society. If we list,
however briefly and abstractly, some of these forces, we shall
see how complete and complex is her grasp of social life – its
groupings and associations, its conflicting interests and pressure
groups, its mechanics and dynamics.

(*a*) *Birth, Rank, Class*. Clearly this set of forces is all-important
as providing an impediment to the Dorothea–Ladislaw union
and as a magnet in the Rosamond–Lydgate marriage. Lower
down the social scale we see how subtly it operates in the
relations between the Garth and Vincy families. We may also
see how strongly divisive a factor these pressures may be, even
in so small a community as Middlemarch. The most obvious
gulf is between town and county; this is most clearly brought
out in chap. 34, where Sir James Chettam, Mrs Cadwallader,
and others, watching Featherstone's funeral from Casaubon's
house, can recognize Vincy but not his wife or family. But
many more subtle examples of this division and the efforts to
bridge it – either seriously as with Dorothea, or comically as
with Brooke – can be found.

(*b*) *Money*. Obviously this is a more important social factor
in the town than in the countryside, though Bulstrode and his
wealth find a parallel in Featherstone. Above all it is one index
of Lydgate's entanglement and downfall. In her cool notation of

apparently insignificant detail, George Eliot is the equal of Flaubert in *Madame Bovary*.

(c) Locality. The native's distrust of the outsider is important; even Bulstrode, long-established in Middlemarch, is still suspect. But more obviously this force functions as a source of latent animus towards Lydgate and of open hostility towards Ladislaw.

(d) Religion. As one might expect, Catholicism does not figure as a direct social factor, though Brooke allows 'an acre of ground for a Romanist chapel'. More surprisingly, Dissent is also scarcely mentioned; the main stress is always on the varieties of Anglicanism, ranging from the old 'High and Dry' Toryism of Cadwallader to the Evangelicalism of Mr Tyke.

(e) Politics. Local politics pervade all aspects of Middlemarch life. But we are never allowed to forget that this provincial story is contained within the broad sweep of national history.

(f) Profession. From the wide range of jobs, the 'manifold wakings of men to labour' exemplified in the novel, we may isolate the medical profession, since it is here that some knowledge of social history illuminates the novel. Much of this information is best provided in the notes to this edition, but one may say something in general of Lydgate's professional role. The doctor is a common fictional figure, but George Eliot is probably the first English novelist to delineate with historical precision the emergence of a new *kind* of doctor.

By the beginning of the nineteenth century the traditional divisions of the medical profession were breaking down, largely due to new demands created by widespread social changes. Traditionally there were three orders – the physicians (today, we should probably think of them more as consultants), the surgeons, and the apothecaries (long since elevated from the humble functions of druggist). More and more doctors held diplomas from both the College of Surgeons and the Society of Apothecaries, and from these surgeon apothecaries emerged a new type of doctor who became the equivalent of the modern general practitioner. Lydgate represents this new type and the hostility he arouses in the physicians of Middlemarch (Dr Minchin and Dr Sprague) and the apothecaries (Toller and

Wrench) reflects in large part that uneasy awareness that the traditional orders, jealously guarded, are being subverted. But Lydgate represents a professional as well as a social advance; his use of the stethoscope and his desire to conduct post-mortems place him in the *avant-garde* of medicine. Ironically, he is saved from an open scandal in the Raffles affair only because Bulstrode, in disobeying his orders, unknowingly reverts to the old-fashioned treatment prescribed by the rest of the profession. One of the great historical events of the period, not mentioned in the novel, is the founding in 1832 of what was to become the British Medical Association. It was originally named the *Provincial* Medical and Surgical Association. Thus, in hoping to advance both medical research and practice in a provincial town, Lydgate is again a prophetic figure; his story is in large part the defeat of the man of the future by the stubborn conservatism of the present.

The range of George Eliot's analysis is thus very wide. But she is always careful to show the interaction of these various factors throughout the society. If national politics and religion merge in the issue of Catholic Emancipation, then local politics and religion merge in the appointment of Tyke as chaplain to the new hospital. Brooke's comic misunderstanding of politics is paralleled by Dagley's distorted notions of what Reform may mean. Gossip is a social lubricant or irritant at all levels, from Mrs Cadwallader through Tantripp and the servants to the inns and streets of Middlemarch. Snobbery is also pervasive; Mrs Cadwallader is echoed by Rosamond. To complete the picture, George Eliot hints at the various forces of social change and upheaval – the Reform Bill and the coming of the railways; this is a world on the move. Above all, throughout the novel George Eliot creates a sense of the reciprocity of man and his environment. Beatrice Webb, in *My Apprenticeship*, tells us that:

For any detailed description of the complexity of human nature, of the insurgence of instinct in the garb of reason, of the multifarious play of the social environment in the individual ego, and of the individual ego on the social environment, I had to turn to the novelists and the poets.

No novel could have so richly rewarded her quest as *Middle-march*.

V

The moral vision embodied in *Middlemarch* creates a corresponding response in the reader. By her method of interweaving concurrent stories, by the proliferation of characters, by the complicated structure of parallels and contrasts, George Eliot bestows upon the reader a wide variety of viewpoints, of changing perspectives, which enlarge our understanding both of the fictional world and of the real world. In this process we constantly revise our judgements and alter the balance of our feelings; we are involved in the protagonists and yet – because of our wider view – we know more than any of them can, so that our sympathies are checked and controlled by our perception of their limitations and blind spots. Bulstrode and Casaubon are analysed with an almost surgical precision; yet at the same time they command our compassion. Any tendency to idealize Dorothea is checked by a cool flow of ironic and qualifying comment.

George Eliot achieves this poised vision in many ways. Locally she does it by her control of language – for example, by her reiterated imagery of the web and other metaphors of connexion, entanglement, and interaction. On a larger scale she achieves it by varying the tempo and intensity of the novel and by playing over a wide range of feelings, setting passages of broad comedy or of subtle wit against pathos and moral seriousness.

But above all, it is by the poise of the omniscient author controlling the action, sometimes acting as a guide, sometimes as an unobtrusive chorus. Only at one point does this even, adult voice falter – in the culmination of the Dorothea–Ladislaw relationship. This *is* a flaw which no critic can satisfactorily excuse; for whatever reason, George Eliot cannot adequately handle the intensities of romantic love. But even this is not so much a positive fault, an ugly blotch; rather it is a blur on a canvas so impressively crowded as to divert our attention elsewhere. And in exploring that canvas we explore ourselves.

If we want an image from *Middlemarch* itself to sum up George Eliot's achievement, then we can do no better than her description of Lydgate's researches into the fundamental structure of organic matter. We may apply, metaphorically, to her what belongs, literally, to him:

He for his part had tossed away all cheap inventions where ignorance finds itself able and at ease; he was enamoured of that arduous invention which is the very eye of research, provisionally framing its object and correcting it to more and more exactness of relation; he wanted to pierce the obscurity of those minute processes which prepare human misery and joy, those invisible thoroughfares which are the first lurking-places of anguish, mania, and crime, that delicate poise and transition which determine the growth of happy or unhappy consciousness.

NOTE

1. The reference is to Professor Briggs's 'Middlemarch and the Doctors', *Cambridge Journal* (1948). [Ed.]

Barbara Hardy

THE SURFACE OF THE NOVEL:
CHAPTER 30 (1967)

There are, no doubt, many ways of organizing a study of detail.
We might proceed by taking one or two striking and symbolic
images and then looking at their local and particular effect in
relation to and in distinction from their function as epitome.
We might choose some striking but apparently isolated images,
and look at them in their local context. We might take the
presentation of minor characters or minor events, or look at
'background' material like description of places, objects, or
gestures. I decided to choose a chapter and look at the various
details it contains. I chose chap. 30 at random since any part
will do to represent the continuous surface of the novel. It so
happens that it is an interestingly mixed chapter, more relaxed
and heterogeneous than, say, chap. 28, which presents Dorothea's disenchanted awakening, or chap. 80, which presents
her vigil after she has seen Ladislaw with Rosamond, or chap.
83, her last scene with Ladislaw. These are all scenes of crisis
in action, but all also highly compressed and pregnant. Chap.
30 is also less blatantly and totally symbolic than other scenes
which do not mark such crises of decision, but are plainly
summaries and potent expressions of idea and feeling, like the
scene in Rome where Casaubon takes Dorothea on a tour of
significant works of art, or the scene of Featherstone's funeral,
or the scene where Mary Garth and Rosamond look together in
the mirror. Chap. 30 does however mark a very important
stage in the action: in it Dorothea is told that Casaubon's illness
is fatal, and must change his way of life, and it ends with Brooke's
decision to invite Ladislaw to Middlemarch. It is morally

important, involving Dorothea's declaration of unselfish love and desire to help, her cry to Lydgate, and his warm but helpless response. It uses symbolism, but in a diffuse and unarresting way, as I shall try to show.

It is difficult to find a chapter in this novel which contains neither a crisis in action nor a crisis in vision. Although the texture is more dense and the epitomes less glaring than in the novels of Henry James, there is very little relaxation of tension in *Middlemarch*, very much less assertive comic play, casual filling-in and local colour than in the Victorian-Gothic structures of Dickens or Trollope. *Middlemarch* has its choric scenes of gossip and crowd-reaction presenting the character of the community, as in the scene of the auction, for instance, or the talk of the women at Mr Brooke's first dinner-party, but these passages are parts, not whole chapters, and usually share the chapter with more crucial and symbolic material. Nearly all the chapters have the same form of organization. There is a dominance of dialogue and action, and this is usually grouped into one, two, or three scenes, separated and steadily bridged by exposition or report. There is a frequent change of scene, of persons, place, and time, but within a fairly restricted framework. We move from one room to another but very often stay in the same house, or move from one part of the day to another but with the same people. Sometimes time is indefinite, faintly and usefully blurred. There are some chapters which have very little exposition, but there are none with no scenic material. Exposition overlaps with scene, for it is dotted with scenic images, and is often vividly and immediately sensational, while scene is seldom purely dramatic but uses commentary and description as well as dialogue. George Eliot's typical chapter, in *Middlemarch*, achieves a loose unity, often with a local concentration of ideas, atmosphere and symbol, as well as of time and place. She often uses her varied and modulated materials to push on time and action *during* rather than *between* chapters.

Chap. 30 begins with a very brief scene between Casaubon, Lydgate, and Brooke, at Lowick, which is followed by the long and central scene between Lydgate and Dorothea. This modu-

lates into a report of Dorothea's thoughts and doings after
Lydgate goes, and eventually, after a longer and rather inde-
terminate interval, presents Brooke writing the crucial letter
asking Ladislaw to come to Middlemarch. The very beginning
of the chapter moves us on from the point at which we left
Casaubon at the end of chap. 29, when he had his first heart
attack. In chap. 30 we are told how 'in a few days' Casaubon
'began to recover his usual condition'. Then there follows an
uncommitted past tense in which Lydgate sits and watches by
the sick man, obviously on more than one occasion. At last a
particular occasion is singled out to make the first scene, in
which Lydgate advises Casaubon 'to be satisfied with moderate
work, and to seek variety of relaxation'. Next comes another
vague past-continuous tense, going back beyond the scene to
various times when Dorothea had been present 'by her husband's
side'. Lydgate 'had determined on speaking to her' and when
Brooke makes the suggestion as they stand 'outside the door' of
Casaubon's sickroom, he decides to do it there and then, asks
for her, is told that she is out, and waits until she comes in.

Then we reach the central scene, long, detailed, chronicling
every word and movement and feeling, co-terminous with the
whole experience and leaping over nothing. It deals very fully
and faithfully with the present but has one or two moving flights
into the past (Dorothea's 'if I had known') and into the future
('For years after Lydgate remembered'). Lydgate goes and time
moves on slowly as Dorothea, still in the library, reads the
letters on the writing-table and then ends by giving Ladislaw's
letter to 'her uncle who was still in the house'. He writes the
reply to Will at Lowick and apparently on the same day: we are
told that 'he went away without telling Dorothea what he had
put into the letter, for she was engaged with her husband, and
– in fact, these things were of no importance to her'.

Time moves on, at first quickly, then very slowly indeed,
foreshortening nothing. Elsewhere this forward progression
covers much larger periods, as for instance in the next chapter,
though here George Eliot uses the same device of picking up
exactly where we left off in the previous chapter and making the

leap within the chapter. In chap. 31 we begin on the evening of
the same day and we have Lydgate off duty with Rosamond, to
whom he talks about the day's happenings – in particular about
Dorothea's reactions and the strong impression they have made
on him. In the following section we return to the indefinite
past-continuous, 'Aunt Bulstrode, for example, came a little
oftener', and thus we proceed a fair distance in time. My
chosen chapter provides less exciting examples of this form of
movement than others, including its successor and its predecessor, but it does reveal what I think is the typical pattern:
overlap or coincidence of time, foreshortening by a past-continuous, movement within rather than between the chapters,
and smooth transition. This kind of structure is one of the things
revealed by a close look at detail.

George Eliot's central events, however, take place within a
unity of time and place, and local unity is another important
feature of her manipulation of time. In this chapter there is
great compression, and in others there is more variety and
movement. Here we have three or four conversations and events,
all involving the same people, and taking place on the same day
in the same house. George Eliot's timing presents not only a
slow and detailed chronicle but a very natural, almost casual,
flow. Events and dialogue appear to be connected by proximity,
not by careful selection. The transitions themselves are often
unexciting, undramatic, and inconspicuous, and the structure is
superficially episodic, not appearing as prologue, main action,
and epilogue, as it usually does in a Jamesian chapter. This
episodic and almost casual appearance *is* only an *appearance*,
since of course selection is taking place all the time. The structure is governed by the relations of proximity, the appearance
suggests the loose unity of 'everything that happened at Lowick
on that day' but crisis is present at each stage. Casaubon is
more or less told to give up his work. Dorothea is informed,
and grasps the loss and desolation for him, and the awful helplessness involved for herself. The action leading up to Ladislaw's invitation, the beginning of another crisis, is all strictly
necessary and plausible. The crises are all revealed and relaxed

by the insensitivity of Brooke, whose suggestions of shuttlecock and Smollett and final almost automatic writing to Ladislaw are splendid instances of what Henry James called the fool's ministrations to the intensities of others. In the first scene Brooke lays bare the intensity he cannot grasp, in the last he shows himself as the only person sufficiently unaware to summon Ladislaw to Middlemarch. He is an ironically chosen maker of destinies. Action pushes ahead at each stage: most important, the reader looks ahead with the characters to the obscure future where Casaubon must relax, where Dorothea will try to help him. This is not just a matter of looking forward, since involved in the look is uncertainty and question: how can he possibly relax, how can she possibly help him? We are left too with the growing attachment of the book title, 'Waiting for Death', to Casaubon and Dorothea as well as to Featherstone.

The book title makes itself sharply felt in this and in the previous chapter, not simply in the subject of the grave illness but also in the emphasis on waiting in general. Looking at single chapters brings out this kind of local emphasis, which I should prefer not to call 'theme' or 'motif', since it scarcely reaches the level of generalization and is really not very conspicuous. However, it is there, and naturally enough. It plays its part in the feeling of the chapter, where watching and waiting are thoroughly explored through many aspects. We observe frustration, fear, anxiety, understanding, insensitivity, love, sympathy, and professional detachment blended with that good humane curiosity informed by imagination. It is not just the action of waiting with which many of the chapters in this book are concerned, but the feelings with which human beings may wait. Lydgate is the first to watch and wait, and we are carefully told that he does this in different ways: he uses the newly invented stethoscope but he also sits quietly by the patient and watches him. His quiet watchful patience, and his conversation with Casaubon about being satisfied with moderate work, are among those details of professional character which make us feel that Lydgate is a good doctor, and that being a good doctor has something to do with being a good man. A little later we

are told that he also watched Dorothea as she watched and
waited:

She was usually by her husband's side, and the unaffected signs of
intense anxiety in her face and voice about whatever touched his
mind or health, made a drama which Lydgate was inclined to
watch. He said to himself that he was only doing right in telling her
the truth about her husband's future, but he certainly thought that
it would be interesting to talk confidentially with her. A medical
man likes to make psychological observations, and sometimes in the
pursuit of such studies is too easily tempted into momentous
prophecy which life and death easily set at nought. Lydgate had
often been satirical on this gratuitous prediction, and he meant now
to be guarded.

Unlike so many watchers in *Middlemarch* Lydgate is concerned
to observe Dorothea, to learn about her, to make no predictions
about her marriage, feelings, and future. His imaginative tact
in this scene shows the delicacy and tenderness in his character
(ironically neighbouring the spots of commonness) which are to
emerge so significantly in the shaping of his and Rosamond's
destinies. This delicacy is brought out more plainly in the
following chapter when he tells Rosamond how moved he has
been by Mrs Casaubon's strong feeling for a man thirty years
her senior, and when Rosamond's brashly conventional and
ignorant rejoinder makes another strand in the web of
irony.

All the characters in chap. 30 watch and wait. Casaubon has
to wait, to try to 'relax', to pass time. Dorothea has to wait,
feeling remorse, responsibility, and helpless love. She who has
been a great collector of lame dogs, and has met the hardship of
finding no lame dogs to nurse in Lowick, now finds herself faced
by a great need and can do little. Here Dorothea finds a cause,
but cannot battle. The only character who is not centrally
involved in watching and waiting is Brooke, whose reactions
frame the central scene, whose role here is his role elsewhere in
the novel, that of the fool who rushes in but avoids all real

commitment. His comments are benevolently maladroit. The ironies of his reference to toy-making (in this house and this family) and the 'it's a little broad, but she may read anything now she's married, you know', are embedded in his flow of well-meaning futile chatter. This barely touches the real conversation between Casaubon and Lydgate, who have little enough in common but are both serious men, here brought together by their understanding of professional seriousness and values. Brooke never actually comes into real communication with anyone in this chapter and his detachment shows at its beginning and at its end.

The decisive event which is comically and ironically framed by Brooke's detachment is Dorothea's reaction to Lydgate's bad news. The form of the chapter reflects in some ways the form of the novel. George Eliot has chosen to call this book 'Waiting for Death', and to spend most of her imaginative energy showing the waiting done by Dorothea. Throughout the novel the significant departures from Dorothea's point of view – 'Why always Dorothea?' – emphasize the normative function this performs. It is she, not Casaubon, who is central in the chapter and in the novel. There are withdrawals, opacities, and foreshortenings in the treatment of Casaubon, very few in the treatment of his wife.

Dorothea comes in to hear the tragic news, from her walk with Celia, radiant and glowing. The 'glow' has been established already, and represents her vitality and her physical youth and health. She comes in from the outside world of health and light, and these vital qualities recede as she goes into the library with Lydgate. What follows is the breaking of the news and a moral crisis. Dorothea does not consciously weigh and choose, as on some occasions before and after, but here spontaneously chooses love. She has stopped resenting, wanting, and criticising, and she thinks of herself in relation to Casaubon only as a possible and frail source of help. She has broken with the past Dorothea who has usually spoken and acted from a sense of her own trials, has stopped listening to her own heartbeats and thinks only of the feeble ones of her husband.

If it is, in George Eliot's terms, an 'epoch' for her, so it is for Lydgate. There is yet another strand in the contrast between Dorothea and Rosamond: 'Women like Dorothea had not yet entered into his tradition.' He makes no rash predictions, but waits with rare sensitive concern, then 'wonders' about her marriage. He is that unusually imaginative man who does not impose categories and who does not gossip. This is a novel where George Eliot is concerned to show how character fits (or does not fit) profession, and how profession shapes character. Lydgate is a fine example of the consistency and subtlety of her psychological and professional detail. Dorothea's spontaneous cry, 'Tell me what I can do?' is to be picked up on several later occasions but here it marks very sharply that naked contact of real feelings which makes a crisis in many different kinds of relationship in the novels of George Eliot.[1] Here Dorothea's helplessness meets Lydgate's helplessness, but the communication makes a living and lasting relation between them.

In action and in feeling, the chapter is crucial, and we see George Eliot underpinning it to past and future, not just in the references to time but also in its symbolic associations. We pick up tones of light and dark from past scenes where Dorothea has stood out from Lowick, from past scenes in the library. We hear tones which are to resound and accumulate in later contrasts between Dorothea and Rosamond, and later scenes where Dorothea's moral energy is seen to be linked with the 'epoch' here marked. If we consider this chapter as 'an organ to the whole' there is abundant material: the recurring antithesis of light and darkness, the particular forms of Lowick and the dim room, the small windows, and the world outside, all connect with many interwoven series of images and symbols in the novel. So too does the cry 'Tell me what I can do?', the significantly expressive use of clothes, and the image of a marble statue. I should like to take some of these familiar structural symbols and to bear in mind both their place in the pattern and their local impact in this chapter.

Only one of these images is made conspicuous by being generalized within the chapter. This is the contrast of darkness and light. I should add that it is also the image which has already been most fully developed before we meet it: in many small metaphors and in the elaborately expressive description of Lowick in chap. 9, and in Ladislaw's violent conspicuous extensions. What additional impressions are made in chap. 30? The library is dark, because it has been left shuttered: 'But there was light enough to read by from the narrow upper panes of the windows.' The light which is let in is described by a tiny arbitrary reminder of its scholarly occupier, which also acts as preparation – if the room were too dark Dorothea would not be able to read Will's letter later on. But there is no immediate question of anyone wanting to read. The 'narrow' is also a detail which seems redundant in the immediate context, but makes a link with the associations already established in the early descriptions of 'small-windowed and melancholy-looking' Lowick. The first description of the library itself, ironically placed in the radiantly optimistic vision of Dorothea before her marriage, mentions 'dark book-shelves', 'curtains with colours subdued by time'. The small windows, bird's-eye views on the walls, and Casaubon's revelation of his own 'sufficiently large' views of women, are contrasted with the bow-window of Dorothea's room, and make their small but unmistakable contribution to the details of visionary symbol. (Chap. 9 is full of imagery of views and darkness and light from which I have merely chosen a few examples.) We are told that Lowick is the kind of house 'that must have children, many flowers, open windows, and little vistas of bright things, to make it seem a joyous home', and we have also met Casaubon's lack of interest in houses for people to live in, and his preoccupation with narrow Egyptian dwellings, tombs and catacombs. The library itself is later to be dubbed 'a caticom' by Tantripp. It is obviously the centre of what Will Ladislaw calls the stone prison and the labyrinth, the room most darkened and subdued by Casaubon's sterile and isolated gloom. Will is of course associated with light and colour, Dorothea with open windows and outward gaze, and the symbolic antithesis of light and dark is to cover many implications of fertility and sterility, breadth and narrowness, life and death – in value and expression natural and common and not confined to this novel or this novelist. How do we read the images of darkness here?

I do not think that we read them primarily as symbols of Casaubon, in spite of the details that attach them to the main pattern of value and feeling. For instance, when Dorothea says to Lydgate, 'You will not mind the sombre light', this is, I think, to be taken at its face-value, with some appropriate and immediate associations with Lydgate's habituation to the valley of the shadow of death. Death does, after all, hang over this book. Her words about the sombre light stand also for Dorothea's acceptance of gloom. But they are primarily an indication of Dorothea's trusting, genuine casualness and informality in dealing with Lydgate in this situation. We are told that Lydgate remembered for years after Dorothea's cry of appeal: 'this cry from soul to soul, without other consciousness than their moving with kindred natures in the same embroiled medium, the same troublous fitfully-illumined life'. Here the dark and the light are generalized and stand for the variegation of human life, and the darkness is that of suffering, death, obscurity, the light perhaps of hope, joy, lucidity. The antithesis acts like the image of the lighthouse in *To the Lighthouse* and does not belong to the Casaubon/Ladislaw or the Casaubon/Dorothea contrast. George Eliot has established a pattern to which she can refer briefly and reliably, as in the easy association in the previous chapter between Casaubon's mood and 'the foggy morning', but it is not a rigidly insistent pattern, and the primary impressions of light and dark in chap. 30 are likely to be falsified if we are concerned only to pluck them out of context.

Another image which we have already met before is the image of a marble statue. When Lydgate tells Dorothea that Casaubon may live for years, with great care, but that 'it is one of those cases in which death is sometimes sudden', Dorothea's physical reactions and feelings are described in this way:

There was silence for a few moments, while Dorothea sat as if she had been turned to marble, though the life within her was so intense

that her mind had never before swept in brief time over an eq[...]
range of scenes and motives.

The most famous of the images of marble lies ahead, in Farebrother's dictum, 'Character is not cut in marble', to which Dorothea makes the incisive reply, 'Then it can be rescued and healed'. But we have met it before, in many forms, in many actual casts and statues. There are the incomprehensible casts brought home by Brooke, 'whose severe classical nudities . . . were painfully inexplicable, staring into the midst of her Puritanic conceptions', and the marbles of Rome, on the wedding-journey, where 'the long vistas of white forms whose marble eyes seemed to hold the monotonous light of an alien world' make on Dorothea an indelible impression. (Incidentally, the accuracy of 'marble eyes' is another instance of a symbol working through precisely realized sensation – 'marble eyes' holding 'monotonous light' is a superb description.) In the Vatican, 'she walked with him through the stony avenue of inscriptions', and she passes on listlessly to the Museum, while he goes to the library. She stands in the hall, where Naumann and Will Ladislaw find her:

Where the reclining Ariadne, then called the Cleopatra, lies in the marble voluptuousness of her beauty, the drapery folding round her with a petal-like ease and tenderness. They were just in time to see another figure standing against a pedestal near the reclining marble: a breathing blooming girl, whose form, not shamed by the Ariadne, was clad in the Quakerish grey drapery. . . .   (chap. 19)

Naumann makes explicit what he sees as the antithesis:

'What do you think of that for a fine bit of antithesis?' said the German, searching in his friend's face for responding admiration. . . . 'There lies antique beauty, not corpse-like even in death, but arrested in the complete contentment of its sensuous perfection: and here lies beauty in its breathing life, with the consciousness of Christian centuries in its bosom.'   (chap. 19)

e examples, and in Farebrother's metaphor too,
ght into contrast with life, not as a form of death
iing fixed, arrested, and unconscious. Look again
phor of marble in chap. 30, remembering that
Naumann are mentioned in the chapter, so that
reson... from the earlier scene might well be expected and
effective:

There was silence for a few moments, while Dorothea sat as if she
had been turned to marble, though the life within her was so intense
that her mind had never before swept in brief time over an equal
range of scenes and motives.

It is a purely local simile, though a few lines later we have a
reminder of Dorothea's 'pallid immobility'. What are we to say
about this image? The art/life antithesis is a very important
subject in *Middlemarch*, not merely because it forms the ambience
for the character and career of Ladislaw, but because George
Eliot is discussing the nature of asceticism and the function of
art, as belonging to the analysis of society, as continuing
Arnold's exploration in *Culture and Anarchy*, as relevant to the
problems of Dorothea's feelings and values. Many characters
are defined and even tested by their response to art, and art
itself is defined and even tested by its relevance and meaning for
human beings of different kinds. If we were making an analysis
of artistic images in the novel, we might well include the simile
in chap. 30, and observe that it belonged to the symbolism of
aesthetic value. If, however, we look at it in its context, it adds
absolutely nothing to that theme, except in automatic reminder,
for what that is worth. What is vivid here in this image is the
local expression of Dorothea's shocked stillness and pallor,
contrasting with the racing pulse of thought and feeling within.
It is an image which shows both the transformation of feeling
and the contrast between outside appearance and inner passion.
It is this local vividness that is primary, not the structural contribution to patterns of imagery and to dominant themes of life
and art. The superficial impression is the most important one.

This is probably a fairly uncontroversial example. More difficult is the symbol of clothes in this chapter. Dorothea first comes in with Celia, 'both glowing from their struggle with the March wind'. When Lydgate speaks to Dorothea, as we have seen, she behaves quite spontaneously, and opens the library door, 'thinking of nothing at the moment but what he might have to say about Mr Casaubon'. She leaves her outdoor clothes on, but a little later takes off her bonnet and gloves. There is the comment that she throws off 'her bonnet and gloves, with an instinctive discarding of formality where a great question of destiny was concerned'. The informality extends also to her action of sitting down, and her 'Sit down' addressed to Lydgate. Her actions and attitudes are typically informal and unselfconscious, but here there is a particular pointing. This is not just Dorothea's usual genuine disregard for social formality, but the informality produced by the crisis, the simplicity and unaffected impatience that are the understandable response. This is also felt after Lydgate has broken the news about Casaubon's illness: 'Lydgate rose, and Dorothea mechanically rose at the same time, unclasping her cloak and throwing it off as if it stifled her.' Here we go beyond the unstudied impatience and spontaneity of the earlier detail: this action of throwing off the cloak is also expressive of violent feeling. In this chapter George Eliot uses Dorothea's clothes not as symbols of value but as changing and highly expressive properties. Clothes are certainly important symbols in this novel, as associated with Dorothea, Celia, Rosamond and Mrs Bulstrode, and in larger traditional ways which draw on the aesthetic and social values with which history has invested clothing, ways which perhaps owe something to Swift and Carlyle. People's attitudes to their clothes symbolize surface and appearance, vanity, exhibitionism, flaunting of sex, of class, over-decorativeness, materialism, extravagance and so on. There are local nuances: Dorothea does not 'deck' herself, Celia and Rosamond do, Dorothea changes from deeper mourning to light, Mrs Bulstrode takes off her ornaments.[2] It is attitudes to clothes, rather than the actual clothes, which are important. This scene in chap. 30 is particularly interesting because in it nothing at all is said about what the clothes are like. It is what is done with them that matters. Dorothea's informal throwing off her garments is in perfect keeping with her neglect of appearances, conventions, propriety, and vanity. It is in perfect keeping with her relationship with Lydgate. And it is in perfect keeping with the grave crisis, when polite formality is too slow and too fussy for deep feeling. Ceremony has broken down. We grasp the expression of these values, but grasp also that the actual gestures are expressive of strong feeling, of impatience, urgency, desire to break out and breathe or do something, need for relief, action, getting down to essentials – this unwieldy list comprises many reactions we might lump together under the reaction from frustration or tension. The last casting off of the cloak is attached to the other gestures and movements in the chapter, and this again is part of the continuum we are likely to ignore and break up if we jump from image to image. Dorothea's attitude to her clothes belongs to the whole presentation of her person and personality and character in this place at this time.

She sets the tone with 'You will not mind this sombre light'. When she addresses Lydgate she is 'standing in the middle of the room' and she does not invite him to sit down for some little time. When she does, she speaks rather abruptly. She begs him to speak plainly, she reacts quickly, her words come out 'like a cry'. The word 'quick' is used of her 'ear' which detects significance in the doctor's tone of voice, and of her 'prevision' of Casaubon's wretchedness. Her voice is described in detail: it is imploring, like a cry, then low, then has 'a childlike despondency' while she actually cries, and her last appeal to Lydgate, 'Think what I can do', is made 'with a sob'. George Eliot is following the detail of voice and movement: we know what Dorothea sounded like, where she stood or sat, how she moved or stayed motionless. We know too how each sound and movement came from the last. The movement of feeling, so much more detailed here than in the framework which begins and ends the chapter, is composed of simple straightforward non-figurative description as well as of metaphors. The metaphor of the marble statue and the cry of 'soul to soul' are placed in a very precise and physical record of movement and speech, some of which is expressive, some apparently there to make a natural flow of acting and doing. People talk, take off their outdoor clothes, come in from walks, notice or do not notice their surroundings, sit down and stand up. Rooms have been changed or left alone since the last time we saw them. The continuum is natural, but it allows for climax. The ordinary actions stop when Dorothea makes her cry for sympathy, which comes quite naturally out of all that has gone before, but strikes the reader, like Lydgate, as a baring of feeling in a crisis presented in decorous and far from unusual terms: after all, people do keep doctors standing up while they put their questions, and do weep in their presence.

After Lydgate goes, the natural track of movement continues, variously and fluently. Although she is alone, she stops crying at the thought that she must keep her tears from Casaubon. She goes to the table, looks at the letters, and reacts to Will's outpoured 'young vivacity' by seeing that it is 'impossible to read' it at that time. The very lack of comment is masterly. Nothing is said about her feelings, she just sees what kind of letter it is and sees that it has nothing to do with the here-and-now. She passes on to give the other letter, addressed to Casaubon, to her uncle. Even the ironical introduction of 'her lack of sturdy neutral delight in things as they are', as Will sees it and puts it, meets the reader unemphatically, with no need for comment on the present crisis which has made everything different, and rendered their debate in Rome theoretic and very far away. It is a most beautiful showing of her control and her commitment, unemphatic and restrained in form as in content.

This central scene is composed of many incidents, tones, and narrative methods. The author's commentary, for instance, is often dramatically appropriate, as in the comments on Lydgate's watching or his withdrawal from rash prediction, or on Dorothea's marble appearance and passionate feeling, or on the process of Brooke's decision to ask Will to Middlemarch, made less by Brooke than by his pen: none of these comments, if we reflect, could have been dramatized or expressed directly through character. The author's voice here, as so often in the later novels, is broken up, and is used functionally, to present and punctuate the dramatic scene. It does not hold up movement but facilitates it, filling in the movement backward or forward in time, standing back and staying silent, condensing urgent feeling into an image, or making a nice stroke of *erlebte Rede*, as in the very last sentence in which Brooke goes away without telling Dorothea what he had 'put into the letter' since 'she was engaged with her husband, and – in fact, these things were of no importance to her'. The many small steps which we take here are made up of some material we call 'dramatic' and some material we tend to call 'undramatic'. My contention is that once we see the continuity and movement, especially of feeling, these divisions seem inappropriate. Voice of author and of characters blend in a naturally moving sequence which gives even to a scene of crisis the appearance and motion of life. The flow attaches us to the parts rather than to the whole, and makes a whole of a stanzaic unit, of the chapter itself.

In this chapter, carefully organized into a fluent but intricate three-part unit, George Eliot has concentrated on crisis and feeling. This is how certain people react to dying, their own and other people's. The detached attitudes of Brooke and Lydgate are delicately observed, and a spectrum of feeling is organized, though Casaubon's unanalysed response makes a stubbornly opaque streak, here as elsewhere. It is one of George Eliot's beautiful movements of decorum, that she withholds the internal commentary of Casaubon, and makes his questions and frustrated comments represent feeling, while the reactions of Lydgate and Dorothea are made fully available to us. She is in a later chapter (42) to follow Casaubon to 'the dark river-brink' in one of the most moving, solemn, and pathetically accurate movements of feeling and reflection, but as yet he is literally the patient, not knowing the implications of Lydgate's watching, which he is later most courteously to praise for its 'scrupulous care', in a phrase which takes us back to this chapter of watching. Other scenes are more strikingly subtle and novel in their

Some readers have been worried by the changes in tone in the Prelude, as if George Eliot's own attitude to Saint Theresa was uncertain and even confused; and this leads naturally into the larger criticism (which I shall discuss in a moment) that her attitude to Dorothea is uncertain. It is true that in the second half of the Prelude, which concerns the later-born Theresa, the transition from irony to sympathy is less clear-cut than in the first; but this is surely natural, and intentional: it is so much easier to sort out our attitudes when dealing with hagiography than in the realistic novel. If we take the first transition as our clue we can surely realise that the same deliberate ambivalence is present in the later paragraphs: a clear perception of the clumsinesses, the ineffectualities, the occasional absurdity of these blundering lives, but an undimmed, unhesitating sympathy for the flame itself, and for what it may with luck achieve. This is the attitude towards Dorothea.

It is affirmed in the very first paragraph of the first chapter, in the opening image through which she is presented:

Miss Brooke had that kind of beauty which seems to be thrown into relief by poor dress. Her hand and wrist were so finely formed that she could wear sleeves not less bare of style than those in which the Blessed Virgin appeared to Italian painters; and her profile as well as her stature and bearing seemed to gain the more dignity from her plain garments, which by the side of provincial fashion gave her the impressiveness of a fine quotation from the Bible, – or from one of our elder poets, – in a paragraph of today's newspaper.

This chapter sets up a view of Dorothea that, through all the shifts of emphasis, is never abandoned. We here see her mainly from the outside: in dialogue with Celia, and in the level commentary of her unruffled author. It is natural therefore that we should first be struck by the critical, ironic tone ('Riding was an indulgence which she allowed herself in spite of conscientious qualms; she felt that she enjoyed it in a pagan sensuous way, and always looked forward to renouncing it'), by the open reference to her love of extremes, by the self-righteousness and 'Puritan toleration' which she shows to Celia during the sharing

psychological analysis, for here George Eliot is relying on impressions already built up and consolidated, though we should notice the new stroke of Lydgate's relationship with Casaubon, forming over the obtuse chatter of Brooke, and that of Lydgate's developing relationship with Dorothea. Both strokes add to character, and are also very important in the creation of local feeling. A character created by George Eliot is made up not only of a carefully arranged sequence of moral choices but also of a variety of feelings. Those feelings are very important in our experience of characters as 'real'. They are not always arranged in the carefully sequential pattern of the moral crisis. For instance, once Lydgate has chosen to vote for Tyke rather than Farebrother, we recognize his susceptibility to the varied pressures of Middlemarch, and we can all eventually nod wisely when he makes a similar choice in the matter of Raffles's death. In this kind of regular development the characters in the novel are much more schematic and steady than real people. But perhaps we accept this kind of moral schematism because it is truthfully presented in the solid and directly expressive forms of feeling. It is not true that Lydgate's strong feeling for Dorothea in chap. 30 changes anything he does: in the very next chapter we see the fatal ease with which he can absorb, or scarcely notice, Rosamond's prettily and dishonestly phrased words about Dorothea and Casaubon. But for the reader he is changed: we have felt, not just been told, that those spots of commonness are really spots in a very delicate and responsive substance, because we have felt his reactions to Casaubon and to Dorothea. This is the full response to character, and it should be made plain that it is a response to feeling which exists in its own right, as it does perhaps most lucidly and movingly in poems which do not give elaborate histories and causalities. In discussing plot and theme and character, we often overlook feeling, but in discussing local detail we stay close to the track of feeling.

When we encounter these characters subsequently, it is with the felt experience behind us. This seems to be important to the total life of the novel. If we compare the scenes of feeling involving Romola and Daniel Deronda, for instance, they will, I suggest, show themselves as lacking in this kind of continuous creation, where all characters respond and move fully, not only in major ways, plainly functional and purposive, but with the implication of total availability. The gestures and tones of Romola and Daniel are fewer and cruder, more intensively symbolic. There is a lack of the kind of detail I have mentioned here, which is so marvellously typical of *Middlemarch*. I cannot substantiate this kind of comparison in a short study nor can I substantiate what I have called the typicality of this kind of detail. As I said earlier, this is a crucial scene, and there are many scenes in the novel where the detail is looser and freer, in feeling, gesture, and sensuousness. This scene contains few objects, for instance. Some of the scenes in Dorothea's room, or in Mrs Garth's kitchen, or in the Lydgates' drawing-room, are filled with prolific examples of the detail which is neither totally symbolic nor painstakingly naturalistic, but which has a superficial vividness which plays a strong part in the life of the novel. The surface is not evenly transparent, the detail sometimes does and sometimes does not create an epitome. The surface is continuous, made up of a complex structure which our larger analysis can only touch on. The divisions in that continuity are many, and the units within book and chapter cannot be appreciated unless we look at them in a close and individual way. It is the detail of sense and feeling, the continuous flow, and the subtle organization within chapters, which I have tried to bring out in this examination of chap. 30 as a specimen of the neglected surface of the novel.

NOTES

1. See my *The Novels of George Eliot* (1959) pp. 104–5.
2. Cf. ibid., p. 104.

Laurence Lerner

DOROTHEA AND THE THERESA-COMPLEX (1967)

Dorothea Brooke is a study of what some psychol[ogists] surely, by now, have labelled the Theresa-complex: a [desire] to do good in the world which is so intense that it mu[st] to some emotional need in the Theresa herself. This [is] announced immediately, in the Prelude, which begin[s with an] account of the young Theresa

walking forth one morning hand-in-hand with her stil[l younger] brother, to go and seek martyrdom in the country of th[e]

Though this account is ironic ('Out they toddled from [the gates of] Avila'), there is nothing ironic about the central descri[ption of] Theresa's flame, soaring

after some illimitable satisfaction, some object which woul[d] justify weariness, which would reconcile self-despair with t[he rap-] turous consciousness of life beyond self.

In the same way, when the passage moves to the 'late[r-born] Theresas', though there is once more a touch of irony ('he[re and] there a cygnet is reared uneasily among the ducklings i[n the] brown pond'), it once more leaves the central sym[bol] untouched:

Here and there is born a Saint Theresa, foundress of not[hing,] whose loving heart-beats and sobs after an unattained goo[dness] tremble off and are dispersed among hindrances, instead of cen[tring] in some long-recognisable deed.

G.E.M.—H

of the jewels; and it is equally natural that when the writing shifts (as it several times does) in favour of Dorothea, it should usually be by a counter-irony, at the expense of Celia, or of a general 'you' or passive voice which disconcertingly identifies the reader with the common run of Dorothea's acquaintances and neighbours:

Women were expected to have weak opinions; but the great safeguard of society and of domestic life was, that opinions were not acted on.

A discriminating reading of the chapter will notice these shifts, and appreciate their delicacy: will perceive that the general impression is more critical than sympathetic, yet will reflect that none of the critical details is wholly to Dorothea's discredit. Yet one's reading should not be merely discriminating, or we shall miss the emotional pressure behind this chapter: to read it knowing *Middlemarch* can bring tears to the eyes. We can see the secret of this in the opening sentences quoted above – in such an image as that of the 'fine quotation from the Bible, – or from one of our elder poets, – in a paragraph of today's newspaper'. It is itself an ambiguous image. Its first impression is no doubt of incongruity; it describes the impression Miss Brooke gave of being out of place, the worthy but slightly boring effect she might have on 'highly civilised society'; but its further resonance is of something deeper and wholly to Dorothea's credit. The same ambiguity emerges from such a detail as the slipping in of 'or from one of our elder poets'. To wrap them up with the Bible in this way has the effect of a perfunctory gesture, the kind of vague, respectful but only half-interested reference Mr Brooke might make to 'fine things – you know'; and so suggests the lack of enthusiasm with which Dorothea's noble appearance might be greeted; yet, again, after we have paused to reflect, we can see the joining of the Bible and the elder poets is massing the evidence that reminds us of the triviality of today's newspaper: the sophisticated comment drops away, and we realise that Dorothea is being – quite simply – compared to all that is fine. Exactly the same double-

ness fits the previous image, of the paintings of the Blessed
Virgin. Now we cannot really doubt that this standard by which
Dorothea with her ignorance matters, and provincial fashion
with its maturity doesn't matter, is the one which George Eliot
really holds. If we know about Marian Evans, we cannot doubt
it; if we remember the simpler irony of *The Mill on the Floss*
('conduct ourselves in every respect like members of a highly
civilised society') we cannot doubt it. But we do not really need
external evidence, we only need to know *Middlemarch* and read
the passages thoughtfully. We shall then feel the passionate
sympathy for Dorothea that lies almost hidden at the heart of
this clear ironic portrait.

So it should not surprise us that although Dorothea's loving
heart-beats and sobs after an unattained goodness lead her to
folly and distress – to her imperceptiveness over Sir James
Chettam's intentions, above all to her disastrous marriage –
they also lead to what we are most to admire about her, to
conduct and feelings that serve as a touchstone for the whole
book. I cannot illustrate this as fully as I would wish, or as the
novel deserves. Let us begin from the account of how Dorothea
receives Mr Casaubon's proposal:

Dorothea trembled while she read this letter; then she fell on her
knees, buried her face, and sobbed. She could not pray; under the
rush of solemn emotion in which thoughts became vague and images
floated uncertainly, she could but cast herself, with a childlike sense
of reclining, in the lap of a divine consciousness which sustained her
own. She remained in that attitude until it was time to dress for
dinner.

How could it occur to her to examine the letter, to look at it
critically as a profession of love? Her whole soul was possessed by
the fact that a fuller life was opening before her: she was a neophyte
about to enter on a higher grade of initiation. She was going to have
room for the energies which stirred uneasily under the dimness and
pressure of her own ignorance and the petty peremptoriness of the
world's habits.

Now she would be able to devote herself to large yet definite
duties; now she would be allowed to live continually in the light of

a mind that she could reverence. This hope was not unmixed with the glow of proud delight – the joyous maiden surprise that she was chosen by the man whom her admiration had chosen. All Dorothea's passion was transfused through a mind struggling towards an ideal life; the radiance of her transfigured girlhood fell on the first object that came within its level. (chap. 5)

The full effect of this passage is lost if we have not just read the letter itself, which is too long to quote ('I am not, I trust, mistaken in the recognition of some deeper correspondence than that of date in the fact that a consciousness of need in my own life had arisen contemporaneously with the possibility of my becoming acquainted with you'). The juxtaposition thrusts at us a violent hint at what we realise steadily as we read on (or remember sadly if we know the book already), the pathetic futility of these hopes of Dorothea's. We guess, or know, that the life opening before her is not to be fuller – or if it is, only in the sense that suffering brings fullness of experience. The higher grade of initiation is into maturity but not happiness. There is direct, even crude irony in the reference to 'the light of a mind she could reverence'. The last two sentences, reminding us that Dorothea was a young girl capable of loving intensely, and therefore all the more eager to marry Mr Casaubon, are really a reminder of the true difficulty of her situation: that because she is a woman, with a woman's feelings and a nineteenth-century woman's prospects, her ardour must – in the words of the Prelude – 'alternate between a vague ideal and the common yearning of womanhood': so that either the latter replaces the former, and disappointment is obvious, or it disguises itself as the former, and disappointment lies in wait.

All this is fairly obvious, for the passage is not complex. What I here want to point out, however, is that the extent of the irony is limited. There is no hint that we are to withdraw our sympathy from the 'rush of solemn emotion' that seizes Dorothea. Her immaturity lies in the uncertainty and dimness of the prospect that she sees before her, but not in the intensity with which she welcomes it. For it is that same intensity which seizes

Dorothea when she exerts her final and liberating influence on Lydgate, when for a moment she is truly Saint Theresa:

Lydgate turned, remembering where he was, and saw Dorothea's face looking up at him with a sweet trustful gravity. The presence of a noble nature, generous in its wishes, ardent in its charity, changes the lights for us: we begin to see things again in their larger, quieter masses, and to believe that we too can be seen and judged in the wholeness of our character.   (chap. 76)

And it is this intensity that sweeps Rosamond to her one moment of true goodness:

Rosamond, taken hold of by an emotion stronger than her own – hurried along in a new movement which gave all things some new, awful, undefined aspect – could find no words, but involuntarily she put her lips to Dorothea's forehead, which was very near her, and then for a minute the two women clasped each other as if they had been in a shipwreck.   (chap. 81)

There is not only the same intensity here – communicated to her from Dorothea – but even the same dimness, the same blur ('some new, awful, undefined aspect'). We cannot doubt, in the light of these passages, that the portrait of Dorothea when 'she fell on her knees, buried her face, and sobbed' is more compassionate than ironic; that foolish as she is, such folly is no necessary consequence of a tendency to rushes of solemn emotion. And we must conclude that the finest moments in *Middlemarch*, those moments which serve as touchstones for the behaviour shown elsewhere in the book, are those in which characters yield to such rushes.

We are told of Dorothea in chap. 10 that

all her eagerness for acquirement lay within that full current of sympathetic motive in which her ideas and impulses were habitually swept along

and in the same chapter Lydgate first meets Dorothea and reacts more or less unfavourably:

'She is a good creature – that fine girl – but a little too earnest,' he thought. 'It is troublesome to talk to such women. They are always wanting reasons, yet they are too ignorant to understand the merits of any question, and usually fall back on their moral sense to settle things after their own taste.'

Lydgate is not swept along by any 'full current of sympathetic motive', and (we see here) would not wish to be. By 'moral sense' he means such a current, something intense and highly charged with emotion: this is clear both from what we know of Dorothea, and from his own contrast with 'reasons'. Now the slow change in Lydgate's attitude to Dorothea is one of the many triumphs of *Middlemarch*. At the beginning, for all his professional idealism, he is aloof and rather patronising to women, and emotionally reserved; and here is his climax:

Lydgate did not stay to think that she was Quixotic: he gave himself up, for the first time in his life, to the exquisite sense of leaning entirely on a generous sympathy, without any check of proud reserve. (chap. 76)

This is the one moment at which Lydgate the man behaves with the dedication and singleness of Lydgate the doctor: the 'spots of commonness' are washed away.

Now this offering of emotional release as the central positive of the book was not merely a decision on George Eliot's part: it was the transcribing into fiction of her own emotional needs. Because Marian Evans had felt 'loving heart-beats and sobs after an unattained goodness', Dorothea's feelings mattered to her more urgently than those of any other character in the book. Several critics have been perceptive enough to observe and (usually) to condemn this.

Best known of these critics is F. R. Leavis, and I shall use his criticism as starting-point for what I want next to say about Dorothea. After enthusiastic praise of the rest of *Middlemarch*, Leavis asserts that 'the weakness of the book . . . is in Dorothea'. He sees this weakness in George Eliot's too sympathetic treatment of Dorothea's 'soul-hunger', in her 'unqualified self-identification' with Dorothea:

Dorothea . . . is a product of George Eliot's own 'soul-hunger' – another day-dream ideal self. This persistence, in the midst of so much that is so other, of an unreduced enclave of the old immaturity is disconcerting in the extreme. We have an alternation between the poised impersonal insight of a finely tempered wisdom and something like the emotional confusions and self-importance of adolescence.[1]

Leavis finds 'unacceptable valuations and day-dream self-indulgences' in the love-affair with Will, and in Dorothea's relations with Lydgate, where we are given a Dorothea 'all-comprehending and irresistibly good'; and he concludes:

Such a failure in touch, in so intelligent a novelist, is more than a surface matter; it betrays a radical disorder. . . . The emotional 'fullness' represented by Dorothea depends for its exalting potency on an abeyance of intelligence and self-knowledge, and the situations offered by way of 'objective correlative' have the day-dream relation to experience; they are generated by a need to soar above the indocile facts and conditions of the real world.[2]

Although Leavis's case against this aspect of *Middlemarch* is well known, I have quoted it here because it has received so much discussion and assent. Mr I. R. Browning actually claims to know what episode in Marian Evans's life most fed this need of hers: the brief affair with John Chapman. Quoting Dorothea's temporary disillusion with Ladislaw, and Romola's permanent disillusion with Tito, he says:

Both these scenes (and there are others like them throughout the novels and stories) betray a deflecting personal identification with the heroine: it is George Eliot who is before us. Anyone well acquainted with her biography will have no difficulty in recognising the *gentle tones* and the *soft eyes* as those of John Chapman.[3]

And it is clear that Leavis is simply articulating a widefelt response when we find similar comments occurring in very different critics: thus Lord David Cecil remarks that George Eliot was not 'wholly immune from the frailties of her sex; like every woman novelist she tends to draw heroes less from life than in the image of her desire'.

Leavis's view has not been accepted by all critics; and it will be convenient to set against it that of David Daiches, who maintains that the Prelude is misleading; that the moral centre of the book is not Dorothea but Mary Garth; that 'doubt remains as to the social usefulness of sainthood'; and that Dorothea is regarded with a steady, critical detachment all through the book.[4] Both critics, for instance, mention the detail of the organ. Mr Casaubon is discussing music, and indicating a certain lofty scorn for pretty playing. He goes on to exempt 'the grander forms of music', which being Mr Casaubon, he describes in a leisurely period:

'As to the grander forms of music, worthy to accompany solemn celebrations, and even to serve as an educating influence according to the ancient conception, I say nothing, for with these we are not immediately concerned.'

'No; but music of that sort I should enjoy,' said Dorothea. 'When we were coming home from Lausanne my uncle took us to hear the great organ at Freiberg, and it made me sob.'

'That kind of thing is not healthy, my dear,' said Mr Brooke. 'Casaubon, she will be in your hands now; you must teach my niece to take things more quietly, eh, Dorothea?' (chap. 7)

This is a perfect exposition, in miniature, of the contrasting attitudes of the three people. We can see why Dorothea accepted Casaubon: for the content of his speech expresses exactly what she thinks about music: she too regards pretty playing as trivial compared with the grander forms. The leisurely period in which he puts it all she will put down to his age and learning, rather than to the fact that his view is even more theoretic than hers – though the betraying detail is there, could she but notice it (as we, on rereading, surely do) in the fact that he feels com-

pelled to add 'according to the ancient conception': for he
prefers to speak, not of his reactions, but of what the fit reaction
has been held to be.

Everyone can agree on Casaubon here; but what of Dorothea
and Mr Brooke? 'We can't help noting,' Leavis says, 'that it is
the fatuous Mr Brooke, a figure consistently presented for our
ironic contemplation, who comments, "That kind of thing is
not healthy, my dear".' Daiches, however, denying the 'unqualified self-identification' with Dorothea, says of Mr Brooke
– quoting this passage – that 'foolish man as he is, [he] often
lays his finger precisely on what is wrong with some conduct
that goes beyond comfortable normal experience'.

It is necessary to oversimplify. There is no paragraph in
Middlemarch whose effect is not carefully integrated into the
whole, and which is not fed by its context. When we disagree
with a good critic, we continually want to say that his quotations are too short: they may seem to mean what he claims, but
if we read on we shall see that they don't quite – and reading
on really means reading the whole of the rest of the novel. I
therefore cannot adequately back up the conclusion which I
take from confronting these two views, but must in the end
appeal (as criticism always must) to the impression made by
the whole book.

But in the simplified terms in which one must work, I can
now state the conclusion clearly. I think that Leavis is right and
Daiches wrong about the balance of the book: Dorothea is its
moral centre. But I think Leavis is wrong, and George Eliot
right, about her soul-hunger.

The other half of Daiches's claim (that Mary Garth is what
Dorothea isn't, the book's moral centre) is even harder to
refute, for in an important sense it is true. Mary is seldom if ever
wrong in her judgements, and there are moments – such as her
refusal to burn the will when Featherstone is dying – when the
author is totally and intensely with her. But on the whole, the
Mary Garth–Fred Vincy story is the least intense, the most
leisurely, the most conventional part of *Middlemarch*: it is the
part Trollope could almost have written. The situation is one

of Trollope's favourites: the young scapegrace, the good girl who sees all his faults but loves him all the same, and the un-heroic, rather worldly clergyman, whom George Eliot prefers to the evangelical Tyke, just as Trollope's well-fed wordlies, we are to feel, do more good in the world than Mr Crawley, the poor and proud fanatic. It is the one part of *Middlemarch* that we are sure will end happily.

Of course Trollope could never have written it: in almost every scene there are punches that he would have pulled, and that George Eliot does not pull. When Fred calls at Stone Court to tell Mary about the bill, we see his egoism with the clarity of George Eliot at her merciless best – and it is a clarity that Mary shares. Fred is genuinely sorry for what he has gone, but his self-reproach is laced with self-pity: he cares that Mary should forgive him, but has not realised that she will not even think about him in her grief for her family. It is not only George Eliot who realises this, it is Mary too:

'What does it matter whether I forgive you?' said Mary, passionately. 'Would that make it any better for my mother to lose the money she has been earning by lessons for four years, that she might send Alfred to Mr Hanmer's? Should you think all that pleasant enough if I forgave?' (chap. 25)

That is outside the range of Trollope: it must cause any male reader to wince (Trollope never attacks his own readers). But to say this is to find Mary's limitation, which I can best describe in terms of my own argument, by saying that she represents the Jane Austen in George Eliot.

She had already come to take life very much as a comedy in which she had a proud, nay a generous resolution not to act the mean or treacherous part. Mary might have become cynical if she had not had parents whom she honoured, and a well of affectionate gratitude within her, which was all the fuller because she had learned to make no unreasonable claims. (chap. 12)

I doubt if this is intended as a deliberate contrast to Dorothea:

the unreasonable claims Mary does not make are selfish ones, whereas those which Dorothea does are claims to be able to do some vast good. All the same it is a contrast: Dorothea could not possibly view the world as a comedy, nor is she in danger of becoming cynical. Now if this account of Mary sounds like any novelist, surely it sounds like Jane Austen, in whom, too, honour and gratitude are the checks of cynicism. What keeps Mary from becoming unattractive – from being 'always right' – is her love for Fred. She does forgive Fred for robbing her parents, and though he does not deserve it, Mary is the better for doing so: she too has her sublimated egoism to conquer, the egoism of seeing through others.

I think the obvious moral shape of *Middlemarch* is also its true shape. Dorothea occupies the Prelude and the final pages; it is she who is the good angel of the climax, the noble nature for which others are the better; it is she with whom George Eliot is accused of 'unqualified self-identification'.

The terms of this accusation are, we may notice, dangerous, for they seem to deal not with the book but with the author. It is true that George Eliot had a Theresa-complex, and that there is a Dorothea in every book; that if Marian Evans (who was ugly) had been beautiful, it would have been with the beauty of Maggie Tulliver; and that (why should we not make the suggestion?) her art is therefore a substitute gratification, granting her vicariously what she could not have in life. But to say this is to say nothing about the merit of the books: as readers, we care not about the similarities between Janet, Maggie and Dorothea, but about the differences. If George Eliot wrote out her own tangles into her stories, we have yet to learn – from the stories themselves – whether she used this emotional pressure to deflect from or add power to the needs of the book.

Leavis does not commit (what Mr Browning, for instance, does) this error of substituting biography for criticism. He is interested in the book's origins only as explanation for a flaw he claims to find in it. If the identification with Dorothea is 'deflecting', this must mean that the author's clear vision has been blinded, that under pressure from her own feelings, she has not told the truth.

What truth? It is easiest to look at the treatment of others, if we are to find the deflecting interest most clearly manifested. If there is such deflection, then those with whom Dorothea comes into contact will be shown more harshly or more softly than the evidence warrants. If the author's sympathy with Dorothea in her marriage flares up too uncritically, we shall protest at the unfair handling of Mr Casaubon; if the need to give her a happy ending is too pressing, then Ladislaw will be passed off as more than the author has managed to make him.

Let us begin with Casaubon, and say at once that in his case the charge is absurd. He is almost the most wonderful thing in *Middlemarch*. Consider the delicate balance that must be struck when he first appears. We must be convinced that Dorothea would wish to marry him, yet we must be aware what he is really like. We are shown Casaubon direct, and also through the eyes of both sisters and (some subtle humour here, that cuts both ways) of Mr Brooke. The most hostile view is Celia's ('Really, Dodo, can't you hear how he scrapes his spoon?'), and we must feel that she is hasty and superficial, yet just: Celia is not malicious or unobservant, and the Casaubon that she sees is a less important part of the man, but a more accurate version of that part, than Dorothea gives of her part. For some time we might feel that Celia's Casaubon is far nearer to George Eliot's than is Dorothea's – until George Eliot makes her startling shift from irony to compassion, in mid-sentence:

One morning, some weeks after her arrival at Lowick, Dorothea – but why always Dorothea? Was her point of view the only possible one with regard to this marriage? (chap. 29)

This is of course a direct assault on the reader, and an unfair one, in so far as the prejudice in favour of 'young skins that look blooming in spite of trouble' is one which George Eliot has herself fostered. It would seem a merely clumsy way of shifting the point of view (and perhaps it is hard to accept it completely) if it had not been prepared for by a number of earlier shifts, less ostentatiously announced: most superbly, in the scene of the Casaubons' first quarrel. This episode (too long to quote) occurs in chap. 20. Dorothea has inquired about her husband's studies, and hoped she may be of increasing use to him.

'Doubtless, my dear,' said Mr Casaubon with a slight bow. 'The notes I have here made will want sifting, and you can, if you please, extract them under my direction.'

'And all your notes,' said Dorothea, whose heart had already burned within her on this subject, so that now she could not help speaking with her tongue.

– and Dorothea's enthusiasm then launches her into an intense plea that he will begin to write the book which will make his vast knowledge useful to the world.

The excessive feeling manifested would alone have been highly disturbing to Mr Casaubon, but there were other reasons why Dorothea's words were among the most cutting and irritating to him that she could have been impelled to use. She was as blind to his inward troubles as he to hers: she had not yet learned those hidden conflicts in her husband which claim our pity. She had not yet listened patiently to his heart-beats, but only felt that her own was beating violently. In Mr Casaubon's ear, Dorothea's voice gave loud emphatic iteration to those muffled suggestions of consciousness which it was possible to explain as mere fancy, the illusion of exaggerated sensitiveness: always when such suggestions are repeated from without they are resisted as cruel and unjust.... Here, towards this particular point of the compass, Mr Casaubon had a sensitiveness to match Dorothea's, and an equal quickness to imagine more than the fact.

Dorothea is not being impertinent nor even, in one sense, thoughtless: her enthusiasm is genuine, and what she says is what she has long pondered, and intends as real praise. The sense of inadequacy that stings Casaubon is his own, because the inadequacy is his own, and we do not condone the quick temper with which he rebukes Dorothea. Yet at the same time this is the scene in which our sympathy first shifts towards him: Dorothea, we learn, 'was as blind to his inward troubles as he to hers'. This calm statement is all important. We do not retract any of our previous judgement of Casaubon: we learn, not that he is a better man than we'd thought, but simply that he is a man who suffers.

I give one other example of the treatment of Dorothea and Casaubon – probably the most moving of all. After Casaubon has learnt of his illness from Lydgate, and repulsed Dorothea's attempts at sympathy, she waits in the corridor to meet him as he goes to bed.

He started slightly on seeing her, and she looked up at him beseechingly, without speaking.

'Dorothea!' he said, with a gentle surprise in his tone. 'Were you waiting for me?'

'Yes, I did not like to disturb you.'

'Come, my dear, come. You are young, and need not to extend your life by watching.'

When the kind quiet melancholy of that speech fell on Dorothea's ears, she felt something like the thankfulness that might well up in us if we had narrowly escaped hurting a lamed creature. She put her hand into her husband's and they went along the broad corridor together.   (chap. 42)

After the scene with Lydgate, and the account of the pride and fear with which Mr Casaubon greeted the knowledge of his danger, his remark to Dorothea has an even greater power than out of context: it is Shakespearean in power. The image of the 'lamed creature', too, clashing with our feelings about Casaubon's earlier behaviour that day, echoes earlier and similar images, for a complex and moving effect. This, we see, is the happiness they might have together – this, and no more. It is the tame rescuing of happiness from bitterness, through a rescuing from egoism, which Mr Eliot offers his fallen couple in *The Cocktail Party*: 'the best of a bad job is all any of us make of it'. Not that George Eliot could ever have said that: Dorothea's higher hopes matter too much to her. It is this which gives the moment such tragic reverberations (Dorothea had hoped for so much more) beyond its human pathos.

One of the triumphs of the scene is the complete conviction which Casaubon carries. We cannot doubt that his behaviour to Dorothea has been cool and even cruel; but we have been made to feel what he has to bear. Perhaps the finest sentence of all gives the measure of his case: Lydgate, we are told, 'was at present too ill acquainted with disaster to enter into the pathos of a lot where everything is below the level of tragedy except the passionate egoism of the sufferer'. Because we have seen that egoism so clearly, we can feel the fineness of this moment of communion, when he responds to Dorothea's companionship.

George Eliot's treatment of Casaubon is one of the first examples in literature of what Lionel Trilling calls 'the double truth'. The phrase comes in his story 'The Other Margaret', in which Stephen Elwin finds himself arguing with his thirteen-year-old daughter Margaret about their coloured servant, also called Margaret. The servant is dishonest and malicious, and contrasts painfully with their previous servant, Milly, who had been a good loyal person. The daughter finds it hard to admit this: she is a passionate liberal, and insists that because the other Margaret is coloured, 'It's not her fault. She's not responsible.' Here is Elwin's reflection on this:

Had he been truly the wise man he wanted to be, he would have been able to explain, to Margaret and himself, the nature of the double truth. As much as Margaret he believed that 'society is responsible'. He believed the other truth too.[5]

– and the other truth is that wrong is wrong, and right is preferable. The Casaubon story seems to me the finest illustration of this point ever written. Never for a moment does George Eliot forget Casaubon's responsibility for the failed marriage; it is he who spurns Dorothea, who is quick to resent, who is locked up in his egoism. Yet from the time when sympathy begins to shift towards him, we are never allowed to look at him through the eyes of Celia, or Mrs Cadwallader, or

Lydgate, even though we know they are right. A compassion is demanded of us – and is given – through whose clamour we can no longer attend to the voice that says 'He is responsible'. Both attitudes are total: they are incompatible, yet they exist alongside each other.

I hardly need to say, after this, that the portrayal of Casaubon is untouched by any of the deflections that may have come from the treatment of Dorothea. Let us turn now to the less clear-cut case of Will Ladislaw. Here, of course, the deflection would, if it is present, lead George Eliot to idealise him, and many critics claim that this is what happens. 'Who can forgive Dorothea,' asks C. S. Lewis, 'for marrying such a sugarstick as Ladislaw?' 'The author, who is evidently very fond of him,' writes Henry James,

has found for him here and there some charming and eloquent touches; but in spite of these he remains vague and impalpable to the end. . . . He is . . . a woman's man.[6]

Now it is certainly not true that (as Leavis maintains) Ladislaw is presented more or less uncritically by the author. George Eliot likes him, but the liking is clear-sighted, not indulgent:

Will was not displeased with that complimentary comparison, even from Mr Brooke; for it is a little too trying to human flesh to be conscious of expressing one's self better than others and never to have it noticed, and in the general dearth of admiration for the right thing, even a chance bray of applause falling exactly in time is rather fortifying.   (chap. 46)

If we replaced 'expressing' by 'behaving', we could attach the sentence to Fred Vincy: it is exactly the tone in which George Eliot speaks of him. And Will during his journalist phase is no more idealised than Fred: 'it is one thing to like defiance,' says George Eliot as Will has to live up to his intentions, 'and another thing to like its consequences'. Even Will at Rome, though treated more sympathetically (for this is the beginning of Will the lover), is clearly enough seen. When his friend Naumann shows him Dorothea leaning against the statue of Ariadne, the love he is not yet conscious of emerges as very convincing ill-temper:

'Only think! he is perhaps rich, and would like to have her portrait taken. . . .'
   'I didn't know they were coming to Rome.'
   'But you will go to see them now – you will find out what they have for an address – since you know the name. Shall we go to the post? And you could speak about the portrait.'
   'Confound you, Naumann! I don't know what I shall do. I am not so brazen as you.'   (chap. 19)

This is detached, surely: we are more conscious of a defensive self-righteousness in Will's remark than of any real indictment of Naumann. And the chapter ends on one of George Eliot's characteristic and impressive generalisations:

Why was he making any fuss about Mrs Casaubon? And yet he felt as if something had happened to him with regard to her. There are characters which are continually creating collisions and nodes for themselves in dramas which nobody is prepared to act with them. Their susceptiblities will clash against objects that remain innocently quiet.   (chap. 19)

Ladislaw has had a bad press from the critics: if he had not been Dorothea's lover, he would have been widely praised as a portrait of a dillettante, drawn with sympathy well laced with irony. But he *is* Dorothea's lover, and in this we can see both the cause and the partial justification for the way critics have treated him. For although George Eliot does not sentimentalise Will noticeably, she does sentimentalise the love between him and Dorothea. The scene in which they finally come together is moving and convincing, and to wish it away would be cynic-ally to refuse one of George Eliot's genuine successes. Yet such a scene does not end things: it should not replace – as it is more or less made to – a human relationship by an idealised ending. After this scene, there is no scrutiny of Dorothea's life. True, we can believe her second marriage was happy: but there is a great difference between a happy marriage realistically portrayed (or, since we are after all near the end of the book, convincingly hinted at), and the glow that suffuses the final pages of a Victorian novel, to the public's satisfaction. Dorothea's second marriage, like that of Adam and Dinah, is merely a happy ending. And just as Adam had to grow shadowy with romance when he took on his final role as a lover, so Ladislaw, splendidly as he is elsewhere seen, blurs slightly as he becomes Dorothea's husband.

The reason for this may not be simply timidity and conventionalism on George Eliot's part, but (in part at least) something more interesting. When *Middlemarch* came out, the *Times* review asserted (with great insistence) that it was not feminist propaganda:

There is a certain school which will find satisfaction in thinking that Dorothea's story involves some special impeachment of the fitness of the present female lot. We do not think that this is at all intended, and if it be intended it is certainly not justified. . . . Her failures and mistakes are not due to the fact of her being a woman, but are simply those which belong to the common lot of human life. . . . The fetters she wore are too common to humanity, but the weight of them is felt far more by men than by woman.[7]

Now the Prelude makes it fairly clear that this is to be a book about woman's lot:

Some have felt that these blundering lives are due to the inconvenient indefiniteness with which the Supreme Power has fashioned the natures of women: if there were one level of feminine incompetence as strict as the ability to count three and no more, the social lot of women might be treated with scientific certitude. Meanwhile the indefiniteness remains, and the limits of variation are really much wider than any one would imagine from the sameness of women's coiffure and the favourite love-stories in prose and verse.

If Dorothea (let us put it at its crudest) could have become a doctor or a teacher, she wouldn't have needed Sir James

Chettam's help to build the cottages; and she wouldn't have married Casaubon. Now there is only one passage which says this, or anything approaching this:

For a long while she had been oppressed by the indefiniteness which hung in her mind, like a thick summer haze, over all her desire to make her life greatly effective. What could she do, what ought she to do?—she, hardly more than a budding woman, but yet with an active conscience and a great mental need, not to be satisfied by a girlish instruction comparable to the nibblings and judgements of a discursive mouse. With some endowment of stupidity and conceit, she might have thought that a Christian young lady of fortune should find her ideal of life in village charities, patronage of the humbler clergy, the perusal of 'Female Scripture Characters', unfolding the private experience of Sara under the Old Dispensation, and Dorcas under the New, and the care of her soul over her embroidery in her own boudoir—with a background of prospective marriage to a man who, if less strict than herself, as being involved in affairs religiously inexplicable, might be prayed for and seasonably exhorted. From such contentment poor Dorothea was shut out.

(chap. 3)

This is feminism, surely: it shows Dorothea 'alternating between a vague ideal and the common yearning of womanhood' – and finding both as unsatisfactory as the author finds them. There seems to her no way that the ideal can be made less vague: that 'thick summer haze' is woman's lot. How understandable then that Dorothea should convince herself that the two will meet in marriage to Mr Casaubon.

Yet the *Times* reviewer was right. George Eliot does not develop this point, and is very anxious to portray Dorothea's lot as belonging 'to the common lot of human life'. During the marriage, it was possible, even necessary, for George Eliot to drive away, or ignore, the feminist hare she had started: for whatever made Dorothea marry Casaubon, the marriage once it has taken place is itself – as a human relationship – her subject. But with Dorothea a widow and in love with Will, the question must arise whether her 'active conscience and great mental need' would really be satisfied in marriage, even happy marriage. The evasive glow with which the marriage is presented is George Eliot's way of avoiding this question.

Not that it is completely avoided: and in the Finale George Eliot allows herself one or two remarks that the comfortable reader had better not linger on too carefully (as the *Times* reviewer no doubt did not):

Dorothea could have liked nothing better, since wrongs existed, than that her husband should be in the thick of a struggle against them, and that she should give him wifely help. Many who knew her, thought it a pity that so substantive and rare a creature should have been absorbed into the life of another, and be only known in a certain circle as a wife and mother. But no one stated exactly what else that was in her power she ought rather to have done.

For Dorothea could neither write novels, nor edit the *Westminster Review*, nor help in the founding of Girton College. The feminist ghost that the author had called up and then banished has briefly returned. That George Eliot was uneasy about this seems clear from the second last paragraph of the novel. As it now stands, this has a reference to the pressure of society that is typical of George Eliot and not at all feminist: the 'determining acts of her life' were 'the mixed result of young and noble impulse struggling amidst the conditions of an imperfect social state'. In the first edition this was spelt out in more detail, and the imperfections of the social state listed; and the second item on the list is 'modes of education which make a woman's knowledge another name for motley ignorance'.[8] In the original manuscript,[9] though there was more detail than now remains, this phrase was not there. She must have added it in proof, then deleted it on a later revision. George Eliot did not, as novelists go, rewrite much; and we can surely conclude that she was uncertain about this paragraph because she could not decide how explicitly she should mention woman's contemporary lot. The uncertain protestations of *The Times*, then, are not surprising: their seeds lay in the author herself. If we feel any embarrassment about Dorothea's second marriage, it may be due as much to this as to a deflecting emotional identification of author with heroine.

Having made this concession, then – and conceding too that there are occasional passages where enthusiasm for Dorothea strikes a false note (for this is a very long book, after all) – I reassert that George Eliot's identification has not caused her to falsify, distort or evade; the personal interest is not a deflecting one. What then do Leavis's criticisms come to? If we look at them again, we can notice that not all his phrases concern truth or falsehood: he speaks of 'immaturity', of 'emotional confusions and self-importance of adolescence', of 'indulgence'. If Mr Brooke or Sir James Chettam or Mr Casaubon were articulate enough, and masters of modern terminology, they would say the same.

The disagreement between Leavis and George Eliot is in fact an ethical one. The heart of Leavis's criticism does not concern falsity in the author's vision, but the value of the Theresa-complex. So it is not surprising that all his criticisms have been anticipated by George Eliot and put into the mouth of one or other of her characters. It is Mrs Cadwallader who describes Dorothea as 'a girl who would have been requiring you to see the stars by daylight' and who says that 'marriage to Casaubon is as good as going to a nunnery'. There is no reason why the reader should not agree with her, as Blackwood, the book's first reader, agreed totally with Celia, yet did not find this a sign of weakness. Most critics who have defended George Eliot against Leavis have done so by accepting his ethical premise, and denying his reading of the treatment of Dorothea. I want to shift the emphasis not towards stressing the irony with which Dorothea is portrayed, but towards defending Saint Theresa against the concept (a central one in Leavis's criticism) of maturity. The presence of a noble nature, generous in its wishes, ardent in its charity, *does* change the lights for us; loving heart-beats and sobs after an unattained goodness ought to have a more complex fate, as the adolescent matures, than simply to be outgrown; and maturity is a virtue within the range of some very dreary people, and beyond the range of some very fine ones. Leavis, in short, has made not an artistic but an ethical criticism. Valuing the Theresa-complex less than George Eliot does, and maturity more, he has passed off his ethical disagreement as if it were the discovery of an artistic flaw. This is why Daiches's defence of the book seems to me the wrong one: he, like Leavis, seems to have a very qualified admiration for Theresas, and so to make the book acceptable has imposed on it a moral that is not quite George Eliot's. I want to put myself with George Eliot against both these critics, even if it means being called immature. There are worse charges.

NOTES

1. *The Great Tradition*, chap. 2, § 2.
2. Ibid.
3. 'The Recriminating Female', *Essays in Criticism* (July 1955).
4. *George Eliot: 'Middlemarch'* ('Studies in English Literature', No. 11).
5. 'The Other Margaret', *Partisan Review* (1945).
6. 'George Eliot: *Middlemarch*' (1873); reprinted in *Nineteenth Century Fiction* (Dec 1953).
7. Review of *Middlemarch* in *The Times*, 7 Mar 1873.
8. Quoted in Gordon Haight's notes to the Riverside edition of *Middlemarch*.
9. Add. MS. 34037, British Museum.

SELECT BIBLIOGRAPHY

The following books and articles are, in the editor's opinion, of particular interest as contributions to the criticism of *Middlemarch*, though for various reasons (such as limitations of space) it was not possible to represent them in the main body of this book.

Jerome Beaty, *Middlemarch from Notebook to Novel: A Study of George Eliot's Creative Method*, University of Illinois Studies in Language and Literature, No. 47 (Urbana, 1960). A study of the composition of *Middlemarch*, and the best guide to issues raised by the joining of 'Miss Brooke' and *Middlemarch*, and the serial publication of the novel. Of major importance to those interested in the practical problems involved in writing the book; but, by virtue of that fact, of only incidental critical value. A summary of the issues treated here at length can be found in Cross's *Life, Letters and Journals of George Eliot*.

Claude T. Bissell, 'Social Analysis in the Novels of George Eliot', *Journal of English Literary History*, xviii (1951) 221–39. Tries to show how in *Middlemarch* (and in *Adam Bede* and *The Mill on the Floss*) social analysis 'helps to determine the choice of material, gives added depth to characterisation and provides one of the ideas by which a diverse and complex world takes on form and meaning'.

David Cecil, 'George Eliot', in *Early Victorian Novelists* (Constable, 1934). Unfortunately too diffuse to quote from at length on *Middlemarch* alone, but contains a lively, general account of the limitations imposed on George Eliot's fiction by her 'negative virtues'.

David Daiches, *George Eliot: 'Middlemarch'* (Edward Arnold, 1963). An introduction to the novel in the 'Studies in English Literature' series. Useful to read in conjunction with Lerner and Leavis for ideas on George Eliot's assessment of Dorothea's character, and a handy short guide on its own.

Sumner J. Ferris, '*Middlemarch*, George Eliot's Masterpiece', in *From Jane Austen to Joseph Conrad*, ed. R. C. Rathburne and

M. Steinmann, Jr (Univ. of Minnesota Press, 1958). For the most part a pedestrian essay, but it does have the merit of suggesting how George Eliot's handling of 'multilateral third-person point of view' may account for her limited success in portraying both Casaubon and Ladislaw.

Barbara Hardy, 'Implication and Incompleteness: George Eliot's *Middlemarch*', in *The Appropriate Form* (Athlone Press, 1964). Gives convincing reasons for George Eliot's failure in presenting the Dorothea–Ladislaw relationship.

John Holloway, 'George Eliot', in *The Victorian Sage* (Macmillan, 1953). A succinct account of George Eliot's social and ethical views as they are revealed in both the authorial intrusions and the dialogue of her fiction. Much of the evidence is taken from *Middlemarch*, and all of it is relevant to an appreciation of the book.

A. T. Kitchel, *Quarry for Middlemarch*, accompaniment to *Nineteenth-Century Fiction*, IV (1950). An annotated edition of George Eliot's notebook composed immediately before and during the writing of *Middlemarch*. Kitchel's introduction and notes, and the notebook itself, provide information about George Eliot's research into political and social life around 1832. Taken with Beaty's study, it gives a clear account of the circumstances of the novel's composition.

George Steiner, 'A Preface to *Middlemarch*', *Nineteenth-Century Fiction*, IX (1955) 262–79. A typical formalist disparagement of nineteenth-century English fiction, treating *Middlemarch* as a good story but not a novel. Critics like W. J. Harvey and John Bayley have shown how wrong-headed this sort of criticism is, but it is instructive to meet it here in its first flush of middle age.

NOTES ON CONTRIBUTORS

QUENTIN ANDERSON is Professor and head of the Department of English at Columbia University, New York. He is author of *The American Henry James*.

DAVID DAICHES is Professor of English at the University of Sussex and author of many literary critical and historical studies, including *Critical Approaches to Literature* and *A Critical History of English Literature*.

BARBARA HARDY is Professor of English at Royal Holloway College, University of London.

W. J. HARVEY, late Professor of English at Queen's University, Belfast, was author of *The Art of George Eliot* and *Character and the Novel*.

ARNOLD KETTLE is Senior Lecturer in English at Leeds University, and the author of *An Introduction to the English Novel*.

FRANK KERMODE is Lord Northcliffe Professor of Modern English Literature at University College, London. For a short time he was an editor of *Encounter*. He is author of *Romantic Image*, *The Sense of an Ending*, and many essays and reviews.

LAURENCE LERNER is Reader in English at the University of Sussex and author of *George Eliot and Her Readers*, three volumes of poetry and a novel.

V. S. PRITCHETT is leading fiction critic of the *New Statesman* and among the most admired of contemporary English short-story writers. He has recently published a biography of his early life, *A Cab at the Door*.

INDEX